Mastering Adobe Premier Pro CS6 HOTSH❂T

Take your video editing skills to new and exciting levels with eight fantastic projects

Paul Ekert

PUBLISHING

BIRMINGHAM - MUMBAI

Mastering Adobe Premier Pro CS6 HOTSHOt

First published: February 2013

Production Reference: 1110213

Published by Packt Publishing Ltd.
Livery Place
35 Livery Street
Birmingham B3 2PB, UK.

ISBN 978-1-84969-478-0

www.packtpub.com

Cover Image by Eleanor Leonne Bennett (eleanor.ellieonline@gmail.com)

Credits

Author
Paul Ekert

Reviewer
Chris Bryant
David Clarke

Acquisition Editor
Erol Staveley

Commissioning Editor
Llewellyn F. Rozario

Lead Technical Editor
Arun Nadar

Technical Editors
Devdutt Kulkarni
Kaustubh S. Mayekar

Project Coordinator
Anugya Khurana

Proofreaders
Amy Guest
Aaron Nash

Indexer
Rekha Nair

Production Coordinator
Nilesh R. Mohite

Cover Work
Nilesh R. Mohite

About the Author

Paul Ekert started getting interested in video editing during the mid 90s when various exciting but crude video editing devices came to market. He soon moved away from this somewhat unreliable technology and transferred to MiroMotion capture cards (Miro were later bought by Pinnacle), which took the radical approach of downloading video from a camera to a PC's hard drive. The default software for these cards was Adobe Premiere. In the late 90s, he started working for a computer supplier, who specialized in building bespoke systems for non-linear editing, predominantly using Adobe Premiere with various hardware combinations supplied by Pinnacle and Matrox. He left this firm to work in the QA department of Pinnacle, one of the leading suppliers of non-linear editing hardware, who were eventually bought by Avid.

In 2005, he left to pursue a career as a freelance writer. Since that time, he has written five books on video editing, one based on Premiere Pro CS3 and another on Premiere Elements 7 (special effects based book). He also wrote one book on Pinnacle Liquid (NLE software) and its follow up, Avid Liquid. During this time, he wrote, filmed, directed, and edited several short films, some of which can be seen on his website. In all, he has over two decades experience in using non-linear editing programs, in particular, Adobe Premiere. A recent (2012) edit that was created using Premiere Pro CS6 (an airshow in Brazil using two GoPro Hero2 cameras) can be seen on youtu.be/OoD9dSyAXC0.

He is interested in most things that come under the heading of geeky. He is never really content to look at something and be impressed with what it does; he always needs to lift the hood, look underneath, and work out exactly how everything works. Of late, he has become fascinated with low-cost animation products such as iClone, and low-cost special effects tools such as HitFilm. He also maintains a long running interest in PC hardware and is always fascinated with various cameras; usually the ones just out of his price range. Find him at trade fairs drooling over them!

He is also a writer of plays, films scripts, novels, short stories, non-fiction books, and the odd poem. Examples of all these can be found on his website, www.PaulEkert.com. During the last few years, he has felt privileged to live a life where he can create and write, and he values the sometimes painful months he spent creating *Ordinary Monsters*, his first published novel (now available for the Kindle). He believes that all writing involves equal amounts of pleasure and pain, just like life. The trick is to enjoy and embrace them both.

About the Reviewers

Chris Bryant, after standing in line for hours to watch Jurassic Park on opening night, was instantly hooked on motion pictures. He also realized at an early age that if you don't want to be filmed, you needed to be the one holding the camera. One of his first paychecks went to purchase an 8 mm camcorder, and his passion for video production has grown ever since. He edited his first video back in high school by chaining together two VCRs to create a thematic introduction to his Senior Project, and was a Media Arts major at Western Connecticut State University.

He eventually went on to start his own company in 2004 (look for Bryant Productions on Facebook) and films a range of promotional and internal training videos for companies nationwide.

For fun, he produces short films, including The Other Half, the first place winner of the 2009 Connecticut Film Festival's "24 Hour Cup 'O Joe Filmmaking Competition". He has experience as a voiceover artist and event videographer.

When he isn't shooting video or editing, he enjoys spending time with his beautiful wife at their home in New York City.

David Clarke started DVC Ltd in 1995, retailing custom-built computer editing systems using Adobe Premiere 1. DVC has expanded to deal with all the major editing programs. He has also produced many training videos on Adobe Premiere Pro and Adobe Encore. He has also run Premiere training courses for Buckingham Palace press office, Fulham football club, and the BBC.

He has directed, edited, and produced effects on the epic, 6-part-adventure-based BBC TV series Dr Who, which included a guest appearance from Jon Pertwee, his last time to play the role of the Doctor.

www.PacktPub.com

Support files, eBooks, discount offers and more

You might want to visit www.PacktPub.com for support files and downloads related to your book.

Did you know that Packt offers eBook versions of every book published, with PDF and ePub files available? You can upgrade to the eBook version at www.PacktPub.com and as a print book customer, you are entitled to a discount on the eBook copy. Get in touch with us at service@packtpub.com for more details.

At www.PacktPub.com, you can also read a collection of free technical articles, sign up for a range of free newsletters and receive exclusive discounts and offers on Packt books and eBooks.

http://PacktLib.PacktPub.com

Do you need instant solutions to your IT questions? PacktLib is Packt's online digital book library. Here, you can access, read and search across Packt's entire library of books.

Why Subscribe?

- ▶ Fully searchable across every book published by Packt
- ▶ Copy and paste, print and bookmark content
- ▶ On demand and accessible via web browser

Free Access for Packt account holders

If you have an account with Packt at www.PacktPub.com, you can use this to access PacktLib today and view nine entirely free books. Simply use your login credentials for immediate access.

Table of Contents

Preface

Adobe Premiere Pro is one of the most popular video editing programs on the market. Its lineage stretches back a number of decades to when the program was given away free with a FireWire or analogue to digital converter card. Since then the program has gone through a number of radical overhauls, not least being CS6, which changed a number of key workflows and altered the main layout to create a very clean looking interface. If you are new to Premiere Pro, or if you have just started to explore the program, or indeed you are coming from a previous version, this book will detail everything you need to know in order to get you up and running as a Hotshot video editor. Take a look at the eight project areas to get an idea of the skills you will be learning. Here you can see that pretty much every aspect of video editing with Adobe Premiere Pro CS6 is covered, often more than once in order for you to practice those new found editing skills. From automatically creating a movie montage, through to editing a short film, a news article, all the way to adding special effects to your Timeline, this book really will make a Hotshot editor out of you.

What this book covers

Project 1, Creating a Movie Montage – The Easy Way, shows you how to take the hard work out of adding many hundreds of clips to a Timeline, and create a montage to the beat of a music track.

Project 2, Cutting a Short Film Without Getting Stung, builds on workflows learned in *Project 1*, but uses those skills to cut a short film using a variety of techniques including three and four-point edits.

Project 3, Protect the Innocent – Interview Edit Techniques, looks at various techniques you will find useful when editing news or documentary footage, such as the J- and L-cuts, and the Extract and Lift functions.

Project 4, See the Bigger Picture – Edit Multiple Cameras, shows you how to synchronize footage that was recorded on nine different cameras, as well as demonstrating a **Picture-in-Picture** (**PiP**) effect.

Project 5, Visual Effects – Muzzle Flashes, Laser Beams, and Clones, takes you through the steps necessary to create these effects using only the filters and effects found in a standard install of Premiere Pro CS6.

Project 6, Visual FX Using Real Media, builds on *Project 5*, but shows you how to replace the effects with real explosions sourced free from the Internet.

Project 7, The Ultimate Do-over – Correcting Visual and Audio Problems, takes a look at just what's involved when someone says, "We'll fix it in post"!

Project 8, Reach the World – Export to DVD, the Internet, and Beyond, looks at the practical steps needed to get your finished project out onto YouTube, or DVD, or wherever else you want to send it.

What you need for this book

This book assumes that you have some familiarity with how PC and Mac programs work. For example you should be comfortable with how to drag-and-drop using the mouse, and how to activate secondary options by holding down the *Shift*, *Alt* (PC) or *option* (Mac), and *Ctrl* (PC) or *command* (Mac) keys. If you are using a Mac with a single button mouse, you should also be aware of the alternative to right-clicking. If you have any doubts about these conventions, you should take a look at your PC or Mac handbook, or if you lack one of those, make a few well-informed searches for some basic "computer usage" tutorials using the search engine of your choice.

This book also assumes that you have installed Adobe Premiere Pro CS6 to your computer and that you are at least capable of launching the program and understanding how to access some of the basic menus. You won't need to know anything further about Premiere Pro CS6, as this book develops along a gentle learning curve, with lots of help and hand holding occurring in the first two projects, and then slightly less help in each of the following ones. Eventually, as you reach the last few projects, you should be able to tackle each task without referring to any of the hints or tips given throughout this book.

Finally, this book also assumes that you have a computer capable of video editing. The minimum specifications for Adobe Premiere Pro CS6 can be found on the Adobe website; however, you should also have at least one extra hard drive attached to your system that is dedicated to storing your video source files. This dedicated video drive can be an internal hard drive, or it can be an external USB or FireWire drive. Whatever it is, it should be as big and as fast as you can afford in order to cope with the large amount of space that video clips demand. All of the source clips that you will download from the Packt Publishing website for use with this book should be stored on your dedicated video drive using the instructions given in each project.

Editing on a computer with just a single drive (a laptop for example) is not recommended as you will experience dropped frames, which appear on screen as a juddering, stuttering playback. If you are undecided about the capabilities of your system, then it's best to ask one of the various dedicated nonlinear video editing dealers for their advice. A good example of a firm with a great deal of knowledge on this subject is DVC based in the UK (www.dvc. uk.com). Take a look at their site even if you are not in the UK, as this is the sort of firm you should be looking for where you live.

Who this book is for

This book is aimed at anyone who wants to edit with Adobe Premiere Pro CS6. You might know very little about the program, or you might have the basic skills and are looking to take them to the next level, or you may be a more experienced user looking to learn how the new workflows in CS6 can be easily accessed. Using these projects, and the sample footage that you can download from the Packt Publishing website, you will learn techniques that can be adapted for use on any type of video project. Using this system it's possible to complete this book in just under a day, assuming you drink plenty of coffee and don't get distracted. Whoever you are, whatever your motives are for learning Premiere Pro CS6, this book will teach you all you need to know in order to improve your workflows. In turn, this will allow you to deliver a accurate frame edit that will really make your projects stand out.

Conventions

In this book, you will find several headings appearing frequently.

To give clear instructions of how to complete a procedure or task, we use:

Mission Briefing

This section explains what you will build, with a screenshot of the completed project.

Why Is It Awesome?

This section explains why the project is cool, unique, exciting, and interesting. It describes what advantage the project will give you.

Your Hotshot Objectives

This section explains the major tasks required to complete your project.

- Task 1
- Task 2
- Task 3
- Task 4, and so on

Mission Checklist

This section explains any pre-requisites for the project, such as resources or libraries that need to be downloaded, and so on.

Task 1

This section explains the task that you will perform.

Prepare for Lift Off

This section explains any preliminary work that you may need to do before beginning work on the task.

Engage Thrusters

This section lists the steps required in order to complete the task.

Objective Complete - Mini Debriefing

This section explains how the steps performed in the previous section allow us to complete the task. This section is mandatory.

Classified Intel

The extra information in this section is relevant to the task.

You will also find a number of styles of text that distinguish between different kinds of information. Here are some examples of these styles, and an explanation of their meaning.

Code words in text are shown as follows: "Browse to your `Images` folder on your designated video drive and import your images."

New terms and **important words** are shown in bold. Words that you see on the screen, in menus or dialog boxes for example, appear in the text like this: "Once Premiere Pro CS6 has finished launching, the **Recent Projects** splash screen appears."

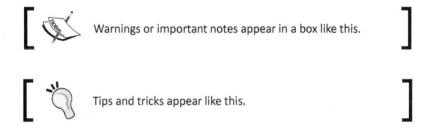

Warnings or important notes appear in a box like this.

Tips and tricks appear like this.

Reader feedback

Feedback from our readers is always welcome. Let us know what you think about this book—what you liked or may have disliked. Reader feedback is important for us to develop titles that you really get the most out of.

To send us general feedback, simply send an e-mail to `feedback@packtpub.com`, and mention the book title via the subject of your message. If there is a topic that you have expertise in and you are interested in either writing or contributing to a book, see our author guide on `www.packtpub.com/authors`.

Customer support

Now that you are the proud owner of a Packt book, we have a number of things to help you to get the most from your purchase.

Downloading the example code

You can download the example code files for all Packt books you have purchased from your account at http://www.packtpub.com. If you purchased this book elsewhere, you can visit http://www.packtpub.com/support and register to have the files e-mailed directly to you.

Errata

Although we have taken every care to ensure the accuracy of our content, mistakes do happen. If you find a mistake in one of our books—maybe a mistake in the text or the code—we would be grateful if you would report this to us. By doing so, you can save other readers from frustration and help us improve subsequent versions of this book. If you find any errata, please report them by visiting http://www.packtpub.com/submit-errata, selecting your book, clicking on the **errata submission form** link, and entering the details of your errata. Once your errata are verified, your submission will be accepted and the errata will be uploaded on our website, or added to any list of existing errata, under the Errata section of that title. Any existing errata can be viewed by selecting your title from http://www.packtpub.com/support.

Piracy

Piracy of copyright material on the Internet is an ongoing problem across all media. At Packt, we take the protection of our copyright and licenses very seriously. If you come across any illegal copies of our works, in any form, on the Internet, please provide us with the location address or website name immediately so that we can pursue a remedy.

Please contact us at copyright@packtpub.com with a link to the suspected pirated material.

We appreciate your help in protecting our authors, and our ability to bring you valuable content.

Questions

You can contact us at questions@packtpub.com if you are having a problem with any aspect of the book, and we will do our best to address it.

Project 1
Creating a Movie Montage – the Easy Way

A movie montage can be used for a variety of purposes; from creating a preview of a wedding video to setting out a trailer for your next film project. Essentially, it's a bunch of clips placed on the Timeline, usually accompanied by some "mood" music that gives an instant taster of the full product. This might sound easy enough, but it's a simple explanation that hides a terrific amount of work needed to create a well-executed montage.

The secret (like most things in life) is in the timing. Premiere Pro CS6 has a number of tricks to help with this and to smooth out the movie montage workflow.

Downloading the example code

You can download the example code files for all Packt books you have purchased from your account at http://www.PacktPub.com. If you purchased this book elsewhere, you can visit http://www.PacktPub.com/support and register to have the files e-mailed directly to you.

Mission Briefing

Your objective in this project is to place a music file on the Timeline, create markers to the beat, organize a rough running order of your clips and photos, and then automate the whole thing to the Timeline, creating edit points at each of the Markers. You'll then fine-tune your sequence using motion effects and the default Adobe transition (**Cross Dissolve**). At the end of the project, you should have created a Timeline that looks as busy as the following screenshot:

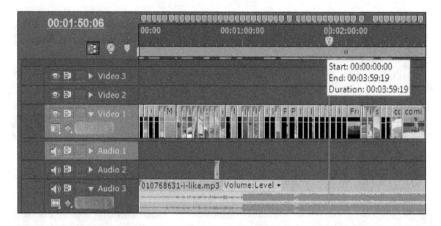

Why Is It Awesome?

A movie montage is a lot of work, but what if you could create the basics with just a few mouse and keyboard clicks? Using Premiere Pro's built-in ability to automate clips to the Timeline is just what this project will teach you to do. Instead of manually dragging or sending a clip to the Timeline, then fiddling around to get it on the beat, you'll use Timeline markers to work out where those beats should be, and subclips to create a little army of media material to send to those beat markers. In all, you should be able to create the basic starting point for a movie montage in a fraction of time it would take to do it manually. Along the way, you'll be introduced to a great editing function, the trim tool, and learn how to alter the flow of time with the **Rate Stretch** tool.

A secondary objective of this project is an attempt to persuade you to use the keyboard shortcuts as much as possible. As useful as the mouse is, it can often lack a degree of accuracy when it comes to video editing. Sometimes, it is the easiest way to do something, but other times, it's a workflow that can slow you down. Sometimes, it can even ruin the look of our project through microscopically inaccurate edit decisions that irritate audiences on a subliminal level. Assign the keyboard shortcuts now, and you will be glad that you did.

At the end of this project, you should have the skills and knowledge that will make creating a movie montage a joy to complete, and not an intense labor of video-editing pain.

Your Hotshot Objectives

The project will be split into eight parts; each one teaching you an essential Premiere Pro CS6 workflow. This project will benefit you more if you follow each task in the following order:

- ▶ Streamlining Premiere Pro CS6 – organizing your media and the interface
- ▶ Music markers matter (placing beat markers on the Timeline)
- ▶ Subclips tame video clips
- ▶ Final preparation (the selection and rejection of your clips)
- ▶ Creating a running order
- ▶ Fine-tuning the edit
- ▶ Correct aspect ratios
- ▶ Finishing touches

Mission Checklist

Before you launch Premiere Pro CS6, you need to make some initial preparations. Begin by gathering together all the various assets you want to include in your movie montage. Assets can be any kind of media that's being used on the Timeline, such as images, audio, and of course, video.

Your first task is locating a musical clip for your montage, and you'll need to think carefully about what sort of music you should use. Most wedding montages will make use of a slow melodic beat, while action montages will have a faster tempo (although you can turn this idea on its head by showing your action sequences in slow motion).

 For an example of music used in a counterintuitive way, take a look at the following aerobatic video edited in November 2012 by the author of this book, at tinyurl.com/cnfvjng.

Whichever creative direction you decide to go in, your next decision should be where to obtain the music from. If the montage is for some kind of public consumption (and let's face it, if it's not why are you bothering?), then you will need to source a clip from one of the many copyright-free sources available on the Internet. Don't even think about using music of your favorite band unless you have a license to use it, which is unlikely.

 In the UK, creators of wedding videos can apply for an **MCPS Limited Manufacture License**; this allows the video maker to use most popular music in their films but for distribution on DVD only. The license assumes, the DVD will not be used at public events, and so it doesn't cover the video being uploaded to YouTube or video-sharing websites. Variations on this type of license are available in most countries around the world.

Pond5 was used as the source of copyright-free music for this project ("i like" by SimilarD at www.Pond5.com, and also, search for item 10768631). This evocatively inspirational musical arrangement costs just $10, lasts for four minutes, and proves in keeping with the material being used in this movie montage. When tracking down the optimal musical arrangement for your movie montage, remember to consider the overall duration; a preview of wedding footage should be around 3 to 4 minutes, while a film trailer will only need to be 60 to 90 seconds. If you have very specific requirements, you might need to consider creating your own music, with pre-composed loops from sources such as Video Copilot's ProScores (tinyurl.com/blp88p).

Pond5 has recently developed a plugin especially for Premiere Pro CS6. Known as a Partner Panel, this plugin will allow you to browse and sample (sometimes even before you buy) video and audio clips available from the Pond5 website.

The next screenshot shows the Pond5 Partner Panel docked to the left-hand side of the interface, with the song "i like" (recommended for this project) highlighted—with the Partner Panel open, just clicking on the file you want will import a sample copy into your **Project** panel for you to add to the Timeline and try before you buy.

Go to www.pond5.com/adobe, where you will find a short video tutorial on how to install the plugin. This video also contains a short demonstration on how to use the plugin inside Premiere Pro CS6, and how to create a docked Partner Panel.

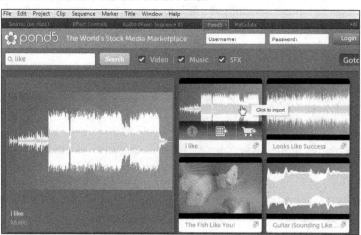

Once you have your music, and with it a clear idea of how long the montage will last (the length of the music clip), you will need to gather together enough assets needed to fill that time effectively. These assets will be the video clips you have previously captured or imported using Premiere Pro CS6 or other applications. You may also want to consider using still images, such as photographs, drawings, and any compositions you have created in other applications, such as After Effects.

Once you have identified the various assets you would like to use, create a new folder on your computer's designated video hard drive; the folder should have a logical name, such as The_Smiths_Wedding_Montage_2012. Once this is done, use your computer's file browser to copy and paste your assets into three separate folders – Audio, Video, Images, as shown in the following screenshot:

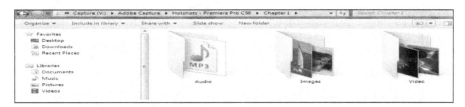

With these steps completed, you are ready to go.

For more information on designated hard drives and the necessity of creating the copies of assets in a separate folder, specifically, when working with Premiere Pro CS6, please see *Preface, Basic Video Editing Tips* in this book.

Users of Mac OS should also read the section of *Preface* that details mouse commands on the PC, and how they translate to the Mac world.

Streamlining Premiere Pro

In this section, you will customize Premiere Pro CS6 to streamline the editing workflow for the project used in this chapter, and many of the others in this book. Specifically, you will customize the general layout of Premiere Pro CS6 to encourage you to use keyboard shortcuts, create new Bins (folders) in the **Project** panel, and finally save this all as a template for use in the future. This task is designed as an **Easy in** feature for you to get used to the style of the book and to double-check whether you have Premiere Pro CS6 set up correctly.

Prepare for Lift Off

Once you are sure all the assets you need are gathered together in three separate folders on your designated video drive, launch Premiere Pro CS6 in the normal way.

Engage Thrusters

You will now set up your interface for easier editing, and save these settings as a reusable template. To do so, follow these steps:

1. Once Premiere Pro CS6 has finished launching, the **Recent Projects** splash screen appears. Then, select the **New Project** icon.

2. Before naming your project, select the **Scratch Disks** tab at the top of the **New Project** window, and confirm whether all scratch disks are set up for optimal performance as stipulated in the following screenshot. In this example the drive letter "V" represents the computers dedicated video drive. More information on using a dedicated video drive can be found in the Preface.

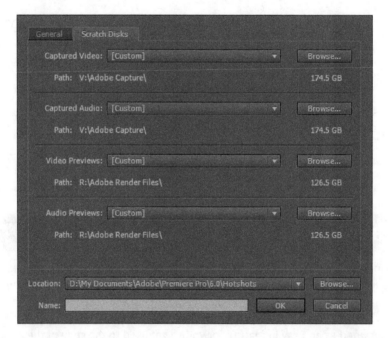

 While you have the previous window open, you should also click the **General** tab, and check if the Mercury Playback settings are correct for your computer. Generally speaking, you will get better performance if Mercury Playback is set to take advantage of your graphics card.

3. Once you are satisfied with the project settings, name this project `Hotshots Template - Montage`, and select a location to save that file. The default Adobe folder in `My Documents` should be fine for this purpose and is recommended for the rest of this book.

4. The **New Sequence** window will now appear. Select the video standard that matches the majority of your video assets (see also *Classified Intel* at the end of this section).

5. The main Premiere Pro CS6 interface will now open, displaying the default editing workspace, as shown in the next screenshot. Here, you can see the **Project** panel and **Timeline** panel sharing a one third/two third portion of the lower interface, while Source Monitor and Program Monitor equally share the upper part of the interface. If your interface is showing something else, use the keyboard shortcut *Alt + Shift +3* (Windows), or *option + Shift + 3* (Mac) to display the editing workspace.

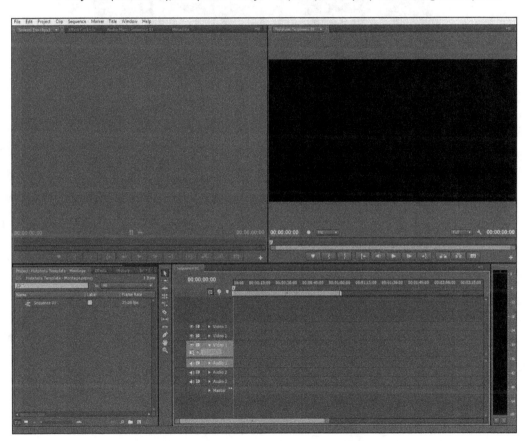

6. Select the **Project** panel by using the keyboard shortcut *Shift + 1*. Selection will be confirmed by displaying a gold border around the **Project** panel.

7. Use the keyboard shortcut *Ctrl + /* or *command + /* to create a new `Bin` folder in the **Project** panel, and name this `Bin` folder as `Video`. Press *Enter* and then *Esc* on the keyboard to exit the renaming function.

8. Repeat step 7 twice to create two more `Bins` folders called `Audio` and `Images`. Your **Project** panel should look like the following screenshot when you have finished:

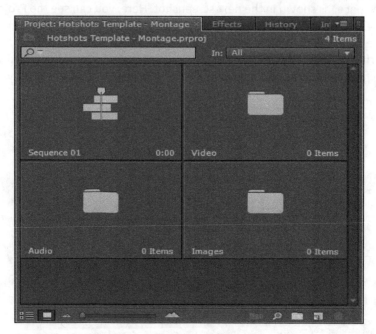

9. From the menu, select **Workspace | New Workspace** and in the **New Workspace** window enter `Editing Optimized`.

When you created your own custom workspace, it will have been assigned a keyboard shortcut. Go to **Windows | Workspace** to see which shortcut combination your workspace has been given.

10. Right-click on the header of the toolbar panel that sits (and takes up valuable real estate) between the **Timeline** and the **Project** panels, and select **Close Panel**. If you prefer to use the mouse for tool selection, ignore this step.

11. Place the cursor between the **Timeline** and the **Project** panels, so that a double-headed arrow appears, then drag to the left-hand side to make the **Timeline** panel larger. Stop before the **Effects** tab disappears.

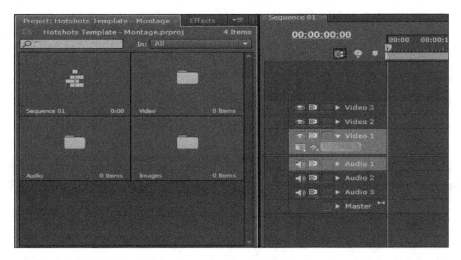

12. Take a moment now to make any other customizations to the general layout of the interface. Once you have finished, press *Ctrl + S* or *command + S* on the keyboard to save this layout.

 By saving this layout as separate Premiere Pro CS6 projects file, it will be available to you whenever you want to create a new montage.

Objective Complete - Mini Debriefing

In this task, you have confirmed that the scratch disks are set for optimal video editing and customized as the workspace towards an optimal editing workflow. You have also created three new bins into which you will later import your assets. More importantly, however, you have begun using keyboard shortcuts to control Premiere Pro CS6. It is important that you at least try to break the habit of using the mouse all the time. Sometimes, it is of course unavoidable or simply easier to use the mouse instead of the keyboard, but overall, keyboard shortcuts can often prove to be more accurate in use than the mouse.

New keyboard shortcuts covered in this task are as follows:

▶ *Shift + Alt +3* (Windows) or *Shift + option + 3* (Mac): This shortcut selects the default CS6 editing workspace

▶ *Shift + 1*: This shortcut selects the **Project** panel as the active panel

▶ *Ctrl + /* (Windows), or *command + /* (Mac): This shortcut creates a new Bin folder in the active **Project** panel

▶ *Ctrl + S* (Windows) or *command + S* (Mac): This is the universal shortcut for saving a project

Classified Intel

Although item 4 of this section asked you to select a video standard that matched the majority of your video assets, it's not going to be a problem if you get this wrong. A new feature of Premiere Pro CS6 is that it will offer to change the Timeline settings of any empty sequence to match the settings it detects in the first clip added to that sequence. However, you need to make sure the first clip on the Timeline represents the majority of clips used in the rest of the sequence; otherwise, you will have to endure unnecessarily long render times.

Music markers matter

You are now ready to do some actual video editing. Let's get started by importing and placing the music clip on the Timeline. You will then create markers to the beat of the music. These will be used in a later step to automatically place your clips on the Timeline to that beat. The audio track is the core of a good montage, so this section may appear relatively simple; it's worth spending some extra time executing the techniques described here.

The first step of this project is also important; there you will use **Save As** to turn your saved Montage-Template into a Montage-Project. It is a simple step, but one that allows you to keep your original Montage-Template for future use.

Engage Thrusters

You will now add markers to the Timeline and edit their position:

1. If it is not already open, reopen the Hotshots Template - Montage file you created in the last task, and then resave it as Hotshots_Montage_X, where X is the subject matter of your montage (**Edit | Save As**).

2. Open the Audio Bin folder without creating a separate **Project** panel by holding down the *Ctrl* or *command* key and double-clicking on the **Bin: Audio** tab.

3. Use the keyboard shortcut *Ctrl + I* or *command + I* to open the **Import** window. Browse to the Audio folder on your designated video drive, and select your music file. Click on **Open** to bring it into Premier Pro CS6.

4. Drag-and-drop your music file to **Audio 3**, then expand the track using the **Collapse-Expand Track** toggle, as shown in the following screenshot:

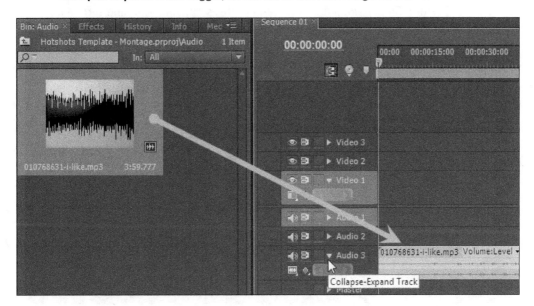

 Expanding the audio track will allow you to see the dips and rises of the music you have selected, creating a handy visual cue for placing your markers. If you want a bigger waveform, place the cursor over the bottom line of the **Audio 3** track (so that it displays a double-headed vertical cursor), and drag-and-drop the track downwards to the required height.

5. Activate the **Timeline** panel using the keyboard shortcut *Shift + 3*, then maximize the panel by pressing Shift + *accent* (accent is the key next to the *1* key and above the *Tab* key). See *Classified Intel* at the end of this task if this doesn't work for you.

6. Zoom the Timeline to the length of the music track by pressing \ (backslash) on the keyboard.

7. Play the music by pressing the *L* key on the keyboard. Each time you hear a change in the beat of the music, hit the *M* key on the keyboard to add a marker at that position on the Timeline. At the end of this step, your Timeline should look something like the following screenshot:

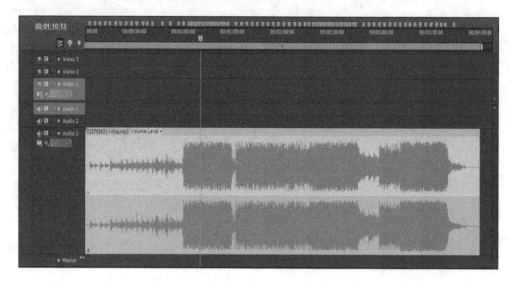

If you make a mistake, press *K* to stop playback and use *Ctrl* + *Z* or *command* + *Z* to undo the last few markers that you placed. Press *J* to rewind back down the Timeline and *L* again to resume playback.

Use of the keys *J*, *K*, and *L* is very important when it comes to frame accurate editing. It's true that playback can be started with the *Spacebar* key and rewinding is accomplished with the cursor keys; however, the position of your fingers on the keyboard is important for a smooth editing experience.

The ideal keyboard position is with the index finger of your right hand hovering over the *M* and *J* keys, with your middle finger over the *K* and *I* keys, and your ring finger over the *L* and *O* keys. Your left hand should be hovering over the *Ctrl* or *command* key (for *Ctrl* + *Z* (Windows), or *command* + *Z* (Mac) to quickly erase mistakes) and the *Tab*, *Shift*, and the *Alt* or *option* keys, which add extra functions to various workflows.

If you work like this for just a short amount of time, you will find that your editing will benefit dramatically. And if you have trouble remembering the keyboard shortcuts, various specially color-coded keyboards can be bought for Premiere Pro, with the more expensive models including a Jog/Shuttle, although at four times the price this is a luxury that you probably need to think about.

8. Review the position of the markers by playing back the sequence. If there are too many markers in any one section, delete the superfluous ones by right-clicking on that marker and selecting **Clear Current Marker** from the context menu.

9. If a marker's position is slightly off the beat, move the marker nearest to the beat by first minimizing the **Timeline** panel (*Shift + Accent*), and then from the menu, select **Window | Markers**. The **Markers** panel should now open in the **Project** panel.

10. Click on the marker you wish to move, and it will appear selected in the **Markers** panel. To move the marker to the right-hand side (up the Timeline), place the cursor under the **In:** value so that it appears as a double-headed horizontal cursor, and with the mouse button held down, drag it to the right-hand side. To move the marker to the left-hand side (down the Timeline), use the **Out:** value and drag it to the left-hand side.

 You can also enter the change directly using numerical values for the markers. Use the Timeline indicator beforehand to work out the values you will need to enter.

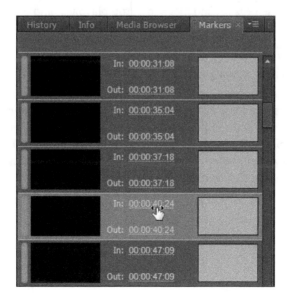

11. Finish by saving your project.

 Audio 1 and Audio 2 tracks are used for the audio content of Video 1 and Video 2 tracks. Even if you don't intend bringing in any audio from your video clips (or maybe you are only using images), it's good practice not to use these tracks for voice over or additional music tracks. The **Master Audio** track is used to track any changes you make to the overall volume level of the sequence. You won't be physically able to place a clip on this track.

Objective Complete - Mini Debriefing

In this simple task, you have added music to the Timeline and created markers to the beat. You also learned how to edit the position of those markers and/or delete them if necessary. Maximizing the Timeline wasn't strictly necessary, but it is a good workflow pattern to hide away anything you don't need to see in order to focus on what needs to be done, in this case, creating accurate markers for your music clip. Take your time completing this section. The more time you spend on the accurate placement of these markers, the better your final montage will look.

New keyboard shortcuts covered in this task are as follows:

▸ *Ctrl + I* or *command + I*: This shortcut opens the **Import** window

▸ *Shift + Accent*: This shortcut maximizes or minimizes the active panel

▸ \ (backslash): This key zooms the Timeline to the length of the project

▸ *M*: This key creates a marker on the Timeline at the Timeline indicator's position

▸ *J*, *K*, and *L*: These keys rewind playback, stop playback, and play back respectively

Classified Intel

If you are using a keyboard outside of the U.S., then you may find certain keyboard shortcuts that do not behave as advertised in the manual. One particular shortcut that gives many non-US keyboard users problems is the accent key. To correct this, open up the keyboard shortcuts from the menu (go to **Edit | Keyboard Shortcuts** for Windows, or **Premiere Pro | Keyboard Shortcuts** for Mac), and type MAX in the search field. Highlight the first in the list (**Maximize** or **Restore Active Frame**), and click on the **Edit** button. Press *Shift + Accent* key (the key next to the number *1* key and above the *Tab* key).

Repeat this for the setting below (**Maximize** or **Restore Frame Under Cursor**), but just press the *Accent* key without holding down *Shift*. Press *Enter* on the keyboard to close this window. Your non-US keyboard should now work as Adobe expects it! Users of Japanese keyboards may have to use the @ key instead of the *Accent* key.

Subclips tame video clips

It's likely that many of your video files, such as AVI or Mov (or whatever) were captured, imported, or made available to you in large chunks; sometimes each clip represents a scene, and sometimes it's a complete dump of a 60-minute tape file. But even if your clips are just a few minutes in duration, it's possible that they are still too long to be used in a montage. Most montages will use clips of 5 to 10 seconds in length, although there is no hard-and-fast rule. In this section, you will tame your video clips by converting them into short subclips, then copy and paste those subclips into a new Montage Bin.

Prepare for Lift Off

As stated earlier, frame accurate video editing is best attempted using as many keyboard shortcuts as possible. However, by default, some shortcuts in Premiere Pro CS6 are left blank, partly to allow you to customize your own workflow and partly because of the difference between U.S. keyboard layouts and the rest of the world. In this section, you will create a **Make Subclips** keyboard shortcut to correct this problem. The suggested shortcut for **Make Subclips** is *0* (the zero key above the letters *O* and *P*). The number zero in this position is used to keep the fingers of your right hand in the same place, so you can use the *J*, *K*, and *L* keys to control playback and use the *I* (In point), *O* (Out point), and *0* (zero) keys to create your subclips.

1. Use the mouse to select **Edit | Keyboard Shortcuts** from the menu.

2. In the search field, type sub.

3. Click on the **Make Subclip...** field, and then click on the **Edit** button at the bottom of the **Keyboard Shortcuts** window. This will place a cursor in the field next to **Make Subclip...**.

4. Press the number *0* (zero) on the top row of keys above the letters *O* and *P* to enter this value as the keyboard shortcut for **Make Subclip...**.

5. Repeat steps 4 and 5 to create a shortcut of *Shift + 0* for the
    Edit Subclip... command.

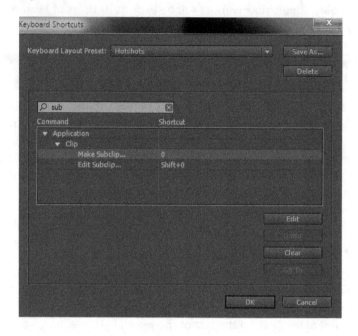

6. Click on **OK** or press the *Enter* key to close this window. You are now ready to go.
    Proceed to the next section of this task, where you will use these shortcuts to
    create subclips from your video files.

Engage Thrusters

You'll now bring in your media and create subclips from longer video clips:

1. Press *Shift + 1* on the keyboard to select the **Project** panel.

2. If you are still in the `Audio Bin` file, click on the `Up One Level` folder button in
    the upper-left corner of the **Project** panel to move to the main **Project** panel.

3. Open the `Video Bin` file inside the **Project** panel by holding down the *Ctrl* or
    command key, and double-clicking on the `Video Bin` file.

4. Use the keyboard shortcut *Ctrl + I* or *command + I* to open the **Import browser**
    window, and browse to the folder on your designated video drive. Here, you should
    find all the video files you copied across at the start of this project.

5. Click on any file in the browser window to select it, then with the *Ctrl* or *command* key held down, click on each file you want to include in your project. If you only have a few files and you want to include them all, you can also use *Ctrl + A* or *command + A* to select all the files in that folder.

6. Now you need to start slicing up the larger files (large is relative when it comes to creating a montage sequence). Begin by double-clicking a long file in your `Bin` folder to send it to the **Source** window.

7. Use *L* to play forward until you find a point where you would like a clip in your montage to begin, and press *K* to stop playback at that point.

> Pressing the *L* key during playback will play your clip back at a faster rate. To slow it back down again, press *J*. Hold down both *K* and *L* to play forward at roughly eight frames per second, or alternatively, hold down just the *K* key, and press and release *L* to move forward one frame.
>
> Use *Shift + J* to rewind the clip at a much slower speed; this is useful if you want to slowly review the placement of your ideal In or Out point. Press *Shift + J* 10 times during normal playback to slow down playback to around one frame per second. You can also use the left and right arrow keys to step forward or backward a single frame at a time. Combine this with the *Shift* key to step forward or backwards in advancements of five frames.

8. Once you have identified the start of your subclip, press the keyboard shortcut *I* to set an In point.

9. Repeat step 7 to find the Out point for this subclip, but this time use the keyboard shortcut *O* to set the Out point.

> There is no hard-and-fast rule for montage clip duration, but typically subclips are around 5 to 10 seconds long, depending on content. Don't worry if your clip is slightly longer or shorter than this; you will be given the chance to correct this later in the project.
>
> Useful though they are, a problem that can occur with subclips is that of insufficient media handles. This problem will be dealt with later in this project. For now, simply put a Media Handle is the extra space (padding at the start and end of a clip) used by transitions on the Timeline. Don't worry if this doesn't mean anything to you right now.

10. You can now create the subclip by using the keyboard shortcut you set at the start of this section (the *0* key above the letters *O* and *P*). Give your subclip a logical name, one that makes sense later in the edit process and press *Enter* to save this subclip to your currently active `Bin` file.

11. Repeat steps 6 through to 10 to create all the subclips you need for your montage.

Avoid naming your subclips `Clip A` or `Clip 1A`, as this can lead to confusion when you come to place them on the Timeline. A better habit is to always give them a logical name and a number, for example, `Waves_1`, `sunset_3`, or `ProjectName_Scene_1_Selection_4`.

Objective Complete - Mini Debriefing

In this task, you learned how to create a brand new keyboard shortcut, divided your clips up into manageable lengths, and once again allowed yourself to work to a frame level of accuracy using the keyboard.

The new keyboard shortcuts covered in this task are as follows:

- ▸ *I* and *O* : These keys set In or Out points of your subclip
- ▸ *J* or *L* (multiple times): These keys fast rewind and fast forward your clip; use the opposite key to slow it back down again
- ▸ *Shift* + *J* or *Shift* + *L*: If the Timeline indicator is stationary, this will play the clip at slower rate in a backwards(*J*) or forwards(*L*) direction
- ▸ *0* (zero) : This key is assigned for **Make Subclip...** command (user defined)

Classified Intel

Subclips serve only as proxy markers to the main media file. Those proxy markers exist in the mind of Premiere Pro CS6 (and indeed a temporary version can be found somewhere inside the application's inner sanctums); but, the original file remains intact and creating a subclip has no permanent effect on the original video clip. However, you can use these subclips in another Premiere Pro project simply by importing that project into your current one.

Final preparation

Choice is as much about rejection as it is about selection. In this section, you'll review your image choices inside a maximized **Project** panel, then copy and paste your final selection across to a new bin (the `Montage Bin` file). You'll finish this section by doing the same with your selection of subclips created in the previous task.

Engage Thrusters

Create a final selection of your clips by following these steps:

1. It's time now to select and reject the media needed for your video `montage.1`. Use *Shift* + *1* to make the **Project** panel the active panel, and move up one level to show all the bins if necessary.

2. Use *Ctrl* + *I* or *command* +*I* to open the **Import** window. Browse to your `Images` folder on your designated video drive and import your images.

3. Use *Shift* + *Accent* to maximize the **Project** panel.

 If the *Shift* + *Accent* key doesn't work for you, make sure you review the *Music Markers Matter* task, *Classified Intel* earlier in this project.

4. With the **Project** panel at its maximum size, make sure the **Icon** view is selected (lower-left corner of the **Project** panel) and review images for duplications or images that say nothing new in comparison to the other images. You can expand the size of the icons by using the **Zoom** tool at the lower-left corner of the **Project** panel.

5. Select the images you want using *Ctrl* + click or *command* + click. Press *Ctrl* + *C* or *command* + *C* on the keyboard to copy these files to your computer's clipboard.

6. Minimize the panel using *Shift* + *Accent* and return to the main **Project** panel area by clicking on the small folder Icon in the upper-right corner of the **Project** panel.

7. Press *Ctrl* + / or *command* + / (forward slash) to create a new Bin file and call it Montage_Name (where Name is the montage you are creating). Press *Enter*, and then *Esc* to exit the rename function.

8. Double-click on the Montage folder to open it in a separate panel.

9. Confirm whether this panel is the active one by looking for the gold border, then press *Ctrl* + *V* or *command* + *V* to paste your images into this bin.

10. Repeat steps 3 through to 9 for the video subclips stored in your Video Bin folder, so you have only your chosen subclips and chosen images in the Montage Bin file. See *Classified Intel* at the end of this task for information on how to review video clips inside the **Project** panel.

11. Close the Montage Bin file when you are finished by clicking on the red cross in the upper-right corner of the window.

Objective Complete - Mini Debriefing

At the end of this task, you should now have all the assets you want to include in your montage saved to one specific Bin. This is important as it will allow you to quickly and easily automate these clips to the Timeline in the next task; however, you need to be sure that only those clips you want to include are added to this Bin. You can add more at a later point if you want to, and subtract some, of course, but you will be making life easier for yourself by only copying across the bare minimum at this stage in the project.

The new keyboard shortcuts covered in this task are as follows:

- ▶ *Ctrl + C* or *command + C*: This shortcut allows you to copy clips to the computer's clipboard
- ▶ *Ctrl + V* or *command + V*: This shortcut allows you to paste clips from the computer's clipboard

Classified Intel

To review video clips in a project Bin, place your mouse cursor over the video clip and move it left or right to invoke hover scrub, a new feature in Premiere Pro CS6. Click inside the icon if you would like to review and even adjust the In and Out points of that clip or subclip. Hover scrub can be toggled on or off by pressing *Shift + H* on the keyboard.

Creating a running order

You are now in a position to create a rough running order of your montage. You'll do this first in the project Bin, using hover scrub to check the clips' content and by moving the clips physically about the bin folder. You will then automate the clips to the Timeline, so they appear at the markers you created in the *Music Markers Matter* section of this chapter.

Engage Thrusters

It's time to use your media to create your montage using the project:

1. Make the **Project** panel active by pressing *Shift + 1* on the keyboard. Confirm whether it is the active panel by looking for the gold border.

2. With the *Ctrl* or *command* key held down, open the Montage Bin file by double-clicking on it.

3. Maximize the panel by pressing the *Shift + Accent* keys.

4. If icons are not already displayed, click on the **Icon View** button in the lower-left corner of the **Project** panel. Adjust the size of the icons using the zoom slider to the right-hand side of the **Icon View** button. Bigger is better, but ideally all icons would be visible in the panel without scrolling.

5. Select the clip you have chosen to display first on your Timeline, either image or video, and place that in the upper-left corner of the panel by dragging it with the mouse.

> When you automate clips from a `Bin` file, Premiere Pro CS6 will place clips on the Timeline in the order they appear in the bin. The first clip will be the one in the upper-left corner of the bin; the second clip will be the one to its immediate right.

6. Repeat step 5 with all other video and image clips until you have a rough running order inside your **Project** panel.

7. When you have completed your rough running order, remove any unused clips from the `Bin` file by clicking on each one and pressing the *Delete* key.

8. Minimize the panel by pressing *Shift + Accent* and ensure the Timeline indicator is at the start of the music clip. Use the mouse or the left arrow key to move it there.

9. Click inside the **Project** panel (this should still be open to the `Montage Bin` file), and then press *Ctrl + A* or *Command + A* to select all clips in the `Bin` file.

10. Click on the **Automate to Sequence** button found in the lower-right area of the **Project** panel.

11. Make sure **Ordering** is set to **Selection Order** and **Placement** is set to **At Unnumbered Markers**. Deselect **Ignore Audio** if you would like to include the audio from your clips in the **Bin: Montage** tab. You can always mute them later if you change your mind, as shown in the following screenshot:

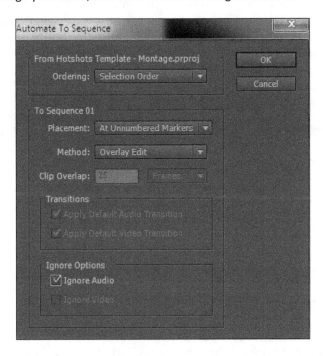

12. Click on **OK** or press *Enter* on the keyboard to send your clips automatically to the Timeline and aligned with your markers.

 If you want an image file or a subclip to appear more than once in your montage, right-click on it and select **Duplicate** from the context menu (fifth down on the list).

Objective Complete - Mini Debriefing

You have now created a montage using the **Project** panel to create a rough running order and the **Automate to Sequence** function to dump that running order onto the musical markers you created earlier in this project. The steps to get here may have seemed somewhat longwinded, but the next time you attempt this, you should find your workflow speed increased significantly. It's a simple yet deceptively powerful method of creating a montage, one of the most used tools to gain the immediate attention of an audience.

Classified Intel

Automate to Sequence is a longstanding feature of Premiere Pro but one that few people seem to realize exists. It has a few quirks, such as it only works with unnumbered markers that are placed on the Timeline rather than markers placed on the clip in the **Source** panel. However, it is a great timesaver for creating montages, as the only alternative would be to add each clip to the Timeline, one at a time, until you are done. Not so bad for a 30-second montage, but somewhat more arduous for a 3 or 4 minute venture using 40 or 50 images and video clips.

Fine-tuning the edit

You've now reached the stage where you need to make some important creative decisions about the timing of each edit point, known as edit **decision points**. A good montage, as has been said earlier in this project, is all about timing, and to complete this task, you will use the trim tool and the speed/duration tool to fine-tune your rough running order into something a little more polished. You will also make use of the shortcut keys *J*, *K*, and *L* that you have used in previous tasks.

Engage Thrusters

Using the Timeline, you will fine-tune your rough assembly edit:

1. Select the Timeline by pressing *Shift + 3* on the keyboard.

2. Play back the sequence by hitting the *L* key. Play the sequence back several times to get a feel for the timing; ignore any gaps in the playback at this point in the task. Once you have an idea of how you want to improve your edit, stop the play back by hitting the *K* key and move onto the next step.

3. You will have probably spotted gaps in the playback shown as a black screen. This is caused by the duration of a clip being insufficient to fill the gap between the beat markers. First of all, find a place where both files on either side of the gap are image files.

4. Place the Timeline indicator over the clip on the left-hand side, and then click on that clip. Open the **trim editor** by hitting *T* on the Keyboard and use *Ctrl* + right arrow (Windows) or *command* + right arrow (Mac) to expand the duration of the image up the Timeline by one frame at a time until it hits up against the next clip in the running order. Use *Shift + Ctrl* + right arrow (Windows), or *Shift + command* + right arrow arrow (Mac) to jump five frames at a time up the Timeline.

When syncing clips to the beat markers, it's likely that you will want to trim a clip towards the next marker rather than trimming the next clip away from a marker. Doing the latter will probably place your cuts badly out of sync with the music.

5. Curing the gaps caused by video subclips is not as simple because, as mentioned earlier in this project, video subclips have a definitive length that lack sufficient media handles, and they cannot be altered in the same way you altered the images in the last steps. However, it can be done using other tools. First, identify a gap that has a video file on the left-hand side of that gap.

6. Click on the clip to the left-hand side of the gap, then select the **rate stretch tool** by pressing *X* on the keyboard. Place the Timeline indicator over the end of the video clip, and it will appear as a red bracket with left and right facing arrows.

7. With the mouse button held down, drag the clip up the Timeline until it hits up against the next clip.

When you've finished with the **Rate Stretch** tool, don't forget to return the mouse pointer to the **Selection** tool by pressing *V* on the keyboard.

Be careful when using the **Rate Stretch** tool, as extending a clip too far will cause it to slow down with noticeable jerkiness during playback. This often stands out and will make your edit look terrible. Short stretches should be fine, but check the playback carefully.

8. If you don't want to alter the speed of a clip, then you can re-edit the subclip's overall duration (thus giving it sufficient media handles for the transition to work with) by selecting a subclip in the **Project** panel (not on the Timeline, that won't work) and pressing *Shift + 0* on the keyboard to open the **Edit Subclip** window.

The previous instruction will only work if you have added the relevant keyboard shortcut as detailed in the *Subclips tame video clips, Prepare for Lift Off* section.

9. Place the cursor under the **End:** field value, so that it appears as a double-headed cursor, and drag it to the right-hand side to extend the duration of that subclip. Press *Enter* to close this window.

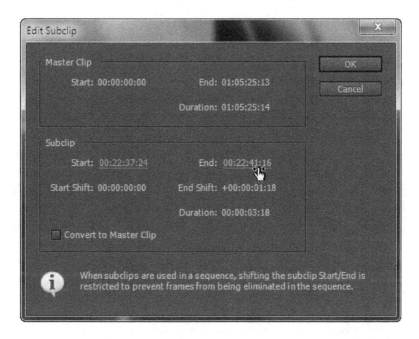

10. Press *Shift + 3* to return the focus to the Timeline, and click on the clip to select it. Make sure the Timeline indicator is over the gap, and then press *T* to open the trim editor.

11. Now use *Ctrl* + right arrow (Windows) or *command* + right arrow (Mac) to expand the duration of the video clip up the timeline one frame at a time until it hits up against the next clip in the running order. Use *Shift + Ctrl* + right arrow (Windows) or *Shift + command*+ right arrow (Mac) to jump five frames at a time up the Timeline.

12. Repeat the various techniques listed earlier to close all the gaps on the Timeline.

 If there is a small flicker of black every now and again, it's likely you have a gap of just a frame or two. Zoom in on the Timeline by pressing the + (plus) key on the main keyboard area (not the number pad area) to catch these gaps, and close them down using the methods detailed in this task.

13. If after playback you can see some poor timing, for example, the marker you placed earlier in this project is not quite on the beat, or you would prefer the cut to be a few frames before the beat, then you can alter this simply using the **Trim** tool. First identify a clip on the Timeline you want to alter.

14. Use the + (plus) key on the keyboard to zoom in on that part of the Timeline.

15. Move the Timeline indicator to exactly where you want the new edit point to land, and press *M* on the keyboard to create a new marker at this point.

16. Select one of the clips below the marker, and press *T* on the keyboard to open the **Trim** tool.

17. If the new marker is up the Timeline (to the right-hand side of the original edit point), press *Ctrl* + left arrow or *command* + left arrow until the edit point matches the new marker. If the new marker is down the Timeline (to the left-hand side of the original edit point), press *Ctrl* + right arrow or *command* + right arrow until the edit point matches the new marker.

18. Repeat this process with each edit point that needs this type of fine-tuning.

> To move a subclip using the previous method, you will need to add more footage to that subclip as detailed in steps 8 and 9 of this task.

Objective Complete - Mini Debriefing

In this section, you have learned some of the more intermediate techniques for editing the In and Out points of clips on the Timeline. Most important is the use of the **Trim** tool and the use of the arrow keys to control those edit points. Once again you have learnt how to do without the mouse and how to create accurate edit points. We will return to the **Trim** tool later in this book and look into more of its powerful features.

The keyboard shortcuts covered in this task are as follows:

- *T*: This key opens the **Trim** tool
- *Ctrl* + left/right arrow or *command* + left/right arrow: This shortcut alters the duration of a clip 1 frame at a time in the **Trim** tool
- *Shift* + *Ctrl* + left/right arrow (Windows) or *Shift* + *command* + left/right arrow(Mac): This shortcut alters the duration of a clip by five frames at a time in the **Trim** tool
- *Shift* + *0*: This shortcut opens the **subclip editor** (when this has been set by the user)

Classified Intel

Use of the **Rate Stretch** tool, as detailed earlier, effectively creates a slow motion clip on your Timeline or a fast forward clip if used in the other direction. A rate stretch on a video clip creating a playing speed of 75 percent or above is not usually detectable by an audience, so long as there is no audio in that video file. Slower than 75 percent and the effect is more noticeable. Slower than 50 percent and the clip becomes somewhat less watchable.

When using the **Rate Stretch** tool, you will hear a change in the audio; higher pitched when the speed is increased, deeper when the speed is decreased. To cancel out this problem on a clip that has been rate stretched, right-click on the clip and select **Speed/Duration** from the context menu. In the **Clip Speed/Duration** window, select **Maintain Audio Pitch**, and your audio will retain its original speed value. However, if the speed change is extreme, lip synchronization will be completely out, so it's only advised to use this option with speed changes between 75 percent and 99 percent.

Correct aspect ratios

The project should now be looking pretty good with a complete montage on the timeline that moves to the music. However, some areas still need some work. For example, the image files may appear too large, and the jumps between some edit points may be too much of a jar. To solve this, you will use the **Motion** effect (a standard effect pre-loaded onto each clip) to scale the images to the correct aspect ratios and scale to frame size. You will also look at some basic pan and scanning of images to add a little motion to your still life images.

 A good timesaving tip is to use Adobe Bridge CS6 to batch re-size your images before you import them into Premiere Pro CS6. See the Adobe Bridge handbook for further details on how to correct aspect ratios using batch commands.

Engage Thrusters

In this task, you will use various tools to correct mismatched aspect ratios:

1. Depending on which camera was used to take your images, they will either be too small or too large for the aspect ratio used by your video. First of all, locate an image on the Timeline that suffers this problem and click on it to select it.

2. Press *Shift + 5* on the keyboard to open the **Effects** controls for that clip.

3. As with all clips in Premiere Pro CS6, the **Motion** effect is applied to the clip as standard. Click on the actual word **Motion** to select that effect.

4. In the **Program** panel (the panel displaying the Timeline output), reduce the zoom level until you can see the white bounding box that indicates the outer area of the image (you may have to reduce the viewing area in Program Monitor to 10 percent to see the bounding box). See the bottom arrow shown in the following screenshot:

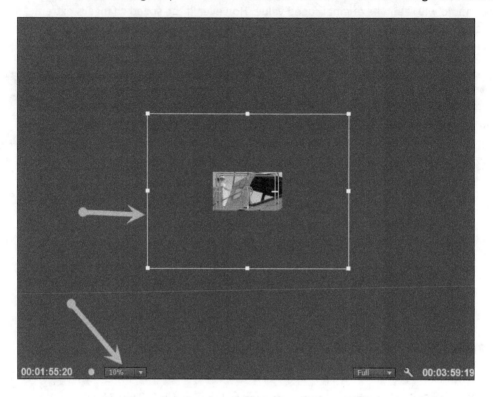

00:01:55:20   10%   Full   00:03:59:19

5. Dial open the **Motion** effect by clicking on the small triangle to the right-hand side of the name tag. Repeat this action to open up the **Scale** slider.

6. Drag the **Scale** slider to the left-hand side to decrease the overall scale of the image. Note that this reduction in scale will happen to both the X and Y dimensions of the image (unless you have accidently deselected the **Uniform Scale** checkbox). Once the scale of the image has been reduced, you can restore the **Program** panel's zoom level to **50%** or more.

7. Your images will probably have a different aspect ratio to the video you are creating, in which case, your image will still be too large on the y axis. Aside from altering the aspect ratio and making anything round into an egg shape, you will be stuck with this. You can, however, alter the position of the picture by placing the cursor under the y axis (the left-most numbers in the **Position** field) until you see a double-headed arrow. With the mouse button held down, drag left-hand side or right-hand side to move the image up or down.

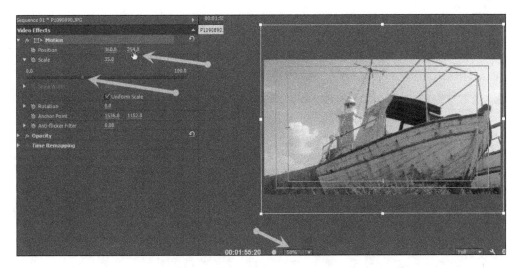

 If you must absolutely see everything in the image, and you are prepared to put up with black bars to the left-hand side and right-hand side of the picture in question (unavoidable with images whose aspect ratio is set to portrait), then simply right-click on the image and select **Scale to Frame Size** from the context menu. If you altered the scale and the position in the motion effect, hit the **Reset** button in the **Motion Effects** panel before or after selecting **Scale to Frame Size**.

8. Repeat steps 1 through to 7 for any other images on the Timeline, or use the **Scale to Frame Size** function. Move onto the next step once you are happy with the results.

9. Now that all your images are being displayed correctly, you can start to add some motion to the images. This is useful for highlighting features in certain images, a sort of zoom effect, or for panning across large panoramic photos that you may have stitched together from several images prior to importing into Premiere Pro CS6. Start by finding a simple image that you would like to add some motion and zoom to as it plays in the sequence. Click on the image you have chosen.

 The following technique works better with images that you have manually scaled down rather than when you have scaled using **Scale to Frame Size**.

10. Place the Timeline indicator anywhere over the chosen image clip, and then move it to the first frame of that clip by pressing the up arrow on the keyboard.

11. In this example, the scale of this image (church bells), has been reduced to **51.6%** at frame 1. At that same frame point, the y axis has been adjusted, so the top of the picture is just outside the top edge of the video-playing area. You may want to set your image to this setting in order to easily follow the next few steps.

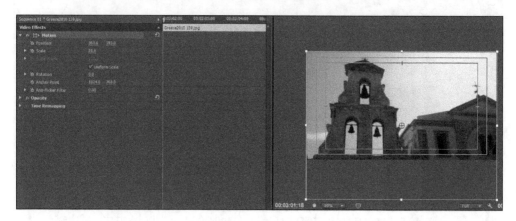

12. Making sure the Timeline indicator is at the start of the clip, toggle animation on for the **Position** and **Scale** values by clicking once on the **Stop Watch** icon for each function. A keyframe has now been created at the start of the clip for **Position** and **Scale**.

13. Move the Timeline indicator to the end of the clip by pressing the down arrow, then pressing the left arrow once, so you can see the last frame of that image. Adjust the **Position** and **Scale** values to suit your needs. In this example, the image has been scaled back to **100%** to create a zoom in effect. The y axis and the x axis were then adjusted to center that zoom on the church bells. This combination creates a zoom and pan effect highlighting the church bells over a smooth 5 second playback period.

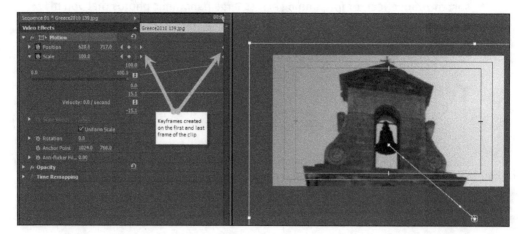

14. Play your version of this back and you may notice the start and end to the zoom are a little sudden. To create a smoother start to the animation, drag a bounding box around the first keyframes in the effects panel with the mouse button held down. This will highlight both keyframes.

15. Right-click on one of the keyframes and select **Temporal Interpolation | Ease Out**.

16. Repeat this for the last keyframes in the effect panel, but select **Temporal Interpolation | Ease In**.

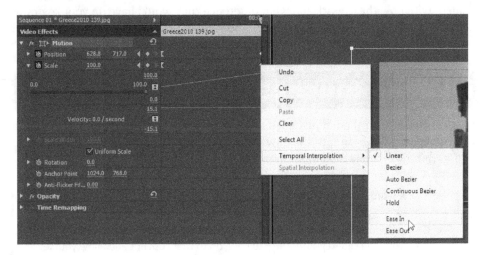

17. Repeat steps 9 through to 16 on each image that you would like to have some kind of motion.

If you have a panoramic photo, perhaps created from several images stitched together, you can create an interesting pan and scan effect using just the **Position** keyframes.

Keyframes are dealt with throughout this book, including the ability to copy and paste keyframes from one media clip to another. This allows you to match up the relative movement and positioning of those clips without having to manually redo it each time.

Objective Complete - Mini Debriefing

You've completed some of your first keyframe techniques in this book. It's a theme you will return to again and again when using Premiere Pro CS6, so it's good to get comfortable with these functions while working on a relatively easy project.

The keyboard shortcuts covered in this task are as follows:

- **Up arrow**: This key moves to the previous edit point (first frame of the selected clip)
- **Down arrow**: This key moves to the next edit point (last frame of the selected clip)

Classified Intel

The options available when right-clicking on a keyframe extend beyond **Ease In** and **Ease Out**. Experiment with how these work and what difference they would have on your keyframe movements by placing an oversized image on the Timeline and adding key frames for pan and zoom. Then, right-click on the keyframes and look at the effect each option gives.

Finishing touches

Your project is nearly finished; it just needs a few final touches, such as some transitions (please, not too many) to smooth the flow of information to your audience. In this section, you will learn how to apply the default transition to your montage.

A word about transitions:

Technically, a straight jump cut, where one clip ends and another starts with no visible transition in place, is a transition—the scene transitions from one clip to another. Try to hang on to that concept and allow yourself to say three times each day; I do not need to add spectacular, tumbling, over-the-top transitions to my movie scenes to make them look good. Although, you might want to think of a shorter version, just so you can get to work on time.

The point I am trying to make is if you watch any movie, outside of extreme comedy genres and a few Spielberg films (Indiana Jones features Saturday Morning sliding transitions), a transition is something that you will rarely see. If you do see one, it will probably be a straight dissolve and there is a good reason for this; it's one of the few transitions that doesn't distract the audience's attention from what they are watching. Adobe has made the dissolve transition the default transition for this reason.

The moral of this story is, use transitions sparingly, even the dissolve, and use other types of transitions only when the genre will support its use.

Engage Thrusters

It's time to add some polish to your project with the selective use of transitions:

1. Find two clips on the Timeline and place the Timeline indicator roughly over the edit point (where the two clips meet on the Timeline).

2. Press *Ctrl + D* or *command + D* on the keyboard to add the default **cross dissolve transition** between these two clips.

[Transitions are normally used for slow moving montages, such as weddings or relaxing holiday videos, or a romantic film. They can also be used in action films but usually only when the montage is set to a slow beat music tempo, and the scenes are being shown in slow motion.]

3. The transition will place itself between the clips (or to one side if one of the clips is a subclip). To alter this, double-click on the actual transition on the Timeline, and this will open the **Cross Dissolve Effect Controls** panel. Change the alignment to **Center at Cut**, **Start at Cut**, or **End at Cut**.

4. To alter the default duration of the cross dissolve, place the cursor just under the **Duration** figure until you get a double-headed arrow; drag to the left-hand side to decrease the duration and to the right-hand side to increase the duration.

5. To fine-tune the start or end points of the transition, toggle on **Show Actual Sources**, then drag the sliders until you are satisfied with the results.

6. When adding a transition between a video file and an image, the transition defaults to **End at Cut**. If you change this to **Center at Cut**, the display can show static frames (repeated frames in Adobe Jargon). This is because there isn't enough video on the tail of the clip to dissolve into the next clip. To correct this, open the **Cross Dissolve Effects** panel as described in step 3, then move the Timeline indicator to one side, so you can see the edit decision point of these clips. Change the alignment to **Center at Cut** if you haven't already done that.

7. In the center, you should see a small gray line indicating the physical end of the clip; the section beyond that is the static frame area (repeated frames). Place your cursor over this line, so that it shows as a yellow bracket with a left or right facing arrow.

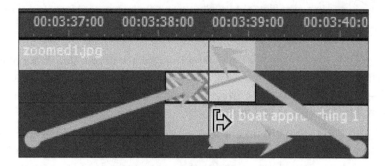

8. With the mouse button held down, drag the tail end of the clip to the right until it reaches the end of the transition. Note that this will move the edit point of this clip a corresponding amount on the Timeline.

9. If you are transitioning between two subclips, you may have to repeat steps 7 and 8 on both tracks in the **Cross Dissolve Effects** panel.

 You can add transitions to multiple clips on the Timeline by dragging a selection around the clips, and then from the drop-down menu, click on **Sequence | Apply Default Transitions to Selection**.

Objective Complete - Mini Debriefing

This task saw the introduction of transitions—a video effect often used and abused by many amateur video makers. Hopefully, through this section, you have learned how to master transitions without letting them master you.

The keyboard shortcuts covered in this task were *Ctrl + D* or *command + D*, which add the default transition to the edit point nearest the Timeline indicator.

Classified Intel

The default transition can be changed to include any of the many (and often for good reasons) unused transitions. Simply open the effects panel by pressing *Shift + 7* on the keyboard, and dial open the video transition folder by clicking on the small triangle. Browse through the transitions until you find one you like (or at least one you can stomach), then right-click on it and select **Set Selected as Default Transition**.

Mission Accomplished

You've now completed the first project in this book and learned some useful organizational skills, the importance of which cannot be understated. The more you organize yourself before you even think about launching Premiere Pro CS6, the less time you'll need to spend on housekeeping the project. And less time spent worrying over where that vital image, music, or video file has hidden itself on your hard drive translates to more time being spent on creativity.

It's a simple formula but often overlooked.

This project also showed you the simple yet powerful technique of taming those huge video files by dividing them into manageable subclips, and you learned how to automate a whole bunch of clips onto the Timeline, automatically aligning themselves to the beat of your chosen music.

You also learned how to correct troublesome keyboard shortcuts on non-U.S. keyboards, and how to add a few useful shortcuts of your own. You finished by adding some transitions to the project and hopefully learnt that when it comes to transitions—less is most definitely more! Keyframing and the trim tool also made brief appearances in this project. Don't worry, we'll go into these tools in more depth in later projects.

Overall, you should have found this project to be an easygoing introduction into some of the more complex functions that Premiere Pro CS6 has to offer. That's a deliberate attempt to ease you into the more advanced workflows that you will begin to discover in the coming projects.

You Ready To Go Gung HO?
A Hotshot Challenge

It's a common saying that films are never finished, they're just abandoned. This points to the fact that whenever a group of creative people get together, they will always want to adjust, trim, and optimize the project in one way or another, often to the point where it's no longer watchable. Films generally only make it to release because of real-life problems like unavoidable deadlines! That being said, this project is just the start of what's possible, and it's time now to take the Gung Ho challenge:

- ▶ Go back over your montage and ask yourself if all of the cuts are really hitting the beat. If not, zoom right in on the Timeline and make macro adjustments to the timing.

- ▶ Look again at the transitions. Do they need to be longer, shorter, or there at all?

- ▶ If you have placed movement on your image files using the **Effects Motion** control, alter the keyframing, **Ease In** and **Ease Out** controls, to see what effect they have, and try some of the other interpolation settings.

- ▶ Last of all, save this project in a safe place as some of the techniques you will learn in later projects, such as **Nested Sequences**, **Motion Titles**, and **Export Options** can and should be added and used with this.

Project 2

Cutting a Short Film without Getting Stung

Premiere Pro CS6 has been designed and refined over the years to make video editing easier, but that doesn't make editing a simple task; you still need a certain degree of know-how and talent to make it happen. Think of how a Formula One car is designed by the best car technicians on the planet, yet only a handful of people in the world can drive one to perfection. Fortunately, making a film with Premiere Pro CS6 isn't as hard as winning a Formula One race, but it still requires preparation, practice, and a little of the aforementioned talent.

You also need to understand the Premiere Pro CS6 editing workflows. Get that under your belt and you are ready to tackle any film project, whether long or short.

Mission Briefing

The primary objective of this project is for you to learn the various workflows Premiere Pro CS6 offers for editing a short film. The aim is to take the clips supplied with this book and create a scene that tells a story lasting around 60 seconds. Once again, as in *Project 1, Creating a Movie Montage – the Easy Way,* you will be encouraged to use as many keyboard shortcuts as possible in order to create a frame-accurate Timeline similar to the following screenshot:

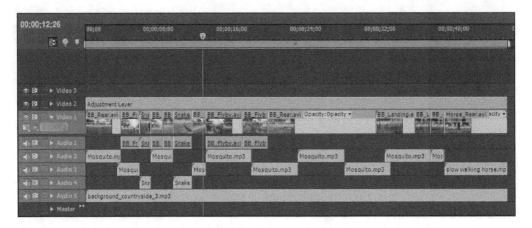

Why Is It Awesome?

Project 2 will build on skills learned in *Project 1*, allowing you to practice those keyboard shortcut workflows, and of course, teach you some new workflows along the way. To do this you'll edit footage specifically produced for this project, creating the opening scene of a short animated film. You'll learn how to cut, trim, edit, and reuse clips in a variety of different ways. You'll also look deeper into controlling the duration of those clips, how to add some basic sound effects, and a color gradient 'movie look' using Premiere Pro's new adjustment layer feature. Don't worry if this means nothing to you yet; all will be explained.

Yes, there will be a certain amount of repetition in this project, but that's deliberate and a clear attempt to hammer home skills and workflows in order for that knowledge to stay with you. Remember: learning a new technique is easy, but remembering a technique is another matter. Project 2 will enhance your learning by repeating workflows from *Project 1* but in a totally different arena; that of making a short film.

The sample footage for this project was produced using a 3D animation program called iClone5 (www.reallusion.com). One of the great things about iClone5 is the ability to add a large number of 'camera' views to any scene, and then render out each camera as a separate viewpoint. The next screenshot shows two of the cameras you will be working with in this project (BB_Rear and Snake_front).

Your Hotshot Objectives

- ▶ Creating a story
- ▶ Three-point edits
- ▶ Combining three- and four-point edits
- ▶ Refining with the Trim tool
- ▶ Correcting various problems
- ▶ Making pictures sing
- ▶ Adding a movie look

Mission Checklist

Before you start this project, there are a number of preparations you need to make. Firstly, open your designated video drive and access the Hotshots folder you created in *Project 1*. Here you should find a folder called Project 1. Create a new folder next to it called Project 2 and inside that new folder, create three folders called Video, Images, and Audio.

With the new folder areas created, visit the Packt Publishing website (www.packtpub.com) and access the companion page for this book (search for Hotshots and then select this Premiere Pro book). Once you are on the correct page, click on the **Support** tab and follow the on-screen instructions for downloading code. The file you will receive is a little on the large size (well it is a video!) but the resulting ZIP file will contain not only the material needed for this project, but also other projects in this book.

Strictly speaking you don't need the Images folder for this project, but it's a good practice to create all three of these folders in an area of your designated video hard drive each time you start a new project.

Video content

Once you have downloaded the ZIP file, extract the contents to a local hard drive. Access the folder containing the extracted content and you should find inside a folder called Project 2. Copy the contents of this folder to the Video folder you created according to what we mentioned in the first paragraph of this section. There are eight video files in total.

When downloading the file, make sure you pick **Save** or **Save As...**, and not **Open** (some browsers default to **Open** for the ZIP files).

Sound effects

For this project you will also need a few sound effects. Sound effects are freely available from the Internet and of course from the world around you. Most smartphones have the ability to record sounds, so make use of this wherever possible to build up your own audio library, not only for this project, but any future ones you might not have considered doing yet. Something to think about—the next time you are standing on a railway station and see a train about to pass at speed, get out that smartphone, stand a safe distance away, and record the audio. Bird song, distant sirens, the polite applause of a crowd; are all there for you to record.

The following sounds are recommended for this project – countryside ambience (birds, wind through trees, that sort of thing, but a gentle summer's day version); an insect buzzing along in flight; a snake hissing (not recommended for self-recording!); pigeon wings flapping; a frog croaking; and a horse walking slowly past (hooves on mud). Once you have gathered these sounds from the Internet or from real-life (apart from the snake!) copy and paste them all into the Audio folder you created inside the Project 2 folder inside Hotshots on your designated video drive.

Many great sound effects can be accessed from SoundDogs.com. Here you can search for the sound you need and then download a 'preview' copy to try inside Premiere Pro CS6 (right-click on the MP3 link, and choose **Save** or **Save Link As...**). These previews are presented at a low (gritty) resolution rate; however, you can buy the full-sound resolution by following the on-screen links. For the sake of learning the core skills in this project, the preview quality should work just fine.

Creating a story

You'll start Project 2 in the same way you started *Project 1*, by making sure everything you need is in the right place, then setting up Premiere Pro CS6 to edit those assets into a short film. However, in this project you will be able to save some time by using the template you created in *Project 1*. You will then use a new feature in Premiere Pro CS6 to work out what sort of clips you are using and to automatically set the timeline sequence to match those clips.

Once this preparation is out of the way, you will quickly use the tools and shortcuts learned in *Project 1* to create a simple story from three of the clips in your Video folder.

Prepare for Lift Off

Once you have completed all the preparations detailed earlier in this chapter, you are ready to go. Launch Premiere Pro CS6 in the usual way and then proceed to the next part of this task.

Engage Thrusters

Set up your project and lay the foundations for your story. Perform the following steps to do so:

1. Once Premiere Pro CS6 has finished launching, the **Recent Projects** splash screen appears. From here, select **Hotshots Template** and select **Montage** from the list.

2. When the project has finished loading, select **File | Save As...** and save this file as **Short Film Project** in the Hotshots folder. If a sequence was automatically created, close it now by clicking on the small X next to the name of the sequence. You should now be looking at a **Project** panel containing three empty bins – **Audio**, **Video**, and **Images**.

If during the last project you used the created template instead of saving the file as a separate project, delete the content of bins and close any open sequences. Do this after you have saved the project in step 2! Once you have done this, create a new sequence by using *Ctrl + N* or *command + N*.

3. Make sure the workspace you created in *Project 1* is active by going to **Window** | **Workspace** (Windows) or **Premiere** | **Workspace** (Mac) and then select the **Editing Optimized** workspace you created in *Project 1*.

 You can also try using the keyboard shortcut assigned to your workspace by Premiere Pro in *Project 1* (hint – if you saved the workspace with the suggested name **Editing Optimized**, it will probably have been assigned the shortcut *Alt + Shift + 5* (WinOS) or *option + Shift + 5* (MacOS)).

4. Select the **Project** panel by using the keyboard shortcut *Shift + 1*. Selection will be confirmed by displaying a gold border around the **Project** panel.

5. Use *Ctrl* + double-click or *command* + double-click to open the Video bin without creating a separate window.

6. Import all eight video files in the Video folder inside Project 2 by pressing *Ctrl + I* or *command + I* to open the **Import** window and browse to the location of the Project 2 folder.

7. Press *Ctrl + N* or *command + N* to create a new sequence. Pick any settings at random; you will correct this in the next step.

8. Rename the sequence **Short Film BB** by right-clicking on the sequence in the **Project** panel and selecting **Rename** from the context menu. Press *Enter* and then *Esc* to exit the Rename function.

9. Drag-and-drop any video clip from the Video bin to the Timeline. Premiere Pro CS6 should now tell you this clip does not match the sequence settings and prompt you to allow the program to match them up. Click on **Change sequence settings** and allow the match to happen.

10. Click on the clip in the Timeline and press *Delete* on the keyboard to remove it from the Timeline.

Matching a sequence to the properties of a clip is a new feature in Premiere Pro CS6 and using it will greatly reduce unnecessary render times. You can also access this function by closing any open sequences, right-clicking on any clip in a bin, and selecting **New Sequence from Clip**. Whichever method you use, avoid unnecessary rendering times by making sure the clip you use matches the majority of the other clips intended for use in your project.

Right-clicking on a clip in a bin and selecting **Insert** or **Overwrite** will not show **Clips Mismatch Warning**. The same is true for **Create Sequence from Clip** and **Automate to Timeline**.

11. With the Timeline set correctly, press *Shift + 1* to activate the **Project** panel, and then use the keyboard shortcut *Shift* + accent (next to the number *1* key and above the *Tab* key) to maximize the **Project** panel. Switch to **Icon View** if it is not already displayed using the **Icon View** switch in the lower-left corner of the **Project** panel. Expand the size of the icons to something you are comfortable working with, using the slider next to the **Icon View** switch.

If the *Shift* + accent key doesn't work for you, see *Project 1* (the *Classified Intel* section of *Music markers matter*) for details on making this work with non-US keyboards.

12. You will now create the basic elements of a short story for this scene using only three of the available clips in the `Video` bin. The story will be insect flies along; insect lands; horse treads on insect. To describe this in video, use the mouse to move the **BB_Rear.avi** file to the upper-left corner of the **Project** panel. Place the **BB_Landing.avi** file next to it. Finally, place **Horse_Rear.avi** next to that file.

13. With the *Ctrl* or *command* key held down, click on each of these three files so that only **BB_Rear.avi**, **BB_Landing.avi**, and **Horse_Rear.avi** are selected.

14. Minimize the **Project** panel by pressing accent on the keyboard.

15. Ensure the Timeline indicator is at the start of the Timeline. Then click on the **Automate to Sequence** icon at the bottom of the **Project** panel.

16. When the **Automate To Sequence** window appears, change **Ordering** to **Sort Order** and leave **Placement** at the default, then uncheck both the **Apply Default Audio Transition** and **Apply Default Video Transition** checkboxes. Click on **OK** or press *Enter* on the keyboard to complete this action.

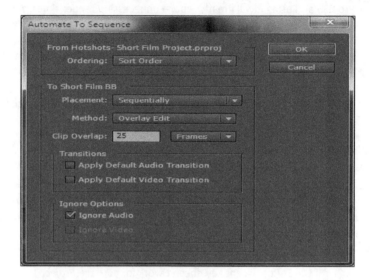

17. Press *Shift + 3* to select the **Timeline** panel, then press \ (backslash) to expand the Timeline to show all the clips present. You should end this section with a sequence that looks something like the following screenshot:

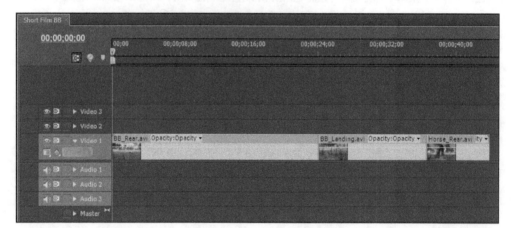

Objective Complete - Mini Debriefing

In this task you have reused the core skills learned in *Project 1* to uncover a new feature in Premiere Pro CS6: automatically matching Timeline properties to the properties of those clips you want to use. You have also sent three clips from the **Project** panel to the Timeline in an order that has created the base line for a short scene. The clips when played back create a beginning, middle, and end to this scene, which are the required elements of a good story.

Play the scene back and you'll find it does indeed tell a story, but it's a simple one that needs embellishment and it has a few problems that will need to be edited away! Move on to the next section to begin doing just that.

Keyboard shortcuts covered in this task are as follows:

- ▸ *Shift* + accent: Maximize the active panel
- ▸ *Ctrl* or *command* + double-click: Open a bin without creating a separate **Project** panel
- ▸ *Ctrl* or *command* + *N*: Create a new sequence
- ▸ *Ctrl* or *command* + \ (backslash): Create a new bin in the **Project** panel
- ▸ *Ctrl* or *command* + *I*: Open the **Import** window

Classified Intel

Although you reused the **Automate to Timeline** function, as you did in *Project 1*, this time you placed the clips onto the Timeline without using markers. This particular workflow is often ignored by Premiere Pro users, and yet it is a quick and effective method of creating a rough assembly of your storyline. When you start to use Premiere Pro CS6 to create your own projects, make sure this is one lesson you don't forget or ignore in a hurry.

Three-point edits

The Timeline is now set to tell a story: the journey of a small insect through the glade where it lives. The insect encounters a snake, a frog (it appears very quickly at around **09;09**), then lands on an ear of corn. Sadly here the insect is trod on by a horse. Such is life. The real problem is some of these events occur too fast to make any impact. In this section you will attempt to correct that lack of impact by using material from the other clips in the Video bin. They will provide alternative camera angles, allowing the viewer to better understand the details of the story. You'll do this by performing a three-point edit, one of the more commonly used editing techniques, and one that works particularly well with keyboard shortcuts.

Engage Thrusters

Use three-point edits to add additional clips to your Timeline. Perform the following steps to do so:

1. Press *Shift + 1* to activate the **Project** panel and use *Ctrl + A* or *command + A* to select all the clips in the Video bin.

2. Right-click on any selected clip and choose **Open in Source Monitor** from the context menu. All of the available clips are now stored in the Source Monitor and available from the selection menu.

> Loading all your clips into the Source Monitor like this will now allow you to access any clip in the Video bin without having to return to the **Project** panel; a handy timesaver.

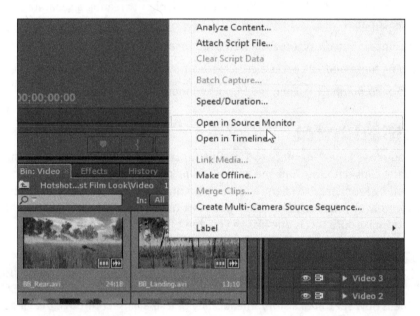

3. You are now ready to begin some editing corrections. On the Timeline, the **BB_Rear.avi** clip is somewhat repetitive. Break the clip up by overwriting part of **BB_Rear.avi** with an alternative camera view. To do this load **BB_Front.avi** into the Source Monitor by clicking on the **Selection** menu in the upper-left corner of the Source Monitor and selecting **BB_Front.avi** from the list, as shown in the following screenshot:

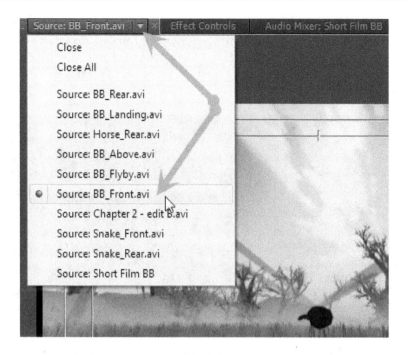

4. With **BB_Front.avi** selected in the Source Monitor, press and hold down the *K* key and with the *K* key still held down, press and hold down the *L* key to move the Source Monitor indicator forward at around 8 frames per second. Continue until you reach the **02;01** point (two seconds and one frame). If you miss this point, hold down the *K* key and use the *J* key to move backward through the clip.

 If you hold down the *K* key and then tap the *J* or *L* key, you will move only one frame backward or forward.

5. When you have the Source Monitor indicator correctly positioned, press *I* (the *I* key between *U* and *O*) on the keyboard to select this as the In point (point 1) for this clip.

6. Hold down the *K* key again and use the *L* key to find the **04;04** point (four seconds and four frames) in this clip.

7. Press *O* (the *O* key) on the keyboard to set this as the Out point (point 2) for this clip.

8. You have selected two of the three points needed for a three-point edit. The third point is where you want the clip to appear on the Timeline. To set this click on the figures in the lower-left corner of the Program Monitor and enter **03;27** to place the Timeline cursor at that point. Press *I* on the keyboard to set this as the Timeline In point (point 3).

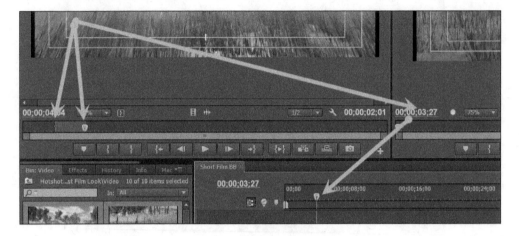

9. Press *Shift + 2* to make the Source Monitor the active panel, then press '.' (period) on the keyboard to send the clip to the Timeline in the **Overwrite** mode. This completes your first three-point edit.

> Pressing '.' (period) on the keyboard instructs Premiere Pro to send the clip from the Source Monitor to the Timeline in the **Overwrite** mode. This does exactly what it says; the new clip will overwrite any frames already on the Timeline, starting at the third point you defined in step 8 and lasting for the duration of the new clip set by you in steps 5 and 7.

10. Now you understand how a three-point edit works, repeat steps 3 to 9 but this time use **Snake_Front.avi** as the source clip. Try it first by performing the suggested parameters given next and send the clip to the Timeline again with the '.' (period) key in order to overwrite the material that is already on the Timeline:

    i.   Select **Snake_Front.avi** in the Source Monitor.

    ii. Set an In point at **00;00**.

    iii. Set an Out point at **01;06**.

    iv. Press *Shift + 3*.

    v.   Set Timeline In point at **06;01**.

    vi. Press *Shift + 2*.

    vii. Send the clip using **Overwrite** (.).

11. To further embellish the confrontation between blue bottle and snake, you will now add two more clips to the Timeline. However, this time you will use **Insert** instead of **Overwrite**. To do this repeat steps 3 to 9 using the suggested clip parameters given next, but use the ',' (comma) key when sending the clips to the Timeline. Note that adding **BB_Rear.avi** is just a preparation step for the next task and demonstrates Premiere Pro's ability to use any clip it wants in multiple instances on the Timeline.

    i.   Select **BB_Front.avi** in the Source Monitor.

    ii. Set an In point at **04;11**.

    iii. Set an Out point at **05;19**.

    iv. Press *Shift + 3*.

    v.   Set Timeline In point at **07;08**.

    vi. Press *Shift + 2*.

    vii. Send the clip using **Insert** (,).

    viii. Select **BB_Rear.avi** in the Source Monitor.

    ix. Set an In point at **05;05**.

    x.   Set an Out point at **06;09**.

    xi. Press *Shift + 3*.

    xii. Set Timeline In point at **08;09**.

    xiii. Press *Shift + 2*.

    xiv. Send the clip using **Insert** (,).

Pressing ',' (comma) on the keyboard instructs Premiere Pro to send the clip from the Source Monitor to the Timeline in the **Insert** mode. This differs from the **Overwrite** mode in that **Insert** shoved any clips to the right of the third point (on the Timeline) up the Timeline, preserving any frames already present. Be careful when using this function, as it can cause audio sync problems.

12. Review and save your project before moving onto the next section. It should look something like the next screenshot. If you have gone wrong somewhere, hit *Ctrl + Z* or *command + Z* to undo your mistake. Save your project before moving on to the next section.

Objective Complete - Mini Debriefing

In this task you've learned the ins-and-outs of a three-point edit (pun intended). This technique is the staple diet of video editors, who spend much of their time creating a rough assembly on the Timeline using multiple camera angles.

You've also covered **Insert**, where the clip is inserted to the Timeline and all the other clips to the right move up to make room; and **Overwrite**, which replaces the frames already on the Timeline with no movement of the existing Timeline clips. You will revisit these functions in later projects.

Keyboard shortcuts covered in this task are as follows:

▸ '.' (period): Overwrite clips on the Timeline with a clip from the Source Monitor

▸ ',' (comma): Insert a clip on the Timeline from the Source Monitor

▸ *I*: Set an In point

▸ *O*: Set an Out point

▸ *K + L*: Move forward at 8 frames per second (when held down)

▸ *K + J*: Move backward at 8 frames per second (when held down)

▸ *Shift + 2*: Set the **Project** panel as active

▸ *Shift + 3*: Set the Timeline as active

Classified Intel

The positioning of the keys you have used; *J*, *K*, *L*, *I*, *O*, '.' (period), and ',' (comma) are all easily accessible under your right hand, allowing you to efficiently complete three-point edits! Your left hand should cover *Ctrl + Z* or *command + Z* to quickly erase any mistakes and *Shift + 1*, *2*, or *3* to switch between the various panels. With practice you should be able to create frame-accurate edits with very little use of the mouse.

If you are having a problem remembering which key does what when using the *J*, *K*, *L* combination, try to think of the *K* key as being a brake that slows down the *L* or the *J* key. Keep your finger on the brake (*K*), and the move forward (*L*) or backward (*J*) will be slower.

Combining three- and four-point edits

In the previous task you performed various three-point edits in order to embellish the conflict between the insect and the snake. However, the insect's escape from the snake is a little sudden, so you will add a portion of another snake clip (**Snake_Rear.avi**), but using a four-point edit in order to control the new clip's duration on the Timeline.

Four-point edits are used to speed up or slow down a clip so that it can fit into a user-defined space on the Timeline. In this case you will use it to slow the content of a clip down by 50 percent, but keep the continuity of the action constant.

After the insect escapes it is also attacked by a frog; however, this is so quick the viewer will never have a chance to see it. To correct this you will combine three- and four-point edits to slow down part of this new clip (**BB_Flyby.avi**) to make the frog's attack a more prominent feature of the scene.

Engage Thrusters

Use the four-point edit technique to add clips to your sequence, changing the speed at the same time. Perform the following steps to do so:

1. In the Source Monitor select the **Snake_Rear.avi** clip.

2. You want to insert part of this clip into the Timeline, but at 50 percent of its actual playback speed in order for the clip to be visible for twice as long. To do this, first find and define the In point (point 1) and the Out point (point 2) for the snake clip using the skills learned earlier in this project. The suggested points are as follows:

   ❑ Set an In point at **02;00**

   ❑ Set an Out point at **03;00**

3. Press *Shift + 3* to make the Timeline active, then press the up or down arrow to send the Timeline indicator to the start of the last **BB_Rear.avi** clip on the Timeline (hint – if you have followed the previous instructions, this should be around **09;14** on the Timeline counter).

4. Define point 3 of this four-point edit by pressing *I* on the keyboard to set an In point at this location on the Timeline.

5. Move the Timeline indicator to **11;19** using any of the methods you have learned so far. Press *O* on the keyboard to set an Out point on the Timeline, and create point 4 of your four-point edit.

6. Press *Shift + 2* to activate the Source Monitor and press the ',' (comma) key to insert **Snake_Rear.avi** onto the Timeline between the two points defined in steps 4 and 5.

7. Because you have defined (in the Source Monitor) a clip that is 1 second in duration and then you defined a gap on the Timeline that is just over 2 seconds in duration, the **Fit Clip** dialog window will appear. Select **Change Clip Speed (Fit to Fill)** and press *Enter* or click on **OK**. The clip will now appear on the Timeline at less than 50 percent of its true speed.

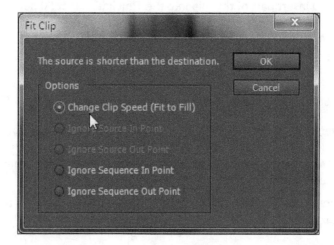

Working out speed increases is simple enough. Here you defined the In and Out points to create a clip of 1 second in duration. On the Timeline you defined the In and Out points of 2 seconds in duration. This creates on the Timeline a space that is twice the size of the clip's set duration, meaning Premiere Pro needs to slow the clip down to slightly less than 50 percent in order for it to obey the rules of a four-point edit.

8. Now you need to address the frog problem! On playback the frog attacks the insect with such speed that it cannot be clearly seen. To remedy this you will add another camera view, but this time adding half the clip as a four-point edit, then the remaining half as a three-point edit. This will create a sequence that shows a seamless slowdown and return to normal speed. To begin, select the **BB_Flyby.avi** clip in the Source Monitor.

9. Define a four-point edit for this clip using any of the methods covered so far. Use the following suggested parameters:

    i.   Set an In point at **03;15**.

    ii.   Set an Out point at **05;15**.

    iii.   Press _Shift + 3_.

    iv.   Set Timeline In point at **13;05**.

    v.   Set Timeline Out point at **17;05**.

    vi.   Press _Shift + 2_.

    vii.   Send the clip using **Overwrite** (.).

    viii.   Select **Change Clip Speed (Fit to Fill)**.

10. Now you need to insert the second half of the clip as a three-point edit. Press _Shift + 2_ to return to the Source Monitor and confirm that the **BB_Flyby.avi** clip is still selected.

11. Define a new set of In and Out points using the following suggested parameters:

    i.   Set an In point at **05;16**.

    ii.   Set an Out point at **08;06**.

    iii.   Press _Shift + 3_.

    iv.   Set Timeline In point at **17;06**.

    v.   Press _Shift + 2_.

    vi.   Send the clip using **Insert** (,).

12. At the end of this task, the middle section of your Timeline should look something like the next screenshot. Use **Undo** if it does not. Save your project when everything is correct and then move on to the next section.

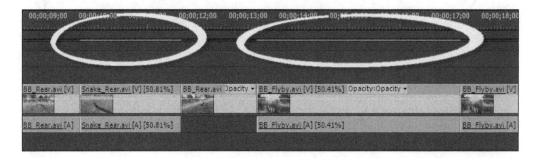

 When you add a four-point edit to your Timeline, a small red line appears above those sections of the Timeline that contain time-stretched clips. This means Premiere Pro CS6 must render these sections of the Timeline before export can be completed. It also means you might see some dropped frames when playing that section of the Timeline back. Whenever you need to render these red areas of the Timeline, simply press *Shift + 3* to set the Timeline as active, then press *Enter* on the keyboard.

Objective Complete - Mini Debriefing

In this section you have discovered how to create a four-point edit from the keyboard and then you went one step further by combining a four-point edit with a three-point edit to show the clip slowing down, then resuming at normal speed. Both types of edits are invaluable to a video editor and it would be in your interest to learn these skills and use them with the keyboard in order to obtain a frame-accurate three- or four-point edit.

Classified Intel

A decrease in speed caused by the four-point edit is often used in video editing to force clips to last a fraction of a second longer, but to fit in with the context of the scene. Clips that are slowed between 75 percent and 99 percent will usually be indistinguishable from 100 percent playback speed. The classic example is perhaps a documentary where you as the editor are supplied with a commentary track that lasts a few seconds longer than the actual video clip. Getting the voiceover re-recorded could be costly; however, just slowing down a clip by a few percent can mask the problem and allow the voice to match the duration of the clip. Only you will know! You will see more of this technique in *Project 3, Protect the Innocent – Interview Edit Techniques*!

Refining with the Trim tool

The scene is now looking a lot better than the original 'story' you created in the first task. It's also about 10 seconds longer. The aim of this project is to create a 60-second scene, the introduction perhaps to a much longer film, so you still have around 10 seconds of action to play with.

In this task you will fill up that time by reclaiming some footage lost during the overwrite of the **BB_Flyby.avi** clip. You'll accomplish this with the Trim tool, and then go on to use the same tool to tidy up some of the other clips on the Timeline. Once again, you will attempt to do as much of this as possible using just the keyboard.

Engage Thrusters

Use the Trim tool to tidy up your edit points. Perform the following steps to do so:

1. Press *Shift + 3* to make the Timeline active, and use the up or down arrow to place the Timeline indicator over the edit point between the **BB_Flyby.avi** and **BB_Rear. avi** clips (hint – this should be around the **19;27** mark).

2. With the Timeline indicator over the edit point between the **BB_Flyby.avi** and **BB_Rear.avi** clips, press *T* on the keyboard to open the Trim tool.

3. By default both the outgoing clip (**BB_Flyby.avi**) and the incoming clip (**BB_Rear.avi**) will be selected; this is signified by a blue border that runs over the top of both clips (as seen in the preceding screenshot). Cycle through the trim modes by pressing *Shift + T* until the right panel (the incoming clip) has a blue border above and below it, the left panel (the outgoing clip) has none, and the bracket on the Timeline is yellow.

4. Hold down the *K* key (and don't release it until you read step 5) and press the *J* key while still in the trim mode. The blue bottle will now fly backwards. Stop by releasing the *J* key on the keyboard (but not the *K* key) when the screen counter in the right-hand side panel reaches **09;20**.

Use the *L* key to move forward if you miss that point (hint – holding down *K + L* or *J* will move forward or backward at 8 frames per second. You can also tap the *L* or *J* key to move one frame at a time in either direction).

If you press *K + J* to move back and if you get the message **Trim Blocked on Video 1**, then you probably have the wrong trim mode selected. Check that the bracket is yellow; if not, use *Shift + T* to cycle through the trim modes.

5. Now release the *K* key. Once you release that key, the clip on the Timeline will expand, moving any clips to the right up the Timeline. This is known as a **ripple edit**.

Pressing *Shift + K* while in the Trim tool will cause Premiere Pro to exit the trim mode and play a section of the Timeline back from a few seconds before the current position of the Timeline indicator. If this keeps causing you problems, remember you can also use the left and right arrow keys.

6. It's time to move on now to the next trim job. Deselect the current trim by clicking anywhere on the Timeline. Then place the cursor over the edit point between **BB_Rear.avi** and **BB_Landing.avi** (hint – at **33;23**). Now press *Shift + K* on the keyboard to show how this edit plays back.

 Depending on the position of the cursor, you may need to press *Shift + K* twice to see the playback. This can also happen the second time you try to press *Shift + K*.

7. Note at the end of **BB_Rear.avi** that the insect begins its landing approach and the camera follows the creature as it dips down. However, in the next clip, **BB_Landing. avi** the insect is flying at the same level as it approaches the grass. To correct this continuity error press *T* on the keyboard to open the Trim tool.

 If the Trim tool opens to the edit point you worked on in step 4, then click anywhere on the Timeline to deselect that edit point and reposition the Timeline cursor again over the edit point described in step 6.

8. Press *Shift + T* to cycle the trim mode to show the left-hand side panel (the outgoing clip) as the active one with a top/bottom blue border and a yellow bracket shown on the left-hand side clip on the Timeline (hint – you may have to go past the red bracket to reach the yellow bracket).

9. Hold down the *K* key and don't release it until instructed, then use the *J* key to move the Out point of the **BB_Rear.avi** clip backwards. Stop when the insect reaches level flight at about **21;00**. Now release the *K* key and note the clip retracts and the other clips follow it down the Timeline.

10. Perform one last trim edit before leaving this section. Begin by clicking anywhere on the Timeline to deselect the last edit point. Then place the Timeline indicator over the edit point between **BB_Landing.avi** and **Horse_Rear.avi**. Press *Shift + K* to playback this edit point.

11. About 10 frames into **Horse_Rear.avi**, the camera begins an upward crane shot and this should really happen from the start of that clip. Worse still, the insect is shown dead on the ground for too long, creating a 'dead' frame space where nothing is happening. Correct this by opening the Trim tool (hint – press *T*).

12. Use the techniques learned before in this chapter to trim **BB_Landing.avi** back to around **7;08** (hint – with the Trim tool open, press *Shift + T* to cycle to the left blue border and left yellow bracket; reduce using *K + J*).

13. Repeat to trim the start of the **Horse_Rear.avi** clip to around **00;12** (hint – with the Trim tool open, press *Shift + T* to cycle to the right blue border and right yellow bracket; reduce using *K + L*).

14. Save your project when you have completed any additional trims you might want to make. Don't forget to render any areas that display as a red line (hint – press *Enter* when Timeline is active).

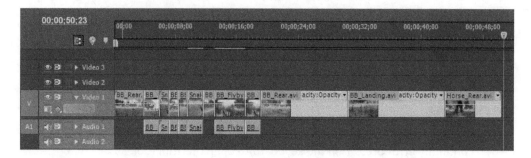

Objective Complete - Mini Debriefing

Once again you have covered skills vital to the work of a video editor. Here you looked at the Trim tool and performed a ripple edit. Understanding how these work will save you an enormous amount of time when you come to work on your own, perhaps more complex, projects.

Keyboard shortcuts covered in this task are as follows:

▶ *T*: Open the Trim tool

▶ *Shift + T*: Cycle through the trim modes

▶ *K + J or L*: Trim backward or forward

Classified Intel

With the Trim tool open, you can press the Spacebar to start a looped playback centered on the edit point. While the playback performs this loop, you can still use the ripple and rolling edit functions covered in this task to trim the clip(s).

Correcting various problems

Playback the scene now and you can see it has really started to come together, but there are still some minor problems that need to be tweaked away. In the **BB_Landing.avi** clip a hoof is visible in the shot before the insect is stomped on. To retain the suspense of the stomp it would be best if the hoof had been hidden from view until the very last second. Likewise, the actual shot of the insect landing on the grass stalk is too brief and should really last a few seconds longer. Using various techniques learned so far in this book you can correct both of these problems.

Engage Thrusters

Use various edit techniques to tweak your Timeline sequence. Perform the following steps to do so:

1. Press *Shift + 3* to set the Timeline as the active panel. Click anywhere on the Timeline to deselect any previous trim edits. Then locate the **BB_Landing.avi** clip on the Timeline and click on it to select it.

2. Use the *J*, *K*, and *L* keys to move the Timeline indicator backward or forward to find the point where a horse hoof first appears in the background (hint – the hoof moves into frame then slides back again, so place the Timeline cursor at the point just before the hoof starts to slide back out of frame, that is, at about **35;18**).

3. With the **BB_Landing.avi** clip selected, press *Shift + 5* to open the **Effect Controls** panel. Dial open the settings for the **Motion** parameters by clicking in the small triangle to the left of the word **Motion**.

4. Click inside the **Scale** parameter and enter a value of around 120.0.

5. Click inside the y-axis parameter (the second **Position** value) and enter a value of around 285.0, as shown in the following screenshot:

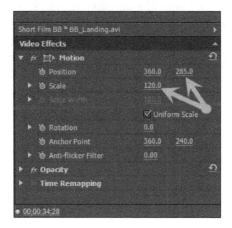

6. The offending hoof should now be out of shot, but the insect landing on the grass stalk is still a little too brief. To solve this you will alter the duration of **BB_Landing.avi**, but only part of it. Start by clicking on the clip to select it.

7. Use a combination of *K + L* or *J* to locate the exact point where the insect lands on the grass stalk (hint – around **35;00**).

8. Press *Shift + 3* to activate the Timeline, then press *Ctrl + K* or *command + K* to razor the clip at this point.

9. Use a combination of *K + L* or *J* to locate the exact point just before the horse hoof appears to crush the insect (hint – around **36;00**).

10. Press *Ctrl + K* or *command + K* to create a second razor cut at this point.

11. Right-click on this new clip (between the slices you have just created) and select **Speed/Duration...** from the context menu, as shown in the following screenshot:

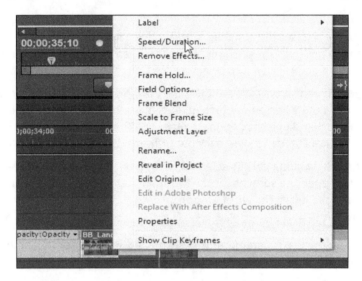

12. The **Clip Speed/Duration** window will appear. Note that it shows the duration of the new 'sliced' clip as **1;20**. Double this by entering a value of 50% in the **Speed** field and then put a check mark next to **Ripple Edit, Shifting Trailing Clips**, as shown in the following screenshot:

 Without the **Ripple Edit, Shifting Trailing Clips** checkbox checked, the **Speed/Duration** effect would have overwritten the next clip on the Timeline and ruined the continuity of the shot.

13. The tail end of **BB_Landing.avi** lasts a little too long. Use a combination of *K + L* or *J* to locate the point just before the last hoof leaves the shot (hint – around **39;06**).

14. Press *Ctrl + K* or *command + K* to razor the clip at this point.

15. Once you are finished, use *Shift + 3* to make the Timeline the active panel, then press \ (backslash) to zoom to the whole Timeline. Make sure the render area bar covers the whole project, and then press *Enter* on the keyboard to render the various slow-motion clips in this sequence. Playback will start automatically once rendering has completed.

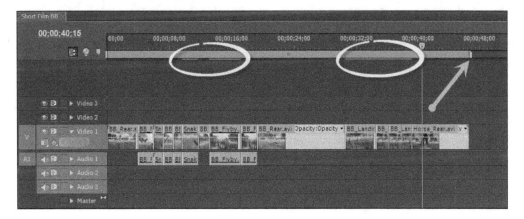

Objective Complete - Mini Debriefing

Video editing is a versatile profession and Premiere Pro CS6 reflects this by providing you with a number of different ways to complete the same task; such as trimming. In this section you learned a number of different ways to trim and refine clips on the Timeline. Which ones you use is all down to the workflow you prefer, although you will probably get a more accurate edit if you stick to those workflows that are keyboard based rather than mouse orientated.

Another technique used here was a variation on positioning the image inside the frame as seen in *Project 1*. As well as creating a better frame of the subject, the **Movement** and **Scale** parameters can also be used to hide objects that have accidently appeared in shot, such as the tip of a dangling microphone, or in this case, a misplaced hoof! You also covered the Razor tool and the **Speed** and **Duration** functions, but use them wisely as they often lack the accuracy of the Trim tool.

Classified Intel

If you need to shorten the duration of a clip but keep the content, you can add a **Speed/Duration** setting in excess of 100 percent. Again, setting a value between `101%` and `125%` will not create a perceivable difference to your audience, but it might make the world of difference to the timing of your sequence.

Making pictures sing

Video tells a story all by itself; even though your short film lacks any kind of sound, it would still get its message across to the viewer. However, that's not good enough for a Hotshot book, so in this section you will add some simple audio effects to the Timeline. These audio effects should have been gathered inside the `Audio` folder on your designated video drive as laid out in the instructions given in the *Prepare for Lift Off* section at the start of this project. If you skimmed that section a bit, but want to add sound, then go back and read it again. Return when you have completed the suggested preparations and gathered enough media to complete this task.

This section shouldn't take you long to complete; it's just going to be a matter of drag-and-drop, with a little bit of trimming. But it's still worth doing as sound adds an extra dimension to your projects, which is worth going the extra distance to achieve.

Engage Thrusters

Add various audio tracks to enhance your Timeline sequence. Perform the following steps to do so:

1. To make this work in a simple fashion, add an extra audio track by right-clicking on the Timeline headers and selecting **Add Tracks...** from the context menu, as shown in the following screenshot:

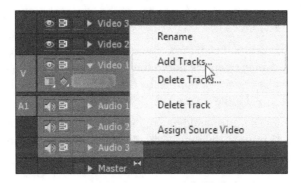

2. Set **Video Track(s)** to 0 and **Audio Track(s)** to 1.

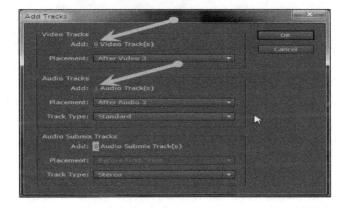

3. Use *Ctrl* + click or *command* + click on the Audio bin in the **Project** panel to open it without creating a new window. Use *Ctrl + I* or *command + I* to open the **Import** window and then import all sound effects stored in the Audio folder for this project. Finally, switch the **Project** panel to **List View** by clicking on the icon in the lower-left corner of the **Project** panel.

It is often easier to deal with long filenames if the **Project** panel is switched to **List View**. Long filenames tend to be common with sound effects and there is no special advantage to using the **Icon View** mode with these types of files.

4. Drag-and-drop your **Background Ambience** sound track to **Audio 4**. This should last for the length of the project; if it does not, then drag it onto the Timeline several times. If the duration is too long, use any of the trim techniques you have learned in this chapter to reduce it.

5. As this is the background clip, the volume doesn't need to be that high. Reduce the volume by dialing open the audio track (use the small triangle next to the name **Audio 4** in the track header), then place the cursor over the yellow volume line so that it displays as a double-headed vertical arrow.

6. With the left mouse button held down, drag this line downwards to reduce the entire volume to around (minus) -10dB. The following screenshot shows how to reduce the volume level of the background ambience track:

7. Add your **Insect** sound effect to **Audio 2**, placing it under every instance where the insect appears on screen. Adjust the volume levels to suit, as described in step 6.

8. Repeat this for the snake, horse, and pigeon sound effects, adding them to **Audio 3**. Sounds of a snake and an insect will probably need to overlap, and placing them on different tracks will allow that to happen.

 When placing clips on the Timeline, they will automatically try to snap to the Out point of a clip next to it, or above/below it. This can make lining up sound effects somewhat tiresome. To temporarily disable this feature, press *S* on the keyboard. Don't forget to toggle it back on when you are finished, as the **Snap To** feature is useful in everyday editing.

9. When you have finished adding your sound effects, go through and change the volume levels of those that need adjustment, as detailed in step 6.

10. Save the project when you are finished and move on to the next section.

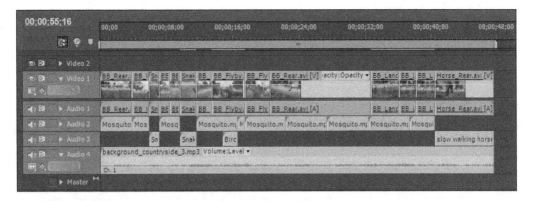

Objective Complete - Mini Debriefing

While this task could never be described as the most technically demanding task in this book, you'll probably be surprised at how much difference adding sound has made to the overall feel of the scene. Hopefully, you will have used this simple section to practice the various skills and keyboard shortcuts you have learned in the less simple sections!

Classified Intel

A quick and easy way of creating special effects with audio is to right-click on any audio effect on the Timeline and select **Speed/Duration** from the context menu. With the help of this feature you can speed up or slow down effects to create the sound you are looking for. You will also find some sound filters in the **Effects** browser.

Adding a movie look

One of the cool things you can do in Premiere Pro CS6 is make your movies look a little less like home videos and a little more like an actual Hollywood movie. You probably can't afford to film under professional lights, or you might have, as in this case, received the footage with no say in how it was filmed. That doesn't matter; you can still use a little creativity to change the tone and look of your footage no matter how it may have been produced.

In this task you will use an adjustment layer, a new feature in Premiere Pro CS6 that allows you to make global changes (like color grades) to the whole sequence without having to copy and paste the settings on to every single clip on the Timeline.

Engage Thrusters

Use an adjustment layer to give your Timeline sequence a movie look. Perform the following steps to do so:

1. Change to the **Effects** workspace by using *Alt + Shift + 6* (WinOS) or *option + Shift + 6* (MacOS).

2. Use *Shift + 3* to select the Timeline as the active panel and press \ (backslash) on the keyboard to zoom in the whole sequence to the Timeline.

3. Use *Shift + 1* to select the **Project** panel as the active panel. Select **File | New | Adjustment Layer...**. When the **Adjustment Layer** window appears, keep the default settings and click on **OK**. The newly created adjustment layer will appear in the **Project** panel.

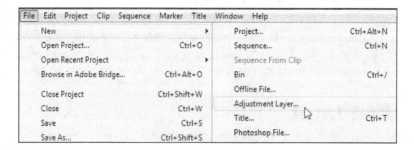

4. Drag-and-drop the adjustment layer from the **Project** panel and onto the start of **Video 2**, then with the left mouse button held down, drag it outwards to match the duration of all of the clips in your sequence.

5. Now you can begin adding effects to the adjustment layer, making global changes to your sequence below. Start by pressing *Shift + 7* to open the **Effects** browser. You will select your effects from here.

6. Let's start by adding some much needed contrast to the scene. In the **Search** field, type in the word `Level`. **Auto Levels** and **Levels** will be revealed to you. Drag-and-drop **Levels** onto the adjustment layer in the Timeline.

 Make sure the Timeline indicator is somewhere around the middle of the scene (showing the sky, trees, and fog) to give you a good idea of the changes you are about to make.

7. Press *Shift + 5* to open up the **Effect Controls** panel and dial open the **Levels** effect by clicking on the small triangle. With the **Effect Controls** panel open, change the following parameters:

    ❑ **(RGB) Black Input Level**: 30

    ❑ **(RGB) White Input Level**: 230

    ❑ **(RGB) Gamma**: 89

    The following screenshot shows the required settings:

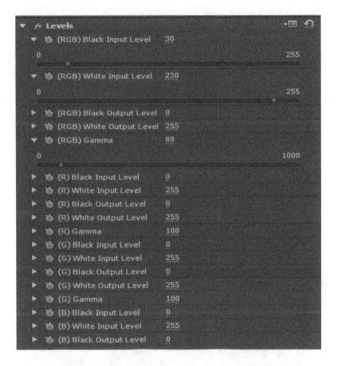

8. The end result should be softening of light levels and some enhancement in detail. To see the changes you have made, toggle the effect on and off by clicking on the **FX** button next to the word **Levels**. Don't forget to toggle it back on again before you move on to the next step.

 Don't worry if this is all looking a little dark right now; you will adjust that in the last steps of this task. For the moment, keep the faith.

9. Press *Shift + 7* to move back to the **Effects** browser, and type `Curves` into the search field. The **RGB Curves** effect will be revealed to you. Drag-and-drop this effect onto the adjustment layer and dial open the controls (you might want to dial shut the **Levels** control area first).

10. Inside the **Master** area, click on the white line twice to create two key points, then drag those key points to create the shape shown in the following screenshot.

> To see the changes the **RGB Curves** effect is creating, check and uncheck the **Show Split View** checkbox. You may find it better to change the **Layout** option (just below the checkbox) to **Vertical**. More information on the **RGB Curves** effect can be found in the Premiere Pro reference guide, which can be downloaded from `http://helpx.adobe.com/pdf/premiere_pro_reference.pdf`.

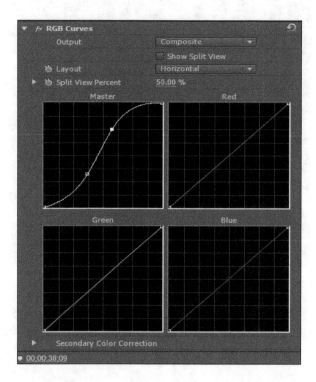

11. The scene is looking very moody; now add a **Gaussian Blur** effect to the adjustment layer. Use the methods given previously, (press *Shift + 7*; type in `Blur`; drag-and-drop; dial open parameters; change **Blurriness** to `50.0`). Don't panic after looking at the result, you will correct it in the next step. Keep the faith!

12. Well now things look very strange, but don't worry, you can tame these stacked effects on the adjustment layer using the **Opacity** parameter to control the strength of the adjustment layer. Start by using *Shift + 5* to make the **Effect Controls** panel the active panel, then dial open the **Opacity** parameter. Make sure the **Keyframe** toggle is off (the small stopwatch icon), then change the **Opacity** value to 50%.

13. While you have the **Opacity** settings open, experiment with the blend mode to see what differences these make to your adjustment layer.

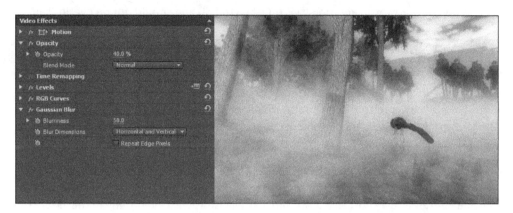

14. Review those effects you have added to your clips and alter them to suit your taste. Once you have finished, press *Shift + 3* to make the Timeline the active panel, then press the *Enter* key to render the sequence.

 To see the overall effect the adjustment layer is having on your sequence, Toggle the layer on and off using **Toggle Track Output Switch** for **Video 2** (hint – the eyeball icon to the left of the track name).

15. Save your project before you complete this task.

Objective Complete - Mini Debriefing

You've now learned how to use two powerful new features in Premiere Pro CS6: the adjustment layer and blend modes in the **Opacity** effect. These two new features, when combined, allow you to create global changes to the look of your film with just a few mouse clicks. Granted, these changes may not look as grand as some effects that can be created in Adobe After Effects CS6, but with practice and using the many filters available as standard in Premiere Pro CS6, the looks you create should only be limited by your imagination and your capability to experiment.

Classified Intel

The blend mode option in the **Opacity** parameters is similar to the one used in photoshop, in that it allows you to choose how the Opacity channel (and in this case the entire adjustment layer) interacts with the video below. Choosing a blend mode is a matter of personal taste more than anything else; it depends greatly on what sort of look you are aiming for. For this short sequence the blend mode **Darken** seems to bring out the shadows while retaining the detail and allowing the fog to have a dreamy but slightly sinister look. Experiment with blend modes; they are a powerful addition to Premiere Pro CS6 and should not be overlooked.

Mission Accomplished

In this project you have created a short film, or at least the opening scene, and learned the various different ways to trim clips on the Timeline. You have also discovered how to create a film look using only those effects shipped with Premiere Pro CS6 as standard. There is no need for expensive plugins with this book!

On top of that you've learned a little bit about the sound capabilities of Premiere Pro and as a bonus you should have created a pretty cool film. That's not a bad list of achievements when you consider how short the short film actually is. As with everything in this book, the actual task completed is just a stepping stone towards learning the core skills needed to be an effective video editor using Premiere Pro CS6.

You Ready To Go Gung HO? A Hotshot Challenge

Once you have your project saved, start again! Create a new sequence and see what you can come up with using the exact same clips, and to see if you can recreate this edit using the keyboard as much as possible (without referring back to the instructions in this project).

When it comes to adding the clips, make your own decisions on how the film should play out, what sort of speed changes you should make, and how stylized your movie look should be. Go crazy and experiment; it really is the best way to learn.

Also note that one clip, **BB_Above.avi**, wasn't used at all in this project. Perhaps you would like to include it in your version? That decision, as the editor in charge, is up to you. If you are feeling adventurous, why not create a flashback version of this film, or a comedy one with strange speed increases.

Whatever you do, I look forward to seeing your movies on YouTube. Don't forget to send me the link to my e-mail address PaulEkert@PaulEkert.com!

Project 3

Protect the Innocent – Interview Edit Techniques

Project 2, Cutting a Short Film without Getting Stung talked about how Premiere Pro CS6 was built to make films, but more accurately it would be best to describe Premiere Pro as a medium for telling a story, and of course stories can take many different forms. In this project you will look at creating a news article for a local TV station. Again you will be using material created specifically for this book, and you will be learning a number of new ways to speed up your editing workflows.

Mission Briefing

Your objective in this project is to learn some of the more commonly used news and documentary editing techniques, such as the J-cuts and L-cuts, accomplished with the Extract and Lift function. You'll also look at plundering the Premiere Pro CS6 effects library to simulate a nighttime look and create some camera shakes (yes sometimes camera shakes is a good thing!).

There will be some repetition from previous projects, but this will be presented in a fresh arena in order for you to practice your new skill sets. To make it a little more of a challenge, the keyboard shortcuts and workflows will often just be hinted at, allowing you to raid your gray cells for techniques learned in the previous two projects. Alternatively you may wish to flick back a few pages and revise up on things you have not yet mastered. Either way, by the time you finish this project, your understanding of the Premiere Pro editing workflows should be reaching a higher level.

The following screenshot gives you an idea of what your Timeline will look like once you have completed this project. Don't worry; you will build this Timeline up with one step at a time.

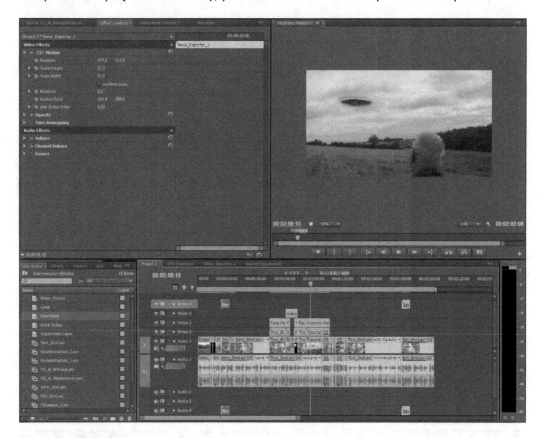

Why Is It Awesome?

In this project you will edit a news report about a man coming home from the pub and witnessing a flying saucer in the night sky. Your job, as an editor, is to tell the story of the idyllic village, the man who saw the UFO, and create a realistic reconstruction of those key events. You'll accomplish all of this using only the material your camera person gave you at the end of the shoot. Reshoots are out of the question, so it's up to you to save the day with what you've got!

Once you've finished, you should have created a news article using various shots including over-the-shoulder shots, reconstruction shots, and even a fake mobile phone shot. And, in the last section you'll learn how to create multilayered titles using Premiere Pro's ability to place one sequence inside another. Again, if this means nothing to you right now don't worry, all will become clear.

Your Hotshot Objectives

The workflows and skills you'll learn in this chapter have been split into the following tasks; some are a little on the long side, but the techniques you will learn makes it worth the effort.

- ▶ Getting the story right!
- ▶ Extracting audio fat
- ▶ Creating a J-cut (away)
- ▶ An L-cut and a UFO!
- ▶ Reconstructing reconstructions
- ▶ Bringing night to day
- ▶ Adding viewpoints
- ▶ Protecting the innocent
- ▶ Adding lower thirds

Mission Checklist

Before you start this project, there are a number of preparations you need to make. Firstly, open your designated video drive and access the Hotshots folder you created in *Project 1*, *Creating a Movie Montage – the Easy Way*. There you should find two folders called Project 1 and Project 2. Create a new folder in the Hotshots folder called Project 3 and inside that new folder, create three folders called Video, Images, and Audio.

With the new folders created, access the folder containing the content you downloaded and extracted in *Project 2*, *Cutting a Short Film without Getting Stung*. You should find a folder inside called Project 3. Copy the contents of this folder to the Video folder you created according to what we said in the first paragraph of this section. There are eight video files in total. Once you have the media copied to the correct location on your computer, proceed to the first task.

Getting the story right!

Once again, in this project you will proceed exactly as you did in *Project 1* and *Project 2*. This is basic housekeeping and ignoring it is like making your own editing life much more frustrating. So take a deep breath, think of calm blue oceans, and begin by getting this project organized. First you need to set the Timeline correctly and then you will create a short storyboard of the interview; again you will do this by focusing on the beginning, middle, and end of the story. Always start this way as a good story needs these elements to make sense.

As you have completed similar tasks in the previous projects, the instructions will be given as the bare minimum. For frame-accurate editing it's advisable to use the keyboard as much as possible, although some actions will need to be performed with the mouse. If you get lost, turn to the first task in *Project 2, Cutting a Short Film without Getting Stung* for hints on how to proceed. Towards the end of this task you will cover some new ground as you add and expand Timeline tracks in preparation for the tasks ahead.

Prepare for Lift Off

Once you have completed all the preparations detailed in the *Mission Checklist* section, you are ready to go. Launch Premiere Pro CS6 in the usual way and then proceed to the first task.

Engage Thrusters

First you will open the project template created in *Project 1*, save it as a new file, and then create a three-clip sequence; the rough assembly of your story. Once done, perform the following steps:

1. When the **Recent Projects** splash screen appears, select **Hotshots Template – Montage**. Wait for the project to finish loading and save this as **Hotshots – Interview Project**. Close any sequences open on the Timeline.

2. Select **Editing Optimized Workspace** that you created in *Project 1*.

3. Select the **Project** panel and open the Video bin without creating a separate window.

 If you would like Premiere Pro to always open a bin without creating a separate window, select **Edit | Preferences | General** from the menu. When the **General Options** window displays, locate the **Bins** option area and change the **Double-Click** option to **Open in Place**.

4. Import all eight video files into the Video folder inside the Project 3 folder.

5. Create a new sequence. Pick any settings at random, you will correct this in the next step. Rename the sequence as **Project 3**.

6. Match the Timeline settings with any clip from the Video bin using the method you learned in *Project 1*, and then delete the clip from the Timeline.

7. Set the **Project** panel as the active panel and switch to **List View** if it is not already displayed.

8. Create the basic elements of a short story for this scene using only three of the available clips in the `Video` bin. To do this, hold down the *Ctrl* or *command* key and click on the clips named ahead. Make sure you click on them in the same order as they are presented here:

   ❑ **Intro_Shot.avi**

   ❑ **Two_Shot.avi**

   ❑ **Exit_Shot.avi**

9. Ensure the Timeline indicator is at the start of the Timeline and then click on the **Automate to Sequence** icon.

10. When the **Automate To Sequence** window appears, change **Ordering** to **Selection Order** and leave **Placement** as the default (**Sequentially**). Uncheck the **Apply Default Audio Transition**, **Apply Default Video Transition**, and **Ignore Audio** checkboxes. Click on **OK** or press *Enter* on the keyboard to complete this action.

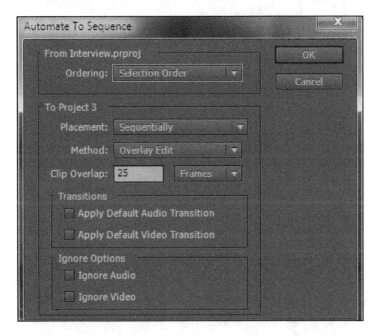

11. Right-click on the **Video 1** track and select **Add Tracks** from the context menu. When the **Add Tracks** window appears, set the number of video tracks to be added as 2 and the number of audio tracks to be added as 0. Click on **OK** or press *Enter* to confirm these changes.

12. Dial open the **Audio 1** track (hint – small triangle next to **Audio 1**), then expand the **Audio 1** track by placing the cursor at the bottom of the **Audio 1** area, and clicking on it, and dragging it downwards. Stop before the **Master** audio track disappears below the bottom of the **Timeline** panel.

> The **Master** audio track is used to control the output of all the audio tracks present on the Timeline; this is especially useful when you come to prepare your timeline for exporting to DVD. The **Master** audio track also allows you to view the left and right audio channels of your project. More details on the use of the **Master** audio track can be found in the Premiere Pro reference guide, which can be downloaded from `http://helpx.adobe.com/pdf/premiere_pro_reference.pdf`.

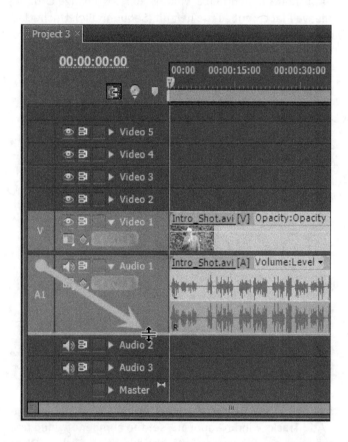

13. Make sure the **Timeline** panel is active and zoom in to show all the clips present (hint – press backslash). You should end this section with a Timeline that looks something like the following screenshot. Save your project (Press *Ctrl + S* or *command + S*) before moving on to the next task.

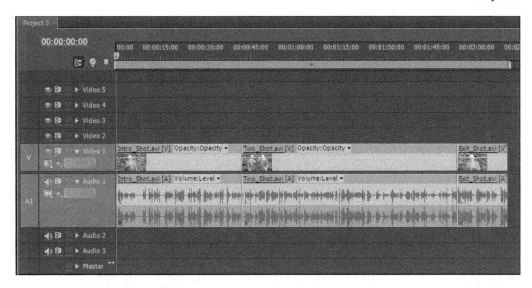

Objective Complete - Mini Debriefing

How did you do? Review the shortcuts listed next. Did you remember them all?

In this task you should have automatically matched up the Timeline to the clips with one drag-and-drop, plus a delete. You should have then sent three clips from the **Project** panel to the Timeline using the Automate to Sequence function. Finally you should have added two new video tracks and expanded the **Audio 1** track.

If you managed all of that without peeking back at *Project 2*, then well done, if not, don't get disheartened, you will have the chance to retest your memory throughout the rest of this project!

Keyboard shortcuts covered in this task are as follows:

▶ \ (backslash): Zoom the Timeline to show all populated clips

▶ *Ctrl* or *command* + double-click: Open bin without creating a separate **Project** panel (also see the tip after step 3 in the *Engage Thrusters* section)

▶ *Ctrl* or *command* + N: Create a new sequence

▶ *Ctrl* or *command* + \ (backslash): Create new bin in the **Project** panel

▶ *Ctrl* or *command* + I: Open the **Import** window

▶ *Shift* + 1: Set the **Project** panel as active

▶ *Shift* + 3: Set Timeline as active

Classified Intel

In this project, the Automate to Timeline function is being used to create a rough assembly of three clips. These are placed on the Timeline in the order that you clicked on them in the project bin. This is known as the **selection order** and allows the Automate to Timeline function to ignore the clips-relative location in the project bin. This is a handy alternative to the methods used in *Project 1* and *Project 2*, but it's not a practical workflow if you have too many clips in your **Project** panel (how would you remember the selection order of twenty clips?). However, for a small number of clips, this is a practical workflow to quickly and easily send a rough draft of your story to the Timeline in just a few clicks. If you remember nothing else from this book, always remember how to correctly use Automate To Timeline!

Extracting audio fat

Raw material from every interview ever filmed will have lulls and pauses, and some stuttering. People aren't perfect and time spent trying to get lines and timing just right can lead to an unfortunate waste of filming time. As this performance is not live, you, the all-seeing editor, have the power to cut those distracting lulls and pauses, keeping the pace on beat and audience's attention on track. In this task you will move through the Timeline, cutting out some of the audio fat using Premiere Pro's Extract function, and to get this frame accurate, you will use as many keyboard shortcuts as possible.

Engage Thrusters

You will now use the Extract function to remove "dead" audio areas from the Timeline. Perform the following steps:

1. Set the **Timeline** panel as active then play the timeline back by pressing the *L* key once. Make a mental note of the silences that occur in the first clip (**Intro_Shot.avi**).

2. Return the Timeline indicator to the start of the Timeline using the *Home* key.

3. Zoom in on the Timeline by pressing the + (plus) key on the main keyboard area. Do this until your Timeline looks something like the screenshot just after the following tip:

 To zoom in and out of the Timeline use the + (plus) and - (minus) keys in the main keyboard area, not the ones in the number pad area. Pressing the plus or minus key in the number area allows you to enter an exact number of frames into whichever tool is currently active.

4. You should be able to clearly see the first area of silence starting at around **06;09** on the Timeline. Use the *J*, *K*, and *L* keyboard shortcuts to place the Timeline indicator at this point.

5. Press the *I* key to set an In point here, then move the Timeline indicator to the end of the silence (around **08;17**), and press the *O* key to set an Out point.

6. Press the # (hash) key on your keyboard to remove the marked section of silence using Premiere Pro's Extract function.

Important information on Sync Locking tracks

The above step will only work if you have the **Sync Lock** icons toggled on for both the **Video 1** and **Audio 1** tracks. The **Sync Lock** icon controls which Timeline tracks will be altered when using a function such as Extract. For example; if the **Sync Lock** icon was toggled off for the **Audio 1** track, then only the video would be extracted, which is counterproductive to what you are trying to achieve in this task!

By default each new project should open with the **Sync Lock** icon toggled on for all video and audio tracks that already exist on the Timeline, and those added at a later point in the project. More information on **Sync Lock** can be found in the Premiere Pro reference guide (tinyurl.com/cz5fvh9), and will be looked at again in a later project in this book.

7. Repeat steps 5 and 6 to remove silences from the following Timeline areas (you should judge these points for yourself rather than slavishly following the suggestions given next):

    i. Set In point at **07;11** and Out point at **08;10**.

    ii. Press # (hash).

    iii. Set In point at **11;05** and Out point at **12;13**.

    iv. Press # (hash).

8. Play back the Timeline to make sure you haven't extracted away too much audio and clipped the end of a sentence. If you need to, summon up your skill sets from *Project 2* and use the Trim tool to restore the full sentence.

 You may have spotted other silences on the Timeline; for the moment leave them alone. You will deal with these using other methods later in this project.

9. Save the project before moving on to the next section.

Objective Complete - Mini Debriefing

At the end of this section you should have successfully removed three areas of silence from the **Intro_Shot.avi** clip. You did this using the Extract function, an elegant way of removing unwanted areas from your clips. You may also have refreshed your working knowledge of the Trim tool. If this still feels a little alien to you, don't worry, you will have a chance to practice trimming skills later in this project.

Classified Intel

Extract is another cunningly simple function that does exactly what it says; it extracts a section of footage from the Timeline, and then closes the gap created by this action. In one step it replicates the razor cut and ripple delete, which you performed in an earlier project.

Creating a J-cut (away)

One of the most common video techniques used in interviews and documentaries (not to mention a number of films) is called a **J-cut**. This describes cutting away some of the video, while leaving the audio beneath intact. The deleted video area is then replaced with alternative footage. This creates a voice-over effect that allows for a seamless transfer between the alternative viewpoints and the original speaker.

In this task you will create a J-cut by replacing the video at the start of **Intro_Shot.avi**, leaving the voice of the newsperson and replacing his image with cutaway shots of what he is describing. You will make full use of four-point edits, and once again, to cement what you have learned in *Project 2*, instructions will be sparse. If you get lost, refer back to *Project 2*.

Engage Thrusters

Create J-cuts and cutaway shots using workflows you should now be familiar with. Perform the following steps to do so:

1. Send the **Cutaways_1.avi** clip from the **Project** panel to the Source Monitor.

2. In the Source Monitor, create an In point at **00;00** and an Out point just before the shot changes (around **04;24**).

3. Switch to the Timeline and send the Timeline indicator to the start of the Timeline (**00;00**). Create an In point here.

4. Use a keyboard shortcut of your choice to identify the point just before the newsperson mentions the "Local village shop". (hint – roughly at **06;09**). Create an Out point here.

5. You want to create a J-cut, which means protecting the audio track that is already on the Timeline. To do this click once on the **Audio 1** track header so it turns dark gray.

6. Switch back to the Source Monitor and send the marked **Cutaways_1.avi** clip to the Timeline using the Overwrite function (hint – press the '.' (period) key).

7. When the **Fit Clip** window appears, select **Change Clip Speed (Fit to Fill)**, and click on **OK** or press *Enter* on the keyboard. The village scene cutaway shot should now appear on **Video 1**, but **Audio 1** should retain the newsperson's dialog. His inserted village scene clip will have also slowed slightly to match what's being said by the newsperson.

8. Repeat steps 2 to 7 to place the **Cutaways_1.avi** clip that shows the shot of the village shop, to match the village church and the village pub on the Timeline with the newsperson's dialog. The following are some suggestions on times, but try to do this step first of all without looking too closely at them:

    ❑   For the village shop cutaway, set the Source Monitor In point at **05;00** and Out point at **09;24**. Set the Timeline In point at **06;10** and Out point at **07;13**. Switch back to Source Monitor. Send the clip in the **Overwrite** mode and set **Change Clip Speed** to **Fit to Fill**.

    ❑   For the village church cutaway, set the Source Monitor In point at **10;00** and Out point at **14;24**. Set the Timeline In point at **07;14** and Out point at **09;03**. Switch back to Source Monitor. Send the clip in the **Overwrite** mode and set **Change Clip Speed** to **Fit to Fill**.

    ❑   For the pub cutaway, send **Reconstruction_1.avi** to the Source Monitor. Set the Source Monitor In point at **04;11** and Out point at **04;17**. Set the Timeline In point at **09;04** and Out point at **12;00**. Switch back to Source Monitor. Send the clip in the **Overwrite** mode and set **Change Clip Speed** to **Fit to Fill**.

The last cutaway shot here is part of the reconstruction reel and has been used because your camera person was unable (or forgot) to film a cutaway shot of the pub. This does sometimes happen and then it's down to you, the editor in charge, to get the piece on air with as few errors as possible. To do this you may find yourself scavenging footage from any of the other clips. In this case you have used just seven frames of **Reconstruction_1.avi**, but using the Premiere Pro feature, **Fit to Fill**, you are able to match the clip to the duration of the dialogue, saving your camera person from a production meeting dressing down!

9. Review your edit decisions and use the Trim tool or the **Undo** command to alter edit points that you feel need adjustments. As always, being an editor is about experimentation, so don't be afraid to try something out of the box, you never know where it might lead.

10. Once you are happy with your edit decisions, render any clips on the Timeline that display a red line above them.

11. You should end up with a Timeline that looks something like the following screenshot; save your project before moving on to the next section.

Objective Complete - Mini Debriefing

In this task you have learned how to piece together cutaway shots to match the voice-over, creating an effective J-cut, as seen in the way the dialog seamlessly blends between the pub cutaway shot and the news reporter finishing his last sentence. You also learned how to scavenge source material from other reels in order to find the necessary shot to match the dialog.

By now you will have noticed the instructions are becoming very sparse indeed, and you have to genuinely remember skills learned in *Project 1* and *Project 2*. Don't get too disheartened if you had to refer back to those projects to jog your memory, this should occur less and less as you progress through this project and the rest of this book.

Classified Intel

The last set of time suggestions given in this task allow the pub cutaway shot to run over the top of the newsperson saying "And now, much to the surprise...". This is an editorial decision that you can make on whether or not this cutaway should run over the dialog. It is simply a matter of taste, but you are the editor and the final decision is yours!

An L-cut and a UFO!

In the last section you created a J-cut using cutaway shots that lead into dialog. The opposite of this technique is to have the dialog lead into a cutaway shot. This is called an **L-cut**.

In this task you will create a simulated shot of a UFO (supposedly shot on a mobile phone) and then insert that shot into the Timeline as an L-cut. To do this you will use a great, but often underused feature in Premiere Pro CS6, Nested Sequences, and you'll do some creative work with the motion and blur effects to sell the shot. This is to make the clip look like a shaky mobile phone recording. You've covered effects like this in *Project 1* and *Project 2*, so again the instructions will be sparse in order for you to put into practice the skill sets you have learned so far.

Engage Thrusters

Create an L-cut and use Nested Sequences to add a UFO scene to your interview. Perform the following steps to do so:

1. You'll start this task by first creating the shot of a UFO that's supposedly been taken on a mobile phone. You'll do this by scavenging part of the **Reconstruction_2.avi** clip and adding some creative filters. Start by sending **Reconstruction_2.avi** to the Source Monitor.

2. Set an In point at the very start of the clip and an Out point after about 24 frames into the clip.

3. Create a new sequence. Name this sequence as **UFO Simulation**. Don't worry about the other settings, just click on **OK** or press *Enter* on the keyboard. Deselect the **Audio 1** track on the newly created sequence with a click to turn it dark gray.

4. Switch back to the Source Monitor and confirm that **Reconstruction_2.avi** is the selected clip and the In and Out points you defined earlier are still marked. If everything looks good, press ',' (comma) on the keyboard to insert this clip onto the Timeline. Switch back to the Timeline and press \ (backslash) to zoom in on the clip.

5. Send the Timeline indicator to the start of the Timeline (hint – press *Home*), then click on **Reconstuction_2.avi** to select the clip on the Timeline and open the **Effect Controls** panel (hint – press *Shift + 5*). Dial open the **Motion** settings (hint – click on the small triangle) to show the **Scale** and **Position** values. Increase the scale of the clip by 330 percent (hint – click inside the **Scale** value and enter 330).

6. You will now create a shaky image (as though taken on a mobile phone while under a bit of stress) by altering the position of the clip after every two frames. Start by toggling animation on for the **Position** parameters (hint – use the stopwatch icon).

7. Click on the actual word, **Motion** in the title area of the effect so that a bounding box appears around the image in the Program Monitor. Place the mouse cursor inside the bounding box, then click-and-drag the image down and to the right. Stop when the UFO is roughly at the center of the frame, as shown in the following screenshot:

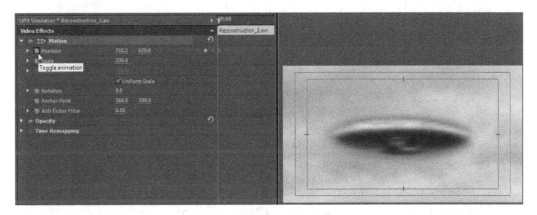

8. Press the right arrow twice to move the Timeline indicator two frames into the clip. Repeat step 7, but this time drag the UFO image so that it goes almost below the bottom of the frame. Stop before a black border (the upper edge of the frame) appears at the top of the display area.

The Timeline indicator will respond to the arrow keys when the **Effects** panel is active. There is no need to return to the Timeline to do this.

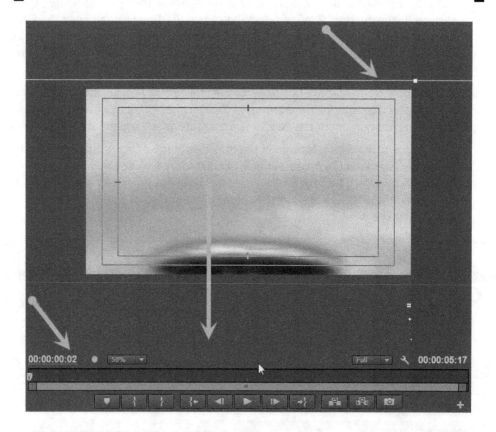

9. Advance another two frames and move the image so that the bottom of the UFO is in the upper-left corner of the display. Repeat the preceding steps and randomly move the UFO about the display while advancing the Timeline indicator two frames after each movement. Don't forget to move forward two frames each time you reposition the UFO. Do this all the way to the end of the clip. Placing the UFO in opposite corners would create an ideal simulation of a nervously held mobile phone. The last movement should return the UFO to the central area of the display.

10. Return to the **Project** panel and create a new adjustment layer. Accept the defaults and press *Enter*, then drag-and-drop the adjustment layer onto **Video 2** and adjust it to the same length as the clip below. (hint – use the zoom controls if necessary).

11. Return the Timeline indicator to the start of the Timeline and then open the **Effects** panel (*Shift + 7*). Type in Blur into the search box. Locate **Directional Blur** from the list and drag this onto the adjustment layer on the Timeline.

12. If not already open, open the **Effect Controls** panel and then dial open the **Directional Blur** settings. Change **Blur Length** to suit your own taste (suggested value is 15).

13. This clip is supposed to have been shot at night, so you need to add a blue filter to recreate a classic 'fake' nighttime look. To achieve this return to the **Effects** panel and type in Tint into the search box. Drag-and-drop the **Tint** effect onto the adjustment layer on the Timeline.

14. Open the **Effect Controls** panel if necessary and then dial open the **Tint** settings. Change **Map to Black** to a dark blue color using the color picker (suggested values can be seen in the following screenshot). Repeat this last step to change **Map to White** to a lighter blue color (suggested hex color number is **# 3D50C5**).

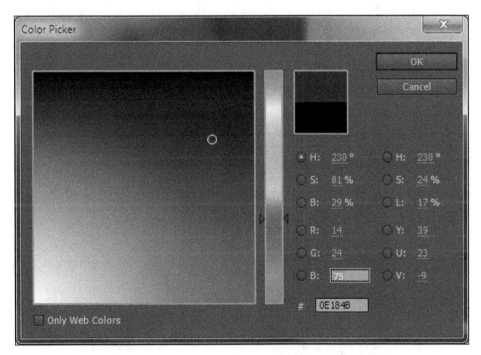

15. Dial open the **Opacity** settings for the adjustment layer and toggle animation off (Stopwatch deselected). Change **Opacity** to a suggested 90 percent value and alter **Blend Mode** to **Linear Light**.

Don't worry too much about how jerky the playback will look, or how brief it is; you will correct those points in the next few steps.

16. Make sure the Timeline is active, then cycle to the `Project 3` sequence by pressing *Shift + 3*, until it is displayed.

17. It's time now to create a J-cut on your Timeline using the UFO simulation sequence. Begin by moving the Timeline indicator to a frame or two before the news reporter says "A flying saucer" (**16;10**). Set this as the Timeline In point. Then move the Timeline indicator to the point just before the next silent area finishes (**19;00**) and set this as the Timeline Out point.

18. Return to the **Project** panel (press *Shift + ?*), right-click on the UFO simulation sequence, and select **Open in Source Monitor**. Make sure the Source Monitor is the active panel and the In and Out points have been set at the absolute start and absolute end of this sequence clip, respectively. Then send the whole of the UFO simulation sequence to the Timeline in the **Overwrite** mode. Alter the value of **Change Clip Speed** (**Fit to Fill**) and press *Enter*.

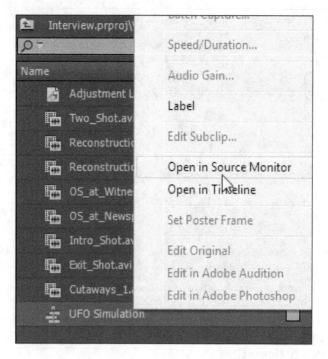

Even though you are sending the whole sequence clip to the Timeline, if you don't set the In and Out points, you will not be given the speed (**Fit to Fill**) option. You must have all four points defined if you want Premiere Pro to recognize this as a four-point edit.

19. Save, render, and playback your Timeline before moving on to the next section.

Objective Complete - Mini Debriefing

This is somewhat a long-winded task for a small result of a 2-second UFO clip, but that's video editing for you. Sometimes the most time-intensive tasks will be all about creating a perfect 2-second sequence.

In this task you revised many of your skills from *Project 1* and *Project 2*, including keyframed movement, scale, and adding effects to an adjustment layer. New to your skill base is creating a nested sequence by placing one sequence inside another. This is a powerful workflow that can be used to stack effects, as seen here, or to assemble the scenes of a film on one Timeline sequence, then use them in another. It can also be used to add a sequence to the Timeline via the Source Monitor in order for you to make use of the four-point edit option, **Fit to Fill**.

Classified Intel

Once in the Source Monitor, the UFO simulation sequence became both a sequence and a clip! This is one of those features in Premiere Pro that for some reason doesn't grab a lot of attention, possibly because the only way to send a sequence to the Source Monitor is by right-clicking and then selecting **Open in Source Monitor**. A double-click will select the Timeline sequence and display it in the **Timeline** panel! It's a shame this workflow gets ignored because it really is a useful way to creatively stack effects without adding loads of video tracks to your main sequence.

Reconstructing reconstructions

In this task you will create a reconstruction of the witness's movements leading up to the UFO sighting. You'll do this by practicing your new found J-cut and L-cut skills, but this time you will be using preset markers to help you work out the optimal In points for your reconstruction clips. Instruction will be brief here to help you revise your newfound workflows.

Engage Thrusters

Use advanced marker functions to create a set of cutaway shots. Perform the following steps:

1. Start by creating markers on the track for every time the witness mentions a location. Press *M* on the keyboard to set the marker at the location of the Timeline indicator. Attempt this first by ear, and then check your markers with the suggested marker locations, given as follows:

    ❑   **Leaving pub**: 45;11

    ❑   **Walking down painless hill**: 47;24

    ❑   **Crossing cow path**: 49;23

    ❑   **Freddy's sheep field**: 51;18

    ❑   **Seeing lights in the sky**: 56;09

2. You now have the potential In and Out points for your reconstruction clips. Return to the **Project** panel and send the **Reconstruction_1.avi** clip to the Source Monitor.

3. Set the In and Out points for this clip to be the duration of the pub shot (around **00;00** to **04;17**).

4. Return to the Timeline and move the Timeline indicator to the first marker on the Timeline by using either *Shift + M* or *Ctrl + Shift + M* or *command + Shift + M*.

5. Set an In point here and then move to the second marker (*Shift + M*) and set an Out point. Return to the Source Monitor and send the clip to the Timeline in the **Overwrite** mode. Set **Change Clip Speed** to **Fit to Fill**.

 If this newly added clip overwrote the audio on **Audio 1**, press *Ctrl + Z* or *command + Z* to undo the action and then make sure the **Audio 1** track is protected by clicking on it once to turn it dark gray.

6. The Timeline should still be the active panel, so while you're there, set an In point at the second marker (your previous Out point) and an Out point at the third marker. Use *Shift + M* to move the Timeline indicator to these markers.

7. Return to the Source Monitor and set the clip to show In and Out points at the start and end of the hill clip (**04;18** to **10;11**). Send it to the Timeline in the **Overwrite** mode. Set **Change Clip Speed** to **Fit to Fill**.

 This last edit creates a somewhat comic effect as the witness moves down the hill in fast forward. If you don't want to have this type of comedy going on, define a smaller section of the hill clip in the Source Monitor.

8. Repeat steps 6 and 7 to set In and Out points at marker 3 (your previous Out point) and marker 4. In the Source Monitor, mark out the last section of the **Reconstruction_1.avi** clip. Send it to the Timeline as before.

9. Time now to add our UFO. With the Timeline still active, create an In point at marker 5 and then set an Out point the old-fashioned way by moving through the Timeline just to the last 'round', as said by the witness (about **01;04;10**).

10. Return to the Source Monitor and load in the **Reconstruction_2.avi** clip using any of the methods you have learned so far.

11. Right-click anywhere inside the Source Monitor and select **Clear In and Out** from the context menu. With the old In and Out points deleted, create a new In point at the very start of the clip and a new Out point just before the UFO leaves the frame (about **04;00**) at the very end of the clip.

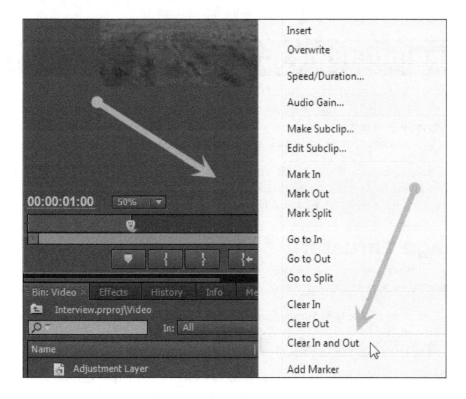

12. Send the clip to the Timeline using **Overwrite**, Set **Change Clip Speed** to **Fit to Fill**.

13. If necessary, render your Timeline, then save your project before moving on to the next section.

Objective Complete - Mini Debriefing

As you can see from your playback, this task presented you with the challenge of creating a reconstruction that matched the dialog of the witness and seamlessly blended it with J- and L-cuts. This used many of the skills you have learned so far, including utilizing markers to identify optimal In and Out points, a skill you picked up in *Project 1*. This is to demonstrate that skills learned in each project can be used in a variety of different ways, and on many different types of projects.

Classified Intel

Markers can also be labeled. To do this just double-click on any marker and a text window will open up allowing you to add a name to that marker and alter its duration. Markers can also be used to create links to web content and to set up your projects for easy export to Encore. This is something you will explore in a later project.

Bringing night to day

A short and sweet section here, many of the reconstruction clips were supposed to be shot at night, but of course they were reconstructed during the day (budget constraints get to everything). In this very brief section you will copy and paste the adjustment layer from the UFO simulation, and add it to the **Reconstruction_1.avi** clips on the Timeline.

This task is here simply to show you that once you have an effect you like, you needn't waste time trying to recreate it, you can simply use copy and paste, regardless of which sequence that effect might have originally be created in.

Engage Thrusters

Create a nighttime scene by copying and pasting an adjustment layer from one sequence to another. Perform the following steps:

1. Click once on the **UFO Simulation** tab on the Timeline to access that sequence.

2. Right-click on the adjustment layer on the Timeline of that sequence and select **Copy** from the context menu.

3. Return to the **Project 3** sequence by clicking on that tab in the Timeline.

4. Move the Timeline indicator to the start of the **Reconstuction_1.avi** clips (**45;11**).

5. Deselect the **Video 1** track by clicking on it to turn it light gray.

6. Make the **Video 4** track active by clicking on it to turn it dark gray.

7. Press *Ctrl + V* or *command + V* to paste the adjustment layer onto **Video 4**.

8. Using the mouse, drag the adjustment layer so it covers all three of the **Reconstruction_1.avi** clips.

9. Finish this section by clicking on **Video 4** to deselect it (turns light gray) then reselecting **Video 1** (turns dark gray). Do not reselect **Audio 1**, leave this as light gray for the moment.

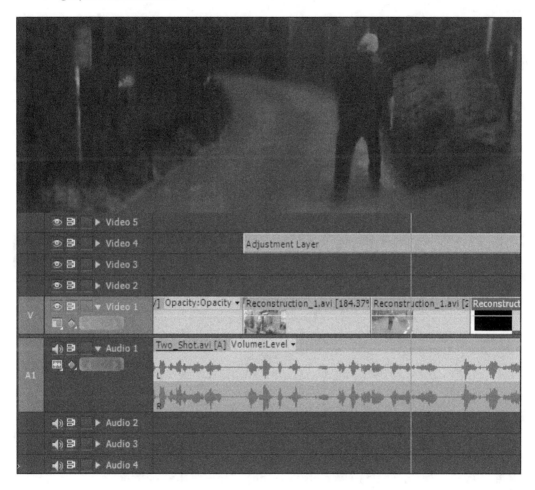

10. Save your project before moving on to the next section of this project.

Objective Complete - Mini Debriefing

As promised this was indeed a very short section, but the effect it creates (a sort of dreamy remembered nighttime) is well worth having, and as is the knowledge of copying and pasting elements from one sequence to another. This method of simulation, or more accurately, faking nighttime conditions has been used for a long time, but it still has the capacity to sell a shot to the audience, although a more sophisticated audience will probably demand real night shots.

One thing to note, the adjustment layer has been placed on **Video 4**, which leaves **Video 5** free for titles. Titles should be placed over an adjustment layer; unless that's the effect you are looking for of course.

Classified Intel

You could have also created a new adjustment layer, and just copied and pasted the effects across to that new layer, but the method used in this task underlines the versatility of Premiere Pro when it comes to reusing clips from any part of your project. The blur filter is used here to enhance the feeling of an event that was 'not clearly' remembered and is not a usual element of nighttime fakery.

Adding viewpoints

You've already added a lot of detail to the interview by using the cutaway shots and reconstruction shots in various J- and L-cuts. However, most interviews you see on TV will flick between the standard two shots (**Two_Shot.avi** is an example of this) and over the shoulder shots to create a sense of intimacy with the people on screen. It's often used to add reaction (nodding) shots from the news reporter.

In this next section you will use two over-the-shoulder clips, **OS_at_Newsperson.avi** and **OS_at_Witness.avi**, to add new viewpoints to your interview. You will achieve this using the Lift function, as well as the ever popular three- and four-point edits.

Engage Thrusters

Here you will create multiple viewpoints by cutting clips with the assistance of the **Audio Waveform** display. Perform the following steps:

1. Locate the **OS_at_Newsperson.avi** clip in the project Video bin and send it to the Source Monitor. Make the Source Monitor the active panel, then use the various keyboard shortcuts you have learned to locate the section where the newsperson asks "Can you tell us anything else about...." (hint – at about **04;06**).

2. When you have located this section of the clip, you will notice the newsperson saying the phrase "Can you tell" twice. Get rid of this slight speech stumble by placing an In point at the start of the second attempt to speak (at around **05;02**).

Trying to find the exact point between the first attempt at saying "Can you tell" and the second attempt can prove tricky when watching for visual cues. Solve this problem by right-clicking anywhere inside the Source Monitor and selecting **Display Mode | Audio Waveform** from the context menu. Then use the + (plus) key on the main keyboard area to zoom in on the waveform displayed in the Source Monitor. You can also access this option by clicking on the **Spanner** icon in the lower-right corner of the Source Monitor.

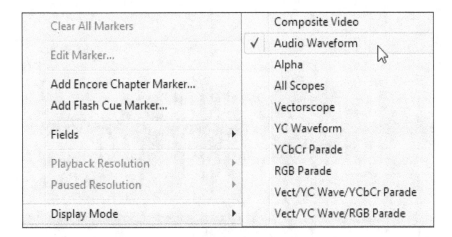

3. Now use the *J*, *K*, and *L* keys to find a point after the newsperson says the word "object" (take note of the waveform shape marked in the next screenshot). When you have located that point, set your Out point. Check your edit decisions by playing from the In point to the Out point by pressing *Ctrl + Shift* + Spacebar or *command + Shift* + Spacebar.

There is a drawn-out pronunciation of the last "T" in that word, be careful not to clip it (see arrows in the following screenshot).

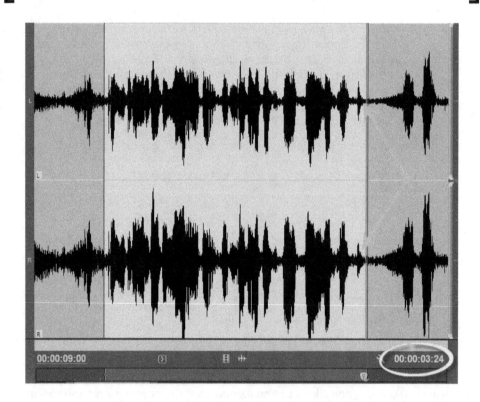

4. With the In and Out points marked, the duration of your edit decision is now displayed in the lower-right corner of your clip (**03;24** in this example). Make a note of the preceding screenshot on a scrap of paper. You will need it in the next steps.

5. Return to the Timeline and use the arrow keys to find the Out point of **Reconstruction_2.avi** (about **01;04;11**). Place a marker at this point (press *M*) then double-click on the marker to open up its properties window. Use the mouse or the keyboard to change the duration amount to match the duration you noted down in step 4. Click on **OK** to close this window.

You should now have a marker split over the duration area you need to clear in order to insert your clip. The duration of this marker is the same as your clip, so set an In point at the marker's left-hand side point and an Out point at the marker's right-hand side point.

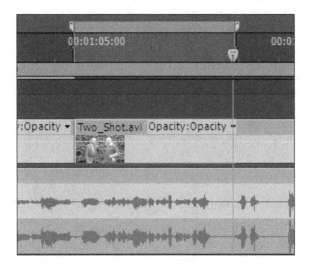

 The In and Out points should appear inside the marker brackets, as shown in the preceding screenshot.

6. Now that you are adding a new viewpoint, you need to remove the audio as well as the video from the Timeline. Click on the **Audio 1** track header area so that it now turns light gray, signifying it is no longer protected.

7. Now use the Lift function to remove this marked section of the Timeline. The keyboard shortcut for Lift is the ';' (semicolon) key.

8. You have now created a gap on the **Video 1** track and the **Audio 1** track. Insert the marked **OS_at_Newperson.avi** clip by first returning the Timeline indicator to the left-hand side of the marker (*Ctrl + Shift + M* or *command + Shift + M*), then returning to the Source Monitor. Send the clip to the Timeline using **Overwrite**.

9. Repeat the preceding steps to add the **OS_at_Newsperson.avi** clip to the Timeline for the line "Well... what sort of noise did it make... for instance". Use the following hints if you get lost:

    i. Use the Source Monitor. Find the phrase "What sort of noise did it make". Mark the In and Out points around it. (hint – use the Source Monitor's ability to display just the waveform of a clip; try to exclude "Well..." at the start of that section and "for instance" at the end).

    ii. Make a note of the duration. (hint – duration should be around **01;17**).

    iii. Place Timeline indicator a few frames before the interviewer says "Well..." (hint – around **01;09;15**).

    iv. Place a marker here (press *M*).

    v. Set duration of marker to match clip. (hint – double click on the marker).

    vi. Place the In and Out points using the marker brackets as a guide.

    vii. Return to Source Monitor. Send clip in the **Overwrite** mode.

10. The edit has been successful, but the next section of the Timeline has a small amount of repetition from the newsperson. Use the **OS_at_Witness.avi** clip to replace this using the suggested settings, given as follows:

    i. Send **OS_at_Witness.avi** to Source Monitor.

    ii. Find the phrase "Oh it was going..." and mark In and Out points around it. (hint – **08;21** to **13;02**).

    iii. Make a note of the duration. (hint – duration should be around **04;07**).

    iv. Place Timeline indicator at the end of the **OS_at_Newsperson.avi** clip on the Timeline. (hint – around **01;11;08**).

    v. Place a marker here (press *M*).

    vi. Set duration of marker to match clip. (hint – double-click on the marker).

    vii. Place the In and Out points using the marker brackets as a guide.

    viii. Return to Source Monitor. Send clip in the **Overwrite** mode.

11. You need to perform this one last time to complete this section of the edit. Using the **OS_at_Newsperson.avi** clip, add one last shot to the Timeline using the following suggestions:

    i.   Load the **OS_at_Newsperson.avi** clip into the Source Monitor.

    ii.   Find the phrase "A little bit like a helicopter". Mark the In and Out points around it (hint – **19;12** to **20;22** will cut out "do you think" from that section of dialog).

    iii.   Make a note of the duration. (hint – duration should be around **01;11**).

    iv.   Place Timeline indicator at the end of **OS_at_Witness.avi** (hint – around **01;15;15**).

    v.   Place a marker here (press *M*).

    vi.   Set duration of marker to match clip. (hint – double-click on the marker).

    vii.   Place the In and Out points using the marker brackets as a guide.

    viii.   Return to Source Monitor. Send clip in the **Overwrite** mode.

12. This edit decision has created a duplication of shots now, with **Two_Shot.avi** repeating some of the dialog from the over-the-shoulder shots. You can cure this using a skill you picked up at the start of this project, Extract! Start by placing an In point at the start of the **Two_Shot.avi** clip on the Timeline (hint – about **01;17;01**). Now move the Timeline indicator just before the witness says "Well...". Place an Out point here. (hint – about **01;20;22**).

13. Use the **Extract** command to remove this section of the Timeline (hint – press #).

14. Render and save your project before you move on to the next section.

Objective Complete - Mini Debriefing

In this section you discovered a way to add different viewpoints to a scene while maintaining continuity with the other shots on the Timeline using markers and three/four-point edits. This technique for editing interviews can of course also be used in films when editing a conversational scene that's filmed from various different angles, possibly at the same time, but likely it will be different takes. Each of these takes will have subtle differences in voice, action, and dialog (people are not machines), and it's your job as a video editor to iron out these differences, get rid of the vocal stumbles, and make it all appear as if every new viewpoint was filmed exactly at the same time. Lack of continuity is one of the big killers for audience attention spans. This technique is also used to control the pace of the dialog, how it switches back and forth, by cutting it to the barebone in order to remove 'dead-audio' time from your final version.

Classified Intel

While the method for using brackets might seem a little convoluted (it is undeniably a fussier method than simply using three- or four-point edits), there may be a time when you need to mark out possible durations on the Timeline and this method will achieve that. The action of creating a marker of a defined duration is of course not limited to working out Timeline areas, as you continue your edit career, you're sure to find more uses for this workflow. The main point of this Task was to demonstrate how Lift and markers can create yet another useful editing workflow.

Protecting the innocent

At the start of the interview the newsperson mentions that the witness would like to have his identity protected. In this task you will achieve that by adding a blur effect over the subject's face using what's called a track matte. Strictly speaking, the lack of motion tracking in Premiere Pro makes this effect somewhat of a challenge, but in this next section you'll see how use of the Premiere Pro CS6 titler application, combined with some simple stock effects, can create the look you are after, one that really will protect the innocent.

Engage Thrusters

Create a blurred face using the Premiere Pro titler. Perform the following steps:

1. Locate the first usage of the **Two_Shot.avi** clip on the Timeline and place the Timeline indicator at the start of that clip (around **37;07**).

2. Press *Ctrl + T* or *command + T* to open up the **New Title** window. Leave all the settings at the default but change the **Name** field to **Face Mask**. Press *Enter* to accept these settings. The titler will now open. You may find it useful to rearrange the layout slightly so that it resembles the next screenshot. Use the mouse to achieve this and expand the main window, and alter the size of the display window.

3. Press *E* on the keyboard to activate the Ellipse tool and then use the mouse to create an ellipse that covers the face of the witness. Click on the small cross in the upper-right corner of the titler to close this window once you are happy with the placement of the ellipse.

Once the ellipse has been created, you can resize and reposition it using the mouse. Just drag any handle to resize, and click/drag anywhere inside the ellipse to move it.

4. In the **Project** panel you will find a newly created **Face Mask** title. Drag-and-drop this onto **Video 3** so the start of the **Face Mask** title is lined up with the start of the **Two_Shot.avi** clip on **Video 1**. Drag the title out to cover the whole of this clip (a duration of about 8 seconds). Playback this section of the Timeline and you will see that the ellipse needs to be animated in order to match the movement of the witness. Start by clicking on the **Face Mask** title to select it, and then press *Shift + 5* to open the **Effect Controls** panel.

5. Make sure the Timeline indicator is at the very start of this clip, then dial open the **Motion** parameters (hint – click on triangle) and toggle keyframes on for the **Position** values using the **Toggle animation** icon (hint – the stopwatch icon). Finish by clicking on the word **Motion** to show the bounding box inside the Program Monitor.

6. Use the left arrow key to move forward to a point where the head of the witness is extended most beyond the ellipse, and then use the mouse (click inside the image) to drag the ellipse back to a point where it covers the head.

7. Repeat step 6, moving through the clip and identifying points where the **Face Mask** ellipse needs to be moved. When you have reached the end of the clip, use the right arrow key to move backwards through the clip and alter the position of the mask as you see fit.

Avoid adding too many keyframes as this can cause Premiere Pro to slow down and become unresponsive. With a segment of this duration you should need no more than around 12 keyframes to control the animation of the face mask. One way to avoid too many keyframes is to make the ellipse slightly larger than the actual head.

8. Once you are happy with the animation of the face mask, it's time to add the blur effect. Start by clicking on the **Two_Shot.avi** clip beneath the title. Hold down the *Alt* or *option* key, and then click-and-drag a copy of the clip upwards to **Video 2**.

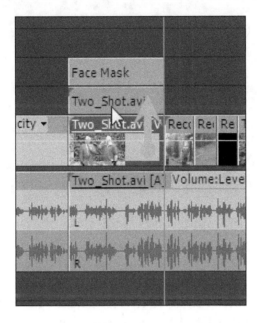

9. Click on the **Two_Shot.avi** copy on **Video 2** in order to select it and then open the **Effects** panel (*Shift + 7*). Type Mosaic into the search field, and then locate the **Mosaic** effect in the Stylize folder. Drag-and-drop this effect onto the clip on **Video 2** (the copy).Open the **Effect Controls** panel (*Shift + 5*) and alter the **Horizontal** and **Vertical** blocks to 75. Check the **Sharp Colors** checkbox.

10. In the **Effects** panel, type in `Matte` into the search field, then locate the **Track Matte Key** at the bottom of the `Keying` folder. Drag-and-drop this effect onto the clip on **Video 2**. In the **Effect Controls** panel for the clip on **Video 2**, alter **Matte** from **NONE** to **Video 3**. The mosaic filter will now be confined within the limits of the ellipse you created earlier in this task.

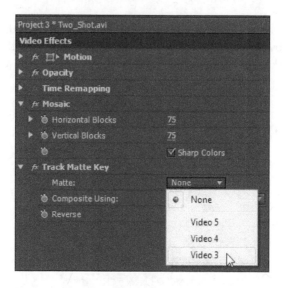

11. There are other clips along the Timeline that need to have a face mask placed over them in order to protect the identity of the witness. Take some time to repeat the preceding steps (hint – the 'Man walking away from the pub' shot will require you to keyframe the **Scale** values as well as the **Position** values).

12. You will need to do some rendering once you have completed this section. Press *Enter* to begin this, and then save your project before moving on to the next section.

Objective Complete - Mini Debriefing

This is a fairly old trick and although it really works best on subjects that don't move around too much (due to the aforementioned lack of motion tracking), it can still create a clean and believable version of this effect. At any rate, it's a handy tool to have when you need to quickly blur out a number plate, a sign on the wall, some unsuitable images, or perhaps a brand name on a T-shirt.

You will need to put in some time getting the keyframe animation smooth and stable, but that's video editing for you, 10 percent inspiration and 90 percent perspiration. Oh, and if you don't like the mosaic effect, try swapping it out for one of the other blur filters.

In this section you also touched briefly on using the titler. This is something you will return to later in this project.

Classified Intel

It's important that you animate the mask before you add a blur or mosaic effect. If you do it the other way around, you may find it an eye-straining exercise to try and match the blurry borders of the matte to the object you are attempting to obscure.

Adding lower thirds

Lower thirds are titles that display in the bottom third of the screen. They usually have a small logo incorporated into them, and have some information on what the viewer is looking at; name of presenter, location, and perhaps what sort of footage they are watching.

In this task you will create a multilayered lower third inside a new sequence, turn that into a nested sequence, and then use it to display your titles on the main Timeline. You have used many of these skills before, but not for creating titles, so the instructions given next will flick backwards and forwards between sparse and detailed, to give you a chance with the new concepts, but to help you revise some skills you really should have learned by now.

Engage Thrusters

Perform the following steps for creating lower third titles for your main Timeline:

1. Switch to the Timeline and create a new sequence (*Ctrl + N* or *command + N*). Call this sequence **News_Reporter_1**.

2. Once the new sequence is created, move back to the **Project** panel and create a black video clip by clicking on the **New Item** icon at the lower-right corner of the **Project** panel, as shown in the following screenshot:

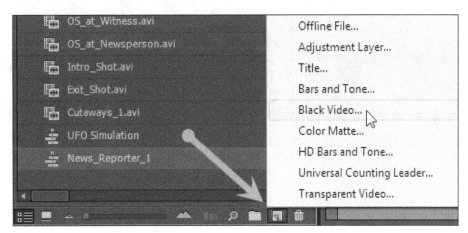

3. Drag-and-drop the black video clip onto **Video 1** and expand it using any of the methods learned so far, so the duration of this clip is around 10 seconds.

4. Open the **Effects** panel and type in Ramp into the search field. Drag-and-drop the **Ramp** effect onto the black video clip on **Video 1**. Move to the **Effect Controls** panel and define a start color that is dark blue by clicking on the small color square and altering the colors in the color picker. Click on **OK** to close the color picker.

5. Repeat step 4 but this time with the end color square and define a color that is very light blue.

6. Return to the **Effects** panel and type in the word Bevel. Drag-and-drop the **Bevel Edges Thick** effect onto the black video clip on **Video 1**. Dial open the parameters for the bevel edges effect and alter **Edge Thickness** to 0.05, **Light Intensity** to 0.50, and **Light Angle** to 25.0. Finish off by finding the **Fast Blur** effect and adding that to the black video clip, use a setting of 50, then find and add **Edge Feather** and use a value of 20.

7. Make sure the Timeline indicator is at the start of the Timeline and dial open the **Opacity** controls. By default Animation toggle should be selected (the stopwatch icon should show as depressed). Change **Opacity** to 0%.

8. Move the Timeline indicator 1 second into the black video clip and then change Opacity to 50%.

9. Move the Timeline indicator to 1 second before the end of the clip (**09;00**) and click on the **Add/Remove Keyframe** icon to create a keyframe to the value of 50% of **Opacity** at the current position. Finish by moving the Timeline indicator to the end of the black video clip and creating a final keyframe by changing **Opacity** to a value of 0%.

When creating keyframes, it is important to note that changes will always occur between one keyframe and the next. In the preceding example, if you had not created a keyframe with the value of 50%, and instead skipped to creating a 0% opacity keyframe at the end of the clip, the opacity value would have altered in gradual steps from the previous keyframe to the last, creating a gradual fade out lasting almost the complete duration of the black video clip. By adding a third keyframe in step 9, you caused the effect to stay at the 50% value from the first keyframe to the second.

10. You are now ready to create the actual title. Move the Timeline indicator to the 1-second mark on the Timeline and press *Ctrl + T* or *command + T* to open the titler. Name it as **News_Person** and press *Enter* to accept the default values.

11. Press *T* to select the Type tool, and then click on one of the font styles. Click inside the blue area and press *Ctrl + Shift + C* or *command + Shift + C* to center the text. Now type in `Jeffery Jefferson` and press *Enter* to drop the cursor down a line. Type in `LNC News`. Click on the Selection tool, and then drag out the textbox to resize and reposition it inside the bevel edges, as shown in the next screenshot. Exit the titler by clicking on the red X.

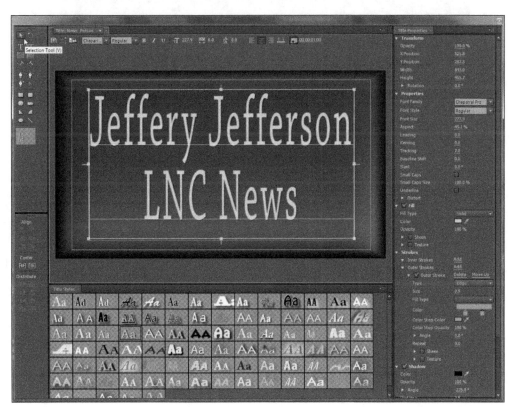

12. Drag-and-drop the **News_Person** title from the **Project** panel onto **Video 2** at the 1-second mark (the Timeline indicator should still be at this position. Leave the Timeline indicator there and open the titler again. Call this title **Lines** and press *Enter* to accept the defaults.

13. Once the titler has opened, press the *L* key to select the Line tool, and then with the *Shift* key held down, draw a straight line under **Jeffery Jefferson** and under **LNC News**. Close the titler when you are done, and then drag-and-drop the **Lines** title from the **Project** panel onto **Video 3** at the 1-second mark.

 Holding down the *Shift* key while drawing a line constrains the line, forcing it to be straight.

14. Hold down the *Shift* key and then click on the **Lines** title on the Timeline, and then on the **News_Person** title to select them both at the same time. Place the mouse cursor at the end of the titles (so that it shows a bracket with an arrow facing left), then drag both clips to the 9-second mark on the Timeline.

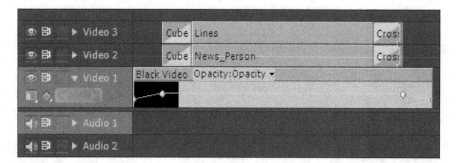

15. Open the **Effects** panel and type in Cube into the search field. Drag-and-drop the **Cube Spin** effect onto the start of the **Lines** title on **Video 3** and repeat to add it to the start of the **News_Person** title on **Video 2**. Double-click on the cube spin at the start of the **Line** title on **Video 3** and check the **Reverse** checkbox in the **Effect Controls** panel.

16. Type in Cross into the **Effects** panel's search field, then drag-and-drop the **Cross Dissolve** effect onto the end of the **Lines** title and onto the end of the **News_Person** title.

17. Click on the **Project 3** tab to display that Timeline sequence, then place the Timeline indicator at the start of the intro, **Shot.avi** (around **12;01**).

18. Switch to the **Project** panel and drag-and-drop the **News_Reporter_1** sequence and place it on **Video 5**. Click on the **News_Reporter_1** clip on the Timeline to select it.

19. Switch to the **Effect Controls** Panel and click on the word **Motion** so that a bounding box appears around the title (reduce the Program Monitor display to 50 percent or less if you cannot see this bounding box). Using the mouse, resize and reposition the title to your own preferences, although of course the tradition is at the bottom third of the screen.

20. Save and render your project before finishing this task.

 If you want to give less of a square feel to your titles, deselect the **Uniform scale** checkbox under the **Scale** parameter.

Objective Complete - Mini Debriefing

In this task you used various Premiere Pro effects to create an interesting background for your title, and you took advantage of the nested sequences function to create a multilayered title in a separate sequence. See the *Classified Intel* section given ahead for details on how that nested sequence can be used again and again, saving more valuable editing time and creating a uniform look to your titles without added duplication of work.

Classified Intel

Once you have created a new nested sequence to make a multilayered title, you can use it for the basis of all your titles in that project. Simply right-click on the nested sequence in the **Project** panel and select **Duplicate** from the context menu. Then rename the duplicate (for example, **Witness_Title_1**), double-click on this to open up the duplicate sequence, and then edit the titles to something else (for example, eyewitness). You will still have to save the title under a different name, but you will at least have saved some time by having the basics in place.

Mission Accomplished

A lot is going on in this project. Here you've picked up skill sets involving the Extract and Lift functions, and have seen how to create special effects using only the stuff Adobe gave you when you first bought Premiere Pro CS6. You've even seen how easy it is to turn day into night and you've also created multilayered titles for lower third use, and have learned how to use nested sequences to save time and effort in their creation.

In addition to this, you've revised many of the editing skills learned in Project 1 and Project 2, hopefully reinforcing those techniques and hammering into you where those keyboard shortcuts are lurking. At this stage of the book you should be able now to edit a variety of different projects, from films to documentaries and most stuff in between.

You Ready To Go Gung HO? A Hotshot Challenge

The project as it stands looks pretty good, but there are many shots that could still be added, most of them from the over-the-shoulder shots at the witness or the news reporter. Return now to this project and try to integrate those clips into your sequence using the techniques described in this project. You'll find that the best place to add them will be between **01;12;19** and **01;47;23**.

Don't forget to add the face blur effect to any shot that shows the witness. Once you are happy with the final edit, add some more titles, for example you could add the title called "Reconstruction" to that segment of the project, and you could add an eyewitness' lower third for the first time the witness is shown on screen.

Lastly, you might want to trawl the Internet for a helicopter sound and use the Rate Stretch tool on it to distort the tone and accentuate the alien feel of the **Reconstruction_2.avi** clip.

Save your project in a safe place when you've finished your Gung Ho challenge, you're bound to have more ideas for improving it.

Project 4

See the Bigger Picture – Edit Multiple Cameras

In *Project 1*, *Creating a Movie Montage – the Easy Way*, you looked at the ways to automate the process of creating a montage edit, and then in *Project 2*, *Cutting a Short Film without Getting Stung* and *Project 3*, *Protect the Innocent – Interview Edit Techniques*, you did everything in a very manual fashion. That's not a bad thing, as most editing is hard manual work, but after all that mental perspiration, this project attempts to give your brain (and your fingers) a little automated rest.

In this project, you will learn how to take clips from nine simultaneous camera angles and get Premiere Pro CS6 to do the hard work of synchronizing them together, allowing you to perform multi-camera editing.

There are two great new multi-camera improvements in Premiere Pro CS6; firstly, the whole process of creating multi-camera editing has been greatly simplified (much to the relief of its userbase), and secondly, the four-camera limit of previous versions has been expanded, and you are now allowed to have a theoretical unlimited amount of cameras!

Mission Briefing

Your objective in this project is to learn how to synchronize camera clips together to create a multi-camera sequence that can be used with the **Multi-Camera Monitor**. You'll then see how easy it is to edit as many cameras as your computer is capable of dealing with. The project will also show you how to edit and fine-tune the multi-camera sequence, and how to enhance it using a **Picture-in-Picture** (**PiP**) effect. You'll also add some transitions and titles just to keep your new-found editing skills from going rusty while you use Premiere Pro's automated multi-camera features. Once you're finished, you should end up with a Timeline that looks something like the following screenshot:

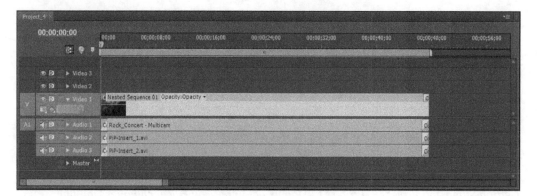

Why Is It Awesome?

This project will help you edit a nine-camera shoot. In addition to that, you will add two more camera angles as insert shots. All the camera footage was created in iClone 5 to simulate a concert, with various different camera angles becoming live at various times during the concert. This has created footage with plenty of editing decisions for you to make. In addition to learning the fundamental principles of multi-camera editing, this project should also provide you with an experience similar to editing a live event. When you reach the task where you need to pick and choose the camera angles, imagine the director sitting behind you saying "cut to camera 4".

Premiere Pro CS6 can cope with as many camera feeds as you want to throw at it, and the temptation when creating an example project like this is to use as many cameras as possible to exploit that fact. However, all this multi-camera goodness comes at a high performance price, and if your computer is not the latest and greatest, you might find it chokes when presented with nine streams of video. If this is the case, then tailor this chapter to your own requirements and use only five or six feeds. If that doesn't work for you, use less. If you get down to two and still have problems, you're probably going to need to upgrade part or all of your computer. Bear in mind, the clips supplied with this project are plain, old NTSC DV clips; if your system struggles with these, imagine how badly it would manage with HD.

Your Hotshot Objectives

The process of creating and editing a multi-camera shoot with Premiere Pro CS6 can throw some users off their seats, so in this project the tasks have been split into small, simple steps to follow these procedures:

- ▶ Organizing your media
- ▶ Creating a multi-camera sync point
- ▶ Activating multi-camera
- ▶ Creating a multi-camera Timeline
- ▶ Editing and tuning multi-cam clips
- ▶ Creating insert clips (PiP)
- ▶ Finishing off

Mission Checklist

Before you start this project, there are a number of preparations you need to make. Firstly, open your designated Video drive and access the Hotshot's folder you created in *Project 1*. Here, you should find the project folders created in the previous projects. Create a new folder called Project 4, and inside that new folder, create three folders named Video, Images, and Audio.

Video

With the new folders created, access the folder containing the content you downloaded and extracted in *Project 2*. You should find a folder inside called `Project 4`. Copy the contents of this folder to the `Video` folder you created at the start of this project. There are 11 video files in total (`Camera_1.avi to Camera_9.avi`, `PiPInsert_1.avi`, and `PiPInsert_2.avi`). Once you have the media copied to the correct location on your computer, proceed to the first task.

Audio

If you want to add a rock track to your project, you'll need to source a piece of music that is 49 seconds long (`SoundDogs.com` is a good place to search), or edit a piece of music from your own audio collection. Just remember that you probably don't have the rights to music obtained from anywhere other than royalty-free music sites, and so, any music you do add to this project can only be for your own personal amusement.

As mentioned earlier, the audio file should be around 49 seconds in length, so you will probably need to edit your choice in a sound application such as **Audacity**. This highly useful program is available as a free download from `audacity.sourceforge.net/download`. Make sure your audio file is of the correct length before moving on to the next section.

If you prefer not to use a separate program to shorten the duration of the audio, simply import the audio into your project, and then use the Source Monitor to define a section of the music required for this project.

If you do decide to add a music track to this project, then follow the *Mission Checklist* section.

Adding an audio track

Use this short task to add an audio track to your project folder. To do, follow these steps:

1. Open the `Audio` folder on your designated video drive.
2. Copy and paste the `Audio` file you wish to use with this project to that folder. Move on to the first task in this project once you have completed these instructions.

Organizing your media

Organizing your media for a multi-camera edit is pretty much the same as setting up any edit, so essentially this task should be a breeze for you. In fact, why not try setting up your project as you've been taught in *Project 1*, *Project 2*, and *Project 3* before you look at the task on the next few pages. Once you have finished setting up your project, read through the instructions to see if you got everything right.

If you still don't feel that confident, you can of course simply follow the instructions as usual. No one is judging you; learn at your own pace, and in a way that feels comfortable. But, above all, just learn! The keyboard shortcuts you should have used appear at the end of this task.

Prepare for Lift Off

Once you have completed all the preparations detailed in the *Mission Checklist* section of this project, you are ready to go. Launch Premiere Pro CS6 in the usual way, and then proceed to the next part.

Engage Thrusters

To organize your project in this short task, follow these steps:

1. Once Premiere Pro CS6 has finished launching and the **Recent Projects** splash screen appears, select Hotshots Template - Montage.

2. When the project has finished loading, save this as Hotshots - Multi-Cam and close any open sequences.

3. Go to **Windows** | **Workspace** | **Editing Optimized** that you created in *Project 1*.

4. Select the **Project** panel.

5. Open the Video bin without creating a separate window.

6. Import all 11 video files in this project's Video folder.

7. Create a new sequence. Pick any settings at random; you will correct this in the next step.

8. Rename the sequence Project_4.

9. Match the Timeline settings with any clip from the Video bin.
10. Delete this clip from the Timeline.

11. Set the **Project** panel as the active panel. Switch to **List View** if it is not already displayed.

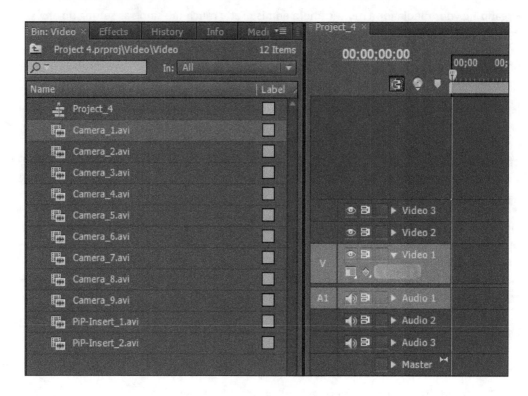

12. Save your project before moving on to the next task.

Objective Complete - Mini Debriefing

How did you do? Were you able to complete this task without reading it through first? Do you remember the keyboard shortcuts listed in the next items? Don't feel too bad if you don't remember everything, but if you don't remember anything, perhaps you need to redo *Projects 2* and *Project 3* to refresh what you have learned.

The keyboard shortcuts covered in this task are as follows:

▶ *Ctrl* or *command* + double-click: This shortcut opens bin without creating a separate **Project** panel

▶ *Ctrl* or *command* + *N*: This shortcut creates a new sequence

▶ *Ctrl* or *command* + / (backslash): This shortcut creates a new Bin folder in the**Project** panel

▶ *Ctrl* or *command* + *I*: This shortcut opens the **Import** window

- ▸ *Shift + 1*: This shortcut sets **Project** panel as active
- ▸ *Shift + 3*: This shortcut sets Timeline as active

Classified Intel

In this project, you dropped a clip on the Timeline to synchronize the Timeline settings with that of the clips being used. This is a good habit to get into, but not strictly necessary when working with multi-camera as the opportunity to match the Timeline to clips will also be available in the next task.

Creating a multi-camera sync point

In this next task, you will address the way in which you can synchronize the various different camera clips, so they display correctly inside the multi-camera interface. Synchronizing cameras is something that's usually accomplished during the live shoot, and often a clapboard might be used, or a light and signal generator would be deployed.

In this project, it's assumed that the concert venue was in darkness, and that a flash gun has been fired at the back of the stage; an audio burst was also sent out precisely at that point in time. In reality, you probably would have either one or the other, or possibly you would have someone stand on stage and clap their hands, assuming, of course, they could be seen and heard by all cameras at the same time.

In this project, you can decide to use either the audio or visual cue to add and name a marker on your clips. This marker will be used to create a sync point that Premiere Pro can use to line up the Video files to play back in synchronization.

Creating a sync-Point marker during a live shoot is problematic. Your choices are usually either a light cue or a sound cue. To effectively use sound as your sync point, all the cameras need to be within a relative distance of the sound-making device (clapboard or tone generator). Those that are too far away could suffer a slight delay in hearing the sound cue.

A light cue is, therefore, a more attractive cue for a video editor. Of course, the problem is how to achieve a light cue. If your crew were on a modest shoot with two or three cameras, then they may have used a flash gun from a camera (or other device with a flash, such as a mobile phone). If this is not practical, for example in a large venue, then it may be possible to have the light engineer give a single blip from one of the ceiling-strobe lights. If all the cameras are running, they will pick this up, and then it's just a matter for the editor to line up the strobe blips from each camera clip.

Engage Thrusters

Create a sync point for you multi-camera clips. Follow these steps:

1. Make sure that the **Project** panel is the active panel.

2. Select all the clips in the `Video` bin by clicking on `Camera_1.avi`, then hold down the *Shift* key and click on `Camera_9.avi`.

3. Right-click on any of the selected clips and select `Open in Source Monitor` from the context menu. This will send all the clips to that area of the interface.

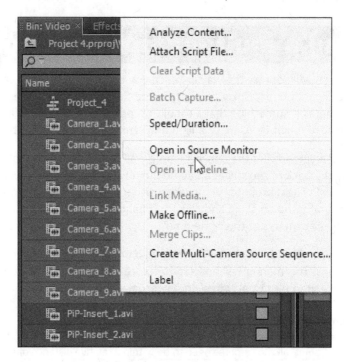

4. Access the `Camera_1.avi` clip by selecting it from the menu in the upper-left corner of the Source Monitor.

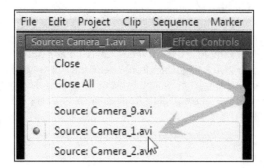

5. Switch the Source Monitor to show the waveform by right-clicking anywhere inside the Source Monitor and selecting **Display Mode** | **Audio Waveform** from the context menu.

6. Scrub through the clip using the *L* key on the keyboard. At a certain point in the clip, you should hear a short tone sound and see the waveform. This is your synchronization point. Each clip will have the same synchronization point at the same point in their timeline. Use the *+* (plus) key on the main keyboard area (not the number pad area) to zoom in on the Source Monitor's play line.

7. Use the *J*, *K*, and *L* keys to position the Source Monitor indicator at the point of the tone sounds. Your Source Monitor indicator should be placed exactly as shown in the following screenshot:

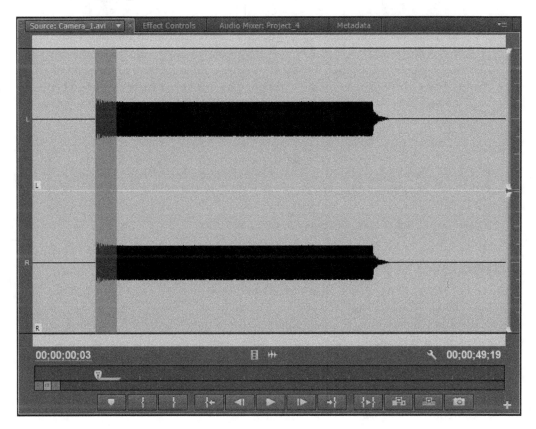

8. Place a marker at this point by pressing *M* on the keyboard.

9. Open the **Marker** properties by double-clicking directly on it. This will display the properties window for that marker. Locate the **Name** field and type `Sync-Point`. Do not close the **Marker** properties window just yet.

10. With the **Marker** properties window still open, highlight the `Sync-Point` text using the mouse, then right-click and select **Copy** to create a copy of this text in your computer's clipboard. Close the **Marker** properties window by pressing *Enter* on the keyboard.

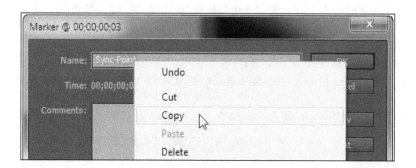

11. Now repeat steps 4 through 9 to create a marker point on each of the camera clips. Use *Ctrl + V* or *command + V* or right-click and select **Paste** to place a copy of the text `Sync-Point` into the **Name** field of each **Marker** properties window that you create and open.

 Each marker must have exactly the same name; using copy and paste will hopefully avoid typo errors that can seriously ruin your multi-cam experience (and a day).

12. Save your project before moving on to the next task.

Objective Complete - Mini Debriefing

At the end of this section, you will have created a set marker at the exact same position on each of the nine-camera clips. You also set a name for that marker by opening up each individual marker, and entering or pasting the name into the correct field. These markers will be used in the next task.

The keyboard shortcuts covered in this task are as follows:

- *Ctrl* or *command + C*: This shortcut copies the selected text into the computer's clipboard

- *Ctrl* or *command + V*: This shortcut pastes the contents of the computer's clipboard into the selected field

- *M*: This shortcut places a marker on the Timeline

- *J*, *K*, and *L*: These shortcuts position the Timeline indicator (in this case, inside the Source Monitor)

- ▶ + (plus): This shortcut zooms in on the Source Monitor's Timeline (main keyboard area)

- ▶ *Shift + 2*: This shortcut sets Source Monitor as active

Classified Intel

These clips are all the same length, and so you could have used a simple In point as your synchronization reference point. However, other multi-camera clips you receive in the future are unlikely to be of the same length and start at exactly the same time, and with such clips, you will need to use the marker method to create a point which Premiere Pro can use to sync up the clips.

Activating multi-camera

In this task, you will use the sync-point markers created in the last task to activate the multi-camera feature of Premiere Pro CS6. This is a fairly simple workflow, but one that seems to be fuddling some users, even though the whole process has been simplified in Version CS6. Although this task is rather short and sweet, it's worth keeping separate, so you can fully understand the last section required to activate and access the multi-camera functions.

Engage Thrusters

Activate the multi-cam camera using your newly created multi-cam clip. Follow these steps:

1. Make the **Project** panel active and switch to **List View** if the `Bin` file is currently set to **Icon View**.

 Switching from **Icon View** to **List View** in step 1 is not a required step when using multi-camera; however, you may find it easier to complete the remaining steps in this task with **List View** selected as the layout for your **Project** panel.

2. Click once on `Camera_1.avi` clip to select it.

3. Hold down the *Shift* key, and then click on `Camera_9.avi` clip. All the clips from one through to nine should now be selected; clips **PiP-Insert_1.avi** and **PiP-Insert_2.avi** should remain unselected. You will use those two clips in another section of this project.

> If you have a low-powered computer, you might want to think about choosing less than the full amount of cameras available in this project. Processing more than four or five streams of video data at any one time can cause problems if your computer is not up to the task; these problems display as a stuttering playback, also known as **dropped-frames**. However, if you are unsure on how many streams your computer can handle, try out all nine to start with, then reduce that amount if you are having playback problems.

4. Right-click any of the nine selected clips and select **Create Multi-Camera Source Sequence** from the context menu.

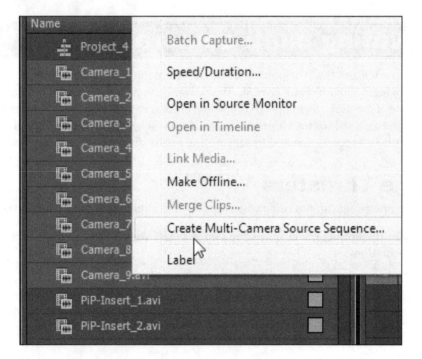

5. Wait for the **Create Multi-Camera Source Sequence** window to open, and then in the **Name** field, type Rock_Concert - Multicam.

6. Click on the **Clip Marker** radio button to select it, the sync point that you created in the last task should be the only option for you to choose. If the window you are working in looks like the following screenshot, then click on **OK** to close it:

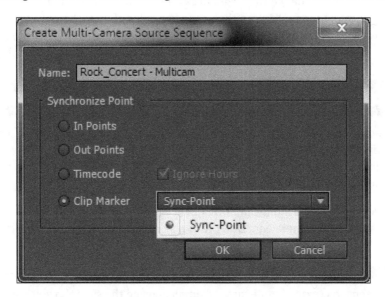

7. A new asset will appear in your Bin file called Rock_Concert - Multicam.

8. Save your project before moving on to the next section.

 Users familiar with previous versions of Premiere Pro will probably be scratching their heads around now and saying "is that it?" Well yes, that is how the process now works in CS6; one that has been greatly simplified from previous versions! There are still a few more steps to be covered before you are completely ready to use multi-camera, but this part is at least a lot easier than it was!

Objective Complete - Mini Debriefing

As promised at the start of this task, this is a fairly straightforward workflow, and you should have few problems following it. In this section, you have created a new type of clip, the multi-camera sequence, which is used exclusively by the **Multi-Cam Monitor**. At the moment, the clips will do little to impress you. In fact, if you drag the clip on to the Timeline, it will show just **Camera 1** in the Program Monitor. Don't worry, you'll be impressed in the next section.

Classified Intel

The multi-camera sequence shares the same color label in the **Bin** area as a normal sequence. If you want to change that, right-click on the multi-camera sequence and select **Label** from the context menu. You can then choose a color of your choice, although the names of those colors may mystify you a little. Whatever happened to blue, green, and red? You may be tempted to select **Cerulean** just to find out what color that actually is.

Creating a multi-camera Timeline

You've created marker points, synced them up, and fed them to the great multi-camera creator that dwells deep within Premiere Pro CS6. You're finally ready to start with actual multi-cam editing. There are different ways to do this, but for the moment, this task will take you through one of the simpler methods.

In this task, you will send the multi-camera sequence to the timeline, activate the multi-camera tool, then create a multi-camera edit. Don't worry, all of that is much easier than it sounds.

Engage Thrusters

Follow these steps to create a multi-camera Timeline using the sync clip you created in the last task:

1. Start by right-clicking on the **Rock_Concert - Multicam** clip and choosing **New Sequence From Clip** from the context menu. Once the new sequence has opened, press the backslash key to zoom the Timeline to the clip.

 If you want to use the optional music track, discussed at the start of this project, open up **Audio 9** now, then drag-and-drop the audio clip on to **Audio 3**.

2. Open the Multi-Camera Monitor by selecting **Window** | **Multi-Camera Monitor** or **Premiere** | **Multi-Camera Monitor**.

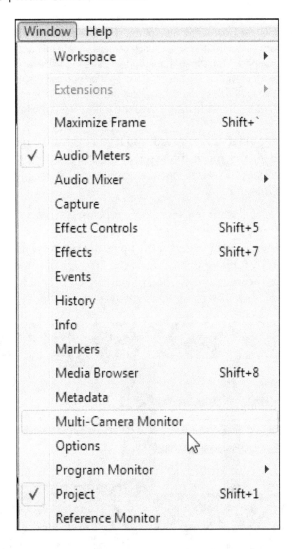

3. The Multi-Camera Monitor should automatically open up with the **Rock_Concert - Multicam** clip displayed inside the matrix. If it is not, click once on the **Rock_Concert - Multicam** clip on the Timeline.

4. Place the mouse cursor over the lower-right corner of the Multi-Camera Monitor and drag it out so that it almost covers the entire Premiere Pro CS6 interface.

When editing with the multi-camera function, it's not actually useful for you to see the Timeline or the two monitors you normally use. In fact, it can be a distraction. When possible, always expand the Multi-Camera Monitor out to its maximum size in order to get a better view of each camera. The bigger the Multi-Camera Monitor, the bigger each camera square will be. If you have docked the Multi-Camera Monitor so that it appears as a tab in the area occupied by the Source Monitor and the Effects Control, then you can maximize it using the accent shortcut. If this keyboard shortcut does not work for you, see *Project 1* for details on getting non-US keyboards to use this new feature in Premiere Pro CS6.

5. Check to see that **Video 1** is selected, and if you have an audio clip on a separate track (the optional rock music discussed at the start of this project), then make sure that audio track has a little speaker icon inside its track header, so you can hear it during your edit.

6. At this point, you will want to check if all your clips are synchronized correctly. Do this by returning the Multi-Camera Monitor's Timeline indicator to the start of the multi-camera clip by pressing the up arrow key. Now use the right arrow key to move slowly forward until you see the first sign of the white square. All nine cameras (or however many you are working with) should show white at the same time. If you have the computer's speaker on, you should also hear the tone.

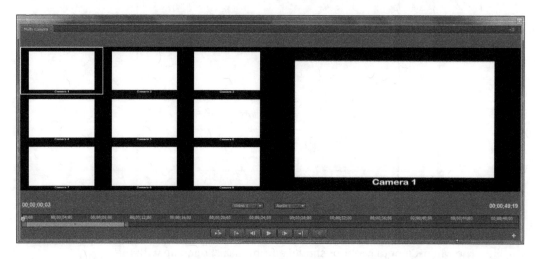

 If one or more white squares appear later or earlier than the others, you need to close the Multi-Camera Monitor, open those clips in the Video bin, and check their relative marker positions. Continue only when this part of the task is 100 percent correct.

7. The clip lasts about 50 seconds; play through it by pressing the Space bar. The main monitor area will display **Camera 1** – ignore this for the moment and pay close attention to the nine smaller squares. Each one of these is overlaid with the label camera x (where x is the number of the camera). Make a mental note of which shots you want to use. Play the clip back several times (up arrow to return the Timeline indicator to the start and then Space bar) before moving on to the next section.

> To get a better view of the various cameras, click on the **Window** options in the upper-right corner of the Multi-Camera Monitor and deselect **Show Preview Monitor**. Don't forget to turn it back on again once you have finished reviewing the material.

8. You will have observed from your playbacks that **Camera 8** goes live earlier than the others. It would be good if the multi-camera sequence defaulted to this camera instead of **Camera 1**. To correct this, reduce the size of the Multi-Camera Monitor, so you can see the Timeline, then right-click on the **Rock_Concert - MultiCam** sequence on the timeline and select **Multi-Camera | Camera 8** from the context menu.

9. Set the Multi-Camera Monitor as the active panel by clicking inside its frame, and expand it back out to cover the whole of your screen.

10. Return the Timeline indicator to the start of the Timeline and then toggle on the **Record** button by pressing *0* (zero) on the keyboard. Watch out for a peculiarity of Premiere Pro CS6, if you leave the record button toggled on, but don't press playback, it can automatically deselect itself – something to check before you go to the next step.

> The number keys you need to use for the last and next steps are the ones just below the function keys on your keyboard. Do not use the number pad area, as this will not select a camera. If you did push it accidently, press *Esc* to deselect that function.

11. Press the Space bar to start playback. As the cameras begin to appear, press the corresponding number on the keyboard to switch to that camera, that is, if you want to cut to **Camera 4**, press the number *4* on the number keys of your keyboard (not the number pad area). Keep selecting different camera shots using the number keyboard shortcuts until the Timeline indicator reaches the end of the sequence. Try to finish on **Camera 2** if possible and avoid making too many fast and frantic camera changes.

> If you prefer to use the mouse over keyboard shortcuts (for whatever reason), then you can also select your new camera angle by clicking inside the square representing the chosen camera. If you have a lot of rapid cuts to make, you may find the mouse method difficult and inaccurate to use.

12. When the Timeline indicator reaches the end of the clip's duration, the multi-camera edit will automatically end, and the edit decisions that you have chosen will appear on the Timeline. Keep the Multi-Camera Monitor open for the moment as you will need it in the next task.

> Don't worry if you felt rushed into choosing camera angles or if you made any mistakes, these will be corrected in the next task. Also, don't feel under pressure to use all the nine cameras in your project. This number of cameras has been supplied to you simply to demonstrate Premiere Pro CS6's new ability to handle more than four cameras in multi-camera, and it is not an indication of how many cameras you need to use in this edit to make a good Timeline. Once again, editing is often more about what you reject than what you select.

13. Save your project before continuing.

Objective Complete - Mini Debriefing

In this task, you have created your first multi-camera edit. If you press the **Play** button again on the Multi-Camera Monitor, you'll see this sequence played back in real time, although, if you have a low-powered computer, there may be a few dropped frames (shown as a jerky movement on screen).

The keyboard shortcuts covered in this task are as follows:

> ▸ / (backslash): This shortcut zooms Timeline to show all clips

> ▸ *0* (zero): This shortcut toggles the multi-camera record to **On**

> ▸ Spacebar: This shortcut begins to playback

> ▸ Numbers 1 to 9: These shortcuts switch to the respective camera number

> ▸ Left and right arrow: This shortcut positions the Timeline indicator (in this case inside the Source Monitor) one frame at a time

Classified Intel

In this task, you selected the cameras using the keyboard shortcuts *1* through *9*. Zero (on the upper numbers) is mapped to toggling the multi-camera record on or off and can't be assigned to a camera number. If you have more than nine cameras (and a super system to play them on), you will need to use the mouse to select camera number from 10 and above. Alternatively, you can open the **Keyboard Shortcuts** option (**Edit | Keyboard Shortcuts**) and type `Multi` into the **Search** field. This will allow you to assign keyboard shortcuts for cameras above the number nine.

Editing and tuning multi-camera clips

It's all a little rushed, isn't it? In any multi-camera edit, you have to make decisions on the fly, a little like you would in a live environment. If you plan to edit in that sort of workplace, then practicing your editing decisions under pressure is a great idea. It's just a pity that Adobe won't allow the Multi-Camera Monitor to work with the arrow keys to create a more relaxed multi-camera experience. However, you can go back and edit those clips as you would on any other Timeline, and you can do that using the Multi-Camera Monitor. This will allow you to replace any camera angles you were not happy with the first time round.

In this task, you will edit the multi-camera edit sequence using the **Replace edit** function in the Multi-Camera Monitor. You will then go on to fine-tune the clips using your old friend, the **Trim** tool.

Engage Thrusters

To refine your multi-camera edit points in this task, follow these steps:

1. Start by returning the Timeline indicator inside the Multi-Camera Monitor to the start of the Timeline by pressing the *Home* key.

2. Reduce the size of the Multi-Camera Monitor by dragging the bottom area of the monitor upwards to reveal the Timeline.

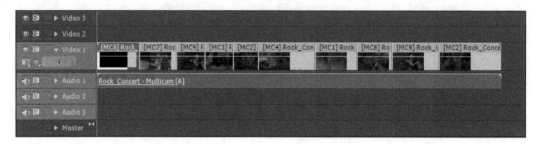

3. Playback the Timeline a couple of times by pressing the *Spacebar* key. Do this until you have an idea of the changes you want to make. Return the Timeline indicator to the start of the Timeline inside the Multi-Camera Monitor when you are ready to move on to the next step.

4. Use the down (**Go to Next Edit Point**) arrow to move the Timeline indicator to the start of a camera you would like to swap for a different view point.

 You can also use the mouse to click on the **Go to Previous Edit Point** and **Go to Next Edit Point** buttons in the Multi-Camera Monitor.

5. Press the shortcut key number associated with the alternative view point (for example, **Camera 5**) or right-click on the multi-camera segment you want to change, and select a new camera angle from the context menu.

 Changes to selected cameras will always occur to the clip on the right-hand side of the Timeline indicator or the clip the Timeline indicator is currently playing through.

If you press the **Play** button while attempting to change the camera angles, the **Record** function inside the Multi-Camera Monitor will automatically be toggled to **ON**, and any changes you make will not be shown until playback is stopped by you or when the Timeline indicator reaches the end of the sequence.

6. Carry on through the sequence by making changes to cameras as you see fit.

7. You may also want to change the start and end points of a camera position. To do so, first close the Multi-Cam Monitor by clicking on the **X** in the upper-right corner.

8. Set the Timeline as the active panel, and place the Timeline indicator over the edit point between each camera position.

9. Press *T* on the keyboard to open the **Trim** tool. To retain synchronization, both panels must have a blue border over the top and bottom area of each trim inlay area.

10. Hold down the *K* key, then use the *J* or *L* key to move the edit point as you have in previous projects. Only release the *K* key once you are sure you have the correct edit. Once the *K* key is released, the edit points will move on the Timeline.

If you are unsure on the process of correctly using the **Trim** tool, return to Project 2, and review the **Trim** tool workflows that you will find there.

11. Review all camera angles and trim as you see fit. If you want to completely change a camera angle for another, reopen the Multi-Camera Monitor and repeat steps 4 and 5. Alternatively, you can use the right-click method mentioned in step 5 to alter a multi-camera segment without reopening the Multi-Camera Monitor.

12. Save your project before moving on.

Objective Complete - Mini Debriefing

In this section, you found out how to correct any rushed decisions you made in the live multi-camera edit arena. Here, this was simply a case of stepping through the edit points with the Multi-Camera Monitor and replacing those clips you wished to change. You also exercised your trim skills to fine-tune your clips without losing synchronicity with the rest of the project.

The keyboard shortcuts covered in this task are as follows:

- ▸ Up and down arrow: This shortcut plays **Previous** and **Next Edit** (when used in the Multi-Cam tool)
- ▸ *T*: This shortcut opens the **Trim** tool

Classified Intel

If you wanted to insert a clip that is totally unrelated to the concert, for example, a shot of the album cover, you can cycle through the trim modes until you see a single red bracket and a single blue border around one of the two trim panels. Any trim you now make would leave a gap for you to insert other material into it. However, this is a rather crude way of editing, a preferable method would be to place the additional material on a track above **Video 1**.

Creating insert clips (PiP)

In this section, you will take the unused camera angles `PiP-Insert_1.avi` and `PiP-Insert_2.avi`, and create a **Picture in Picture** (**PiP**) effect. This allows you to have a small window over the main play area, one that gives an alternative view of the action, for example a crowd reaction shot, without cutting away from the main action. To do this, you will use one of Premiere Pro's preset PiP effects.

There are a number of PiP effects to choose from, and by all means, if you prefer to use an example other than the suggestions listed in this task, please do. It is your project after all!

Engage Thrusters

To add PiP clips in this task, follow these steps:

1. Start by dragging-and-dropping `PiP-Insert_1.avi` onto **Video 2**. Make sure the start of the clip lines up with the very start of the Timeline. Your carefully constructed multi-camera sequence is now totally obscured by the `PiP-Insert_1.avi` clip.

These clips were also created as part of a synchronized set as can sometimes happen in a multi-camera shoot. Often these insert shots are incomplete and unsuitable for a multi-camera Timeline, however, there's no reason they can't be used to create a series of inset cutaway shots.

2. Use *Shift + 7* to open the **Effects** browser, and type `pip` into the **Search** field.

3. A number of cool preset PiP effects will be revealed to you in the **Effects** browser.

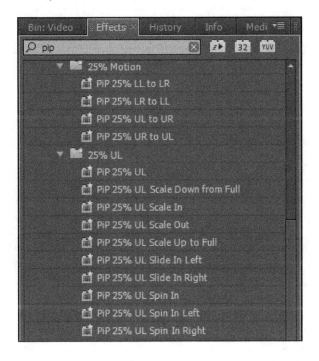

4. Locate the **PiP 25% UL Slide in Left** effect. Drag-and-drop this effect onto the `PiP-Insert_1.avi` clip on **Video 2**.

5. Playback the Timeline, and you will see the clip slides in before anything is visible. Correct this by clicking on the `PiP-Insert_1.avi` clip to select it, and then press *Shift + 5* to make the **Effects Controls** panel active.

6. Dial open the **Motion** parameters and the two keyframes controlling the slide-in will be visible.

7. With the left mouse button held down, drag a bounding box around the two keyframes to select both. Both keyframes should now be displayed as gold.

 Zoom in using the + (plus) key if you cannot clearly see both keyframes.

8. Move the Timeline indicator to the point where some action is visible from the active camera and in the PiP insert function (at least 3 or 4 seconds into the playback).

9. Click-and-drag the right keyframe until it meets with the Timeline indicator (with both keyframes selected, the left keyframe will follow the right one when you move it).

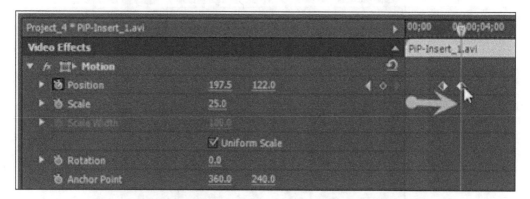

10. Move the Timeline indicator to a point where you want the PiP to slide back off the screen (10 or 15 seconds), then press the **Add/Remove Keyframe** button to add a keyframe.

11. Move the Timeline indicator 10 or 15 frames further up the Timeline, then click on the word **Motion**. A bounding box will appear around the PiP.

12. Use the mouse to click-and-drag the PiP off screen.

If the clip exits too slowly, move the two key frames you just added a little closer together (you only have to move one). If it is too fast, move them further apart.

13. Finish off by opening the **Opacity** parameters, toggling off keyframes (stopwatch deselected), then reduce opacity to around **75%**.

14. Repeat the previous steps, but add `PiP-Insert_2.avi` to **Video 3**, and experiment with a different PiP effect from Premiere Pro's extensive library.

15. Save your project before moving on to the next section.

Objective Complete - Mini Debriefing

In this section, you used a relatively minor technique to create cool inserts. The workflow for these PiPs is fairly simple to get them in and running, but fine-tuning them can absorb a lot of time. However, it is worth spending some extra time getting the exact position, opacity, and size just right for your project.

The keyboard shortcuts covered in this task are as follows:

▸ *Shift + 7*: This shortcut opens the **Effects** browser

▸ *Shift + 5*: This shortcut opens the **Effects Controls** panel

Classified Intel

If you want to bring the PiP back on later in the Timeline, don't forget to add a keyframe before moving the PiP, otherwise, the movement will be between the last exit keyframe and the next entrance keyframe you create. This creates a very slow PiP entrance. If you accidently do this, copy the last exit keyframe (select keyframe, then press *Ctrl + C* or *command + C*), and then paste this keyframe (*Ctrl + V* or *Command + V*) after you have moved the Timeline indicator in the **Effects Controls** panel.

Finishing off

This is a short and sweet section. In this section, you will finish off by bundling this whole sequence up into a nested loop, then extracting the flash and tone area at the start of the clip, as they are no longer needed. You will then add some transitions to fade out the clip. If you feel really on the edge, then you could try performing this without reading the task instructions later. There's always the undo key to erase your mistakes!

If you don't feel that sure of your editing skills just yet, read on.

Engage Thrusters

To add some final polish to your project in this short task, follow these steps:

1. Set the Timeline as the active panel by pressing *Shift + 3*, then use the mouse to drag a bounding box around all the clips in this sequence (including the PiP inserts and your audio track if you added one).

2. Right-click on any of the selected clips and choose **Nest** from the context menu.

3. Set an In point at the very start of the Timeline by pressing *I* on the keyboard.

4. Set an Out point when the inlay shows some action (somewhere around the 2-second mark) by pressing *O* on the keyboard.

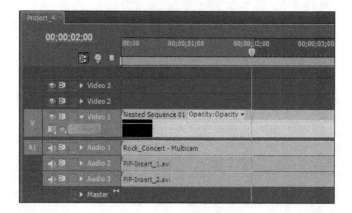

5. Extract that section of the Timeline using the **Extract** function (the # key). The light flash and audio tone will be deleted from the Timeline, and the clips will all shuffle up to **00;00;00;00**.

6. Make sure the Timeline indicator is at the very start of the Timeline, then press *Ctrl + D* or *command + D* to add a cross dissolve to the start of the sequence. Then, press *Ctrl + Shift + D* or *command + Shift + D* to add an audio fade in (**Constant Power**) to the audio tracks being used.

7. Move the Timeline indicator to the very end of the Timeline and press *Ctrl + D* or *command + D* to add a cross dissolve to the end of the sequence. Then press *Ctrl + Shift + D* or *command + Shift + D* to add an audio fade out (**Constant Power**) to the audio tracks being used.

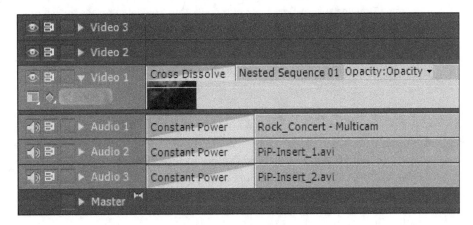

8. You now have audio fades and video fades on all of your tracks. Save your project in a safe place before finishing this project.

The previous screenshot shows the **Cross Dissolve** audio fade that is slightly shorter than the **Constant Power** audio fade below, and there is a good reason for this. The correct project settings for the clips used in the previous Timeline is 30 frames per second (fps). However, the computer that Premiere Pro CS6 was installed on is a U.K. system and as such, Premiere automatically defaults all video transitions to 25 frames per second, regardless of the what fps is being used on the Timeline (on an NTSC system it defaults to 30 frames per second).

However, the audio transitions are defined as seconds and not frames, so we will always default to one second no matter what fps your Timeline is set to.

Are you confused? Actually, it's simple to work out. All you need to do is remember to manually adjust your default transition settings (**Edit** | **Preferences** | **General**) to reflect the Timeline fps you are using. For example, if you are using a Timeline set to 50 frames per second, then the default transition setting should be changed to 50, if you want your transitions to have a duration of one second. If left at 25 or 30, the default transition on a 50-fps timeline would be around half a second. It's easy, huh? But, plenty of people get caught out on this, including, as the previous screenshot shows, the author of this book.

Objective Complete - Mini Debriefing

As promised, this was short and sweet, but necessary to demonstrate how the workflows you have learned can, with just a few key presses and mouse clicks, turn a pretty cool project into a finished project! Save this project somewhere safe; you are likely to have ideas on how to improve it by the time you reach the end of this book.

The keyboard shortcuts covered in this task are as follows:

▶ *Shift + 3*: This shortcut sets the Timeline as the active panel

▶ *I*: This shortcut sets the In point

▶ *O*: This shortcut sets the Out point

▶ *#* (hash): This shortcut extracts the defined area

▶ *Ctrl* or *command + D*: This shortcut adds the default video transition to the selected track

▶ *Ctrl* or *command + Shift + D*: This shortcut adds the default audio transition to the selected track

Classified Intel

If the duration of the **Cross Dissolve** audio fades does not suit you, double-click on one, then in the **Effects Controls** panel, alter the duration value, either with the mouse or by directly entering into the value area.

Mission Accomplished

If you had been using an earlier version of Premiere Pro, then this project would likely have been many pages longer. It's a great testament to the developers at Adobe that this project is as short as it is. There is, of course, much more to multi-camera concept, but the workflow listed in this project will get you up and running on the majority of the multi-camera projects.

The techniques you have learned here are valuable enough, but you probably won't really experience multi-camera work until you have created your own. Try to do this on a simple project first; something short and easy to edit. In this project, creating a sync point was fairly easy, because the material you were supplied with was set up to be simple to work with. On real-life multi-camera shoots, you may find this is not the case.

You Ready To Go Gung HO? A Hotshot Challenge

The project looks pretty good in its current form, but there's still room for you to go all Gung Ho on it. Titles, for example, would be a great addition, but they would need to have some kind of motion added to them in order to suit the rock concert's atmosphere. You could also experiment with the **Time Stretch** tool on the PiP insert clips, and perhaps look at adding a color grade movie look as you did in *Project 2*; something to accentuate the red colors seen throughout this video.

Experiment using the skills you have learned so far, drag in an adjustment layer, try out some of those effects in the **Effects** browser and see what they actually do, and how they interact with the **Blend** mode in the **Opacity** settings.

Move on to the next project only when you have spent at least an hour or two being creative with this one.

Project 5

Visual Effects – Muzzle Flashes, Laser Beams, and Clones

In the various projects leading up to this point in the book you have looked at techniques and workflows used in editing situations you are likely to come across in nearly every type of project. Project 5 is a diversion away from that, where you will look at creating a special effects scene using many of the techniques you might have seen on the big screen.

However, in an effort to keep this book accessible to all Adobe Premiere Pro CS6 users, the entire project will be created using only those effects and tools available in the standard version. This will mean creating your own muzzle flashes and laser bolts, and also a variation on the bleach bypass look favored by many film makers.

Mission Briefing

Your objective in this project is to complete a short **science fiction** (**SF**) scene using only those effects found in the stock version of Premiere Pro CS6. No third-party plugins or downloaded material will be used in this project; the exception being a pre-composed animated MechBot. All the other effects in this project will be created by you using workflows you already know, but in ways you have yet to explore. Once you have finished with this project, you will end up with a short film similar to the following screenshot:

Why Is It Awesome?

This project will take you through a range of video effects available to every Premiere Pro CS6 user, but we will look at them in a fresh way, showing you how to create cool-looking special effects without the need to buy expensive third-party plugins or composite material such as muzzle flashes. With some imagination and a little time this project will show you how to create a cool-looking scene with just the tools available to every Premiere Pro CS6 user. Make no mistake; this project isn't a pushover. It requires giving attention to detail and a fair amount of time tweaking keyframes in order to create a believable special effects scene. But the investment in time is worth it.

The alien robot shown in the following screenshot was animated using iClone, rendering the final images against a blue background.

Using iClone in this way, to create short animations of machines that either do not exist or you cannot afford to use (helicopters for example), is the ideal way of integrating 3D objects with live action.

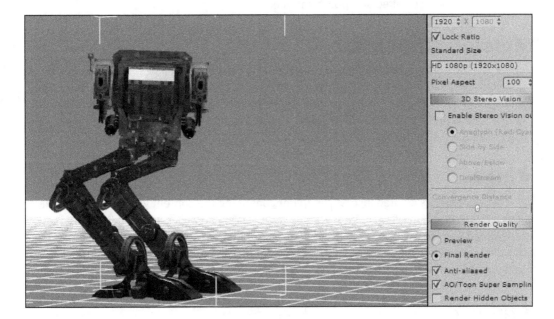

Your Hotshot Objectives

The following tasks have been divided up to represent the sort of workflow you would likely use when creating a special effects scene:

- Organizing your project media
- Key in the alien robot
- Creating an army of clones

- ▸ Creating a laser beam of doom
- ▸ Creating a lightning spectacular (freeze frame and lightning ball)
- ▸ Creating a muzzle flash
- ▸ Adding sound effects
- ▸ Adding various effects to polish the scene

Mission Checklist

Before you start this project, there are a number of preparations you need to make. Firstly, open your designated video drive and access the `Hotshots` folder you created in *Project 1, Creating a Movie Montage – the Easy Way*. There you should find the project folders created in the previous projects. Create a new folder next to it called `Project 5` and inside that new folder, create three folders called `Video`, `Images`, and `Audio`.

Video

With the new folders created, access the folder containing the content you downloaded and extracted in *Project 2, Cutting a Short Film without Getting Stung*. You should find a folder inside called `Project 5`. Copy the contents of this folder to the `Video` folder you created according to what we mentioned in the first paragraph of this section. There are four video files in total.

Audio

Repeat the same steps as given in the preceding section, but this time open the `Audio` folder in the `Project 5` content pack. Copy the contents of this folder to the `Audio` folder you created according to what we mentioned in the first paragraph of this section. There are two audio files in total. Once you have the media copied to the correct location on your computer, proceed to the first task.

If you want additional sound effects, you'll need to source; a pistol shot and an automatic rifle shot. If you want to go all Gung Ho on this project, you might look to find some dramatic music that is 30 seconds or so in duration (`SoundDogs.com` is a good place to search). Just remember that you don't have the rights to music not obtained from royalty-free music sites and so the music can only be used for your own personal amusement.

Organizing your project media

Organizing your media for a special effects scene is similar to that of creating any other edit, the exception being the amount of tracks you will need to complete the special effects. However, as we have seen in previous projects, it's often easier to utilize Premiere Pro's ability to nest one sequence inside another in order to avoid having too many Timeline tracks to organize effectively. You can also use the Nest feature to simplify the Timeline further, and remember that any alterations that are made to the original sequence will be updated automatically inside its nested counterpart.

However, as this part of the task is pretty much the same as others that you have encountered in this book, you are encouraged to set up your project as you've been taught in *Project 1, Creating a Movie Montage – the Easy Way*, *Project 2, Cutting a Short Film without Getting Stung*, *Project 3, Protect the Innocent – Interview Edit Techniques*, and *Project 4, See the Bigger Picture – Edit Multiple Cameras*, before you look at the task on the next few pages. Once you have finished, read through the instructions to see if you got everything right. The exception in this project is using the **Background.avi** clip to match sequence settings to the properties of the clip. Once the **Background.avi** clip has been dragged onto **Video 1**, you don't need to delete it as it will be used in the next step.

If you still don't feel that confident, you can of course simply follow the instructions as usual. The keyboard shortcuts you should have used are given at the end of this task.

Prepare for Lift Off

Once you have completed all the preparations detailed in the *Mission Checklist* section of this project, you are ready to go. Launch Premiere Pro CS6 in the usual way and then proceed to the next part.

Engage Thrusters

Organize your project and add the **Background.avi** clip to the Timeline. Perform the following steps to do so:

1. Once Premiere Pro CS6 has finished launching and when the **Recent Projects** splash screen appears, select **Hotshots Template | Montage**. When the project has finished loading, save this as `Hotshots - Special Effects 1` and close any open sequences.

2. Select **Editing Optimized Workspace** you created in *Project 1*.

3. Select the **Project** panel and open the `Video` bin without creating a separate window. Import all four video files in the `Video` folder inside `Project 5`. If you have any audio files to import, do so now, then return to the `Video` bin.

4. Create a new sequence and call it **MechBot_Sequence**. Pick any settings at random, you will correct this in the next step.

5. Match the Timeline settings by dragging-and-dropping the **Background.avi** clip onto **Video 1**. Click on **Change sequence settings** when this option window appears.

6. Set the **Project** panel as the active panel. Switch to **List View** if it is not already displayed. This isn't necessary for the next task, but you may find it easier to view the files in **List View**.

7. Save your project before moving on to the next task.

Objective Complete - Mini Debriefing

How did you do it? Were you able to complete this task without reading it through first? Could you remember the keyboard shortcuts listed next? Don't feel too bad if you couldn't remember everything, but if you couldn't remember anything, perhaps you need to re-do *Project 2* and *Project 3* to refresh what you have learned.

Keyboard shortcuts covered in this task are as follows:

▶ *Ctrl* or *command* + double-click: Open bin without creating a separate **Project** panel

▶ *Ctrl* or *command* + *N*: Create a new sequence

▶ *Ctrl* or *command* + \ (backslash): Create new bin in the **Project** panel

▶ *Ctrl* or *command* + *I*: Open the **Import** window

▶ *Shift* + *1*: Set the **Project** panel as active

▶ *Shift* + *3*: Set Timeline as active

Key in the alien robot

In this task you will bring in the 3D animation of a mechanized robot (**MechBot.avi**) onto your Timeline, then you will use the blue screen key to remove the blue background it was rendered against. You'll also use keyframes to bring the robot to life and set markers to help you best work out where those keyframes need to be. This part will utilize skills you should already know well from the previous projects.

Engage Thrusters

Add the MechBot to your Timeline and remove the blue background. Perform the following steps to do so:

1. Make sure the **Project** panel is the active panel. Then double-click on **MechBot.avi** to send it to the Source Monitor.

2. Make sure the Source Monitor is the active panel, then use the J, K, and L keys to scrub through the **MechBot.avi** animation. As the walk motion begins to reach the end, you need to place a marker (press M) just at the point when the left foot contacts the ground (around **02;18**).

3. With the marker in place, make the Timeline the active panel, then send the Timeline indicator to the end of the clip using the down arrow. Press O on the keyboard to set an Out point at this location.

4. Make the **Video 1** and **Audio 1** tracks inactive by turning the track headers dark gray (hint – click on the header). Now make **Video 2** and **Audio 2** active by turning them light gray (**Audio 2** may already be active by default). Finish this step by dragging the **V** marker upwards onto **Video 2** and the **A1** marker downwards onto **Audio 2**, as shown in the following screenshot:

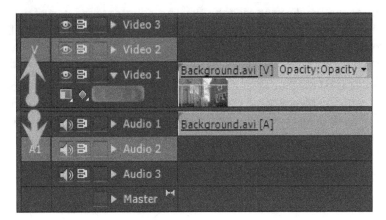

Making the tracks inactive (dark gray) will prohibit changes occurring to them through commands such as *Ctrl + K* or *command + K* to slice a clip. Only active tracks (light gray) will be affected by such commands. However, just setting a track to dark gray is not enough to tell Premiere where you want it to send your Source Monitor clips when using the **Overwrite** or **Insert** mode. To do this you need to map the tracks using the **V** and **A1** markers. These can be dragged up or down the tracks order and doing so, maps that track for Source Monitor **Overwrite** and **Insert** mode commands. This can be changed at any time during the edit of your project.

You should be aware that the **V** and **A1** markers will only appear in the header area if you have a clip loaded into the Source monitor that contains both video and audio.

5. Return to the Source Monitor and insert the **MechBot.avi** clip onto the Timeline using the **Overwrite** mode (press '.'). Your Timeline should look something like the next screenshot; if it does not, review steps 3 and 4 before continuing.

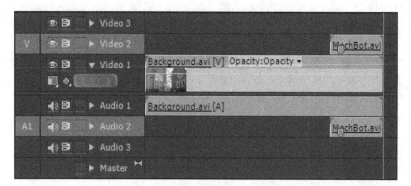

6. Return to the Timeline and send the Timeline indicator to the start of the **MechBot.avi** clip using the up arrow. You need to remove the MechBot's blue-colored background. This will be done using the classic blue screen removal technique. Start by opening the **Effects** browser (*Shift + 7*) and typing in the word `Key` into the search field.

7. This will reveal the Blue Screen Key filter in the `Keying` folder. Drag-and-drop this effect onto the **MechBot.avi** clip on **Video 2**. Set the **Effect Controls** panel as active (*Shift + 5*), then dial open the blue screen key parameters and adjust the settings to remove the blue background, but keep the model intact. Suggested parameters would be as follows:

    ❑ **Threshold**: 35%

    ❑ **Cutoff**: 35%

These setting are shown in the following screenshot:

 When removing a blue screen, you may find that activating **Mask Only** (in the blue screen key parameters area) will help you create a clean key. This replaces the subject with a white silhouette. If there are any areas of the background that show through this silhouette, use the **Cutoff** slider to improve that situation.

8. Return to the Timeline and zoom in on the **MechBot.avi** clip (use the + key) and use the *J*, *K*, and *L* keys to position the Timeline indicator over the clip marker you placed on the **MechBot.avi** clip in step 2.

9. Press *Shift + 5* to open the **Effect Controls** panel if it is closed, then click on the word **Motion** in the **Effects** panel to highlight a bounding box around the **MechBot.avi** clip.

 You may need to drop the zoom level in the Program Monitor to 50 percent in order to view the bounding box around **MechBot.avi**.

10. Place the mouse inside the Program Monitor and drag the **MechBot.avi** clip over to the right and downwards, so that it appears roughly, as shown in the following screenshot:

11. Open up the parameters for Motion (small triangle next to the effect's name) and make **Toggle Animation** ON for **Position** and **Scale** to set keyframes at this point in the Timeline.

12. Set the Timeline as the active panel, then move the Timeline indicator to the start of the **MechBot.avi** clip (up arrow). Alter the **Scale** parameter to 75% to create a scale keyframe at this position in the Timeline.

13. Place the mouse inside the Program Monitor again and this time drag the MechBot downwards and to the left, so that it appears roughly, as shown in the next screenshot. This will create a new keyframe at the start of the clip for the **Position** parameter.

The position path followed by the **MechBot.avi** clip should be a slight slope from the first keyframe to the last in order for the feet to be hidden from view during the life of the clip. Getting animated feet to stay in contact with the floor can be time consuming and will often spoil the overall effect, so try to hide animated feet wherever possible in your own projects.

14. With the **Timeline** panel active, press the \ (backslash) key to zoom the Timeline to the longest clip.

15. Render and save your project before moving on to the next task.

Objective Complete - Mini Debriefing

At the end of this task you will have added the **MechBot.avi** clip to the Timeline, removed the blue screen background using the Premiere Pro CS6 Blue Screen Key filter, then animated the clip using just four keyframes (two for **Position** and two for **Scale**) in the **Motion** parameters. Don't worry about the unrealistic placement of the MechBot; you will correct that in the next task.

Classified Intel

Green and blue screen removal are classic tools of all special effects editors, although in Premiere Pro CS6 the green screen removal tool is obvious by its absence in the list of keying filters. For images that require a green background to be keyed out (or any other color) use the Ultra Key filter. Inside the parameters of this effect you will find an eye-drop tool that can be used to sample the background color of your clips and plenty of parameters to help key in your shots. Ultra Key also integrates with the Mercury engine to give real-time playback.

Creating an army of clones

In this task you will create an army of two clones (not much of an army admittedly) using the Crop and Garbage Matte tools. The Garbage Matte tool unsurprisingly does what it says, it masks, or Matte's out, those parts of the image that are not good to you; the Crop effect performs a similar function, although its parameters are more tightly restricted (as you will see in this example). You'll also use the Garbage Matte tool to create the illusion of the MechBot stepping out from behind the wall of the building and the Crop filter to create the illusion of clones.

Before you do any of that, you need to mark your clips in order to set the timing of events. Clones are often used in film making to create the sense of having more extras on the set than you can actually afford, but the timing of conversations and events need to be carefully controlled, both when the scene is shot, and now here when it is being edited. To do this you will use your trusty clip marker.

Engage Thrusters

Here you will create clones from two separate shots. Perform the following steps to do so:

1. Set the **Project** panel as active and switch to **List View** if the bin is currently set to **Icon View**. Use the keyboard shortcut *Ctrl + N* or *command + N* to create a new sequence. Call this sequence **Main Project**. Don't worry about which presets to use.

2. Drag-and-drop **MechBot_Sequence** from the **Project** panel to **Video 1** on the Timeline. If you have rendered this sequence in the last task, it should appear here as rendered. If not, render the Timeline now. Press \ (backslash) to zoom the Timeline to this clip.

If the **Clip Mismatch** window appears, select **Change sequence settings** so the Timeline matches your **MechBot_Sequence**.

3. Open the `Video` bin without creating a separate window, then use *Ctrl* + click or *command* + click to select the **Guard_01.avi** and **Guard_02.avi** clips in the **Project** panel. Right-click on either of the selected clips and choose **Open in Source Monitor**.

4. Set the Source Monitor as active, then select the **Guard_02.avi** clip using the menu in the upper-left corner of the panel. Use the *J*, *K*, and *L* keys to find the spot just before the guard points down screen (around **09;04**). Press *M* to place a marker at this point. Repeat this to place a marker at the point where the guard reacts to something behind him (around **26;07**).

5. Now repeat step 4 to place a marker on the **Guard_01.avi** clip at a point just before the guard raises his rifle (around **10;18**).

6. Set the Timeline as the active panel and use the *J*, *K*, and *L* keys to find the point where the MechBot's left foot steps clear off the wall (around **48;05**). Press *M* to set a marker at this point. This will be the event that "Guard_02" is reacting to.

7. Drag-and-drop the **Guard_02.avi** clip from the Source Monitor anywhere onto **Video 2**. Once you release the clip, the markers will be visible. Drag the clip along the Timeline so that the second marker on this clip maps to the Timeline marker.

8. Drag-and-drop the **Guard_01.avi** clip onto **Video 3**. Once released, the clip markers will show up. Line up the first marker on this clip to the first marker on the **Guard_02.avi** clip. By the end of this task your Timeline should look something like the following screenshot:

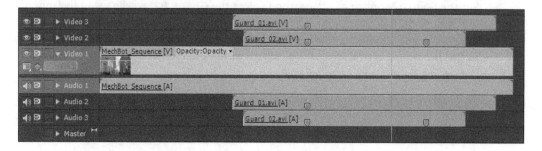

9. At last it is time for you to add some masks in order to reveal your clones and the MechBot in all their glory. Start by setting the **Effects** browser as the active panel, and then enter Crop into the search field. Drag-and-drop the **Crop** effect onto the **Guard_01.avi** clip on **Video 3**.

10. Move the Timeline indicator to about half way through the **Guard_01.avi** clip on **Video 3** and then click on that clip to select it. Set the **Effect Controls** panel as active and dial open the **Crop** parameters if they are not already open. Click on the word **Crop** to make the crop bounding box visible, which by default covers the entire frame of the Program Monitor.

 You may need to zoom the Program Monitor out by 50 percent to see the bounding box.

11. Use the mouse to grab and adjust the top and right-hand side areas of the Crop. When you are done, your Program Monitor should look something like the next screenshot.

 Make sure you don't crop too far into the guard's movements, scrub through the Timeline to make sure you haven't clipped any part of his body or his rifle, or that of his neighbor.

12. Finally, you will create a Matte to block out the building and create the illusion of the MechBot stepping out from behind the side of the wall. Start by finding the **Garbage Matte** effect in the **Effects** browser (type in `Matte` in the search field), then drag-and-drop **Sixteen-Point Garbage Matte** onto the **Guard_02.avi** clip on **Video 2**.

13. The **Guard_02.avi** clip should automatically have selected itself and **Sixteen-Point Garbage Matte** should be open in the **Effect Controls** panel. Click on the **Sixteen-Point Garbage Matte** text to show the Garbage Matte's bounding box in the Program Monitor.

14. Use the mouse to drag each Garbage Matte point to the right of the Program Monitor to follow the shape of the wall and roof behind which the robot is currently hiding. When you have finished, your Matte should look something like the next screenshot. Scrub through the Timeline when finished, to reveal the MechBot stepping out from behind the wall.

> If you are unhappy with the animation of the MechBot, double-click on the **Mechbot_Sequence** on **Video 1** and make your changes in the sequence that opens. Any changes you make here will be automatically updated in the main sequence.

15. Render and save your project before moving onto the next task.

Objective Complete - Mini Debriefing

Play back the scene now and it has started to look a little more impressive. Using two types of Mattes, the **Crop** effect and **Sixteen-Point Garbage Matte**, you have created an army of two guards (actually the same actor) and revealed a robot stepping out from behind a wall. Already this scene is starting to sell itself, but as with all special effects scenes, there is still plenty to do!

Classified Intel

Mattes and crops can be stacked over each other and keyframed to reveal on-screen objects over time. They are powerful tools, and when used correctly, have many uses.

In this example a **Crop** effect was used on the **Guard_01.avi** clip (the left-hand side guard) and a Garbage Matte was used to reveal the MechBot stepping out from behind the wall. This choice was picked for this project simply to show off how the problem of masking or revealing areas of the screen can be solved in various ways using Premiere Pro CS6. However, the **Crop** effect does leave some nasty lines on the windows (clouds are cut horizontally in half), which shows the limitations of this effect. You may decide to go back and delete the **Crop** effect in favor of a Garbage Matte (Sixteen Point is recommended). As an editor the decision is yours. Perhaps something to consider when you reach the last task and go all Gung Ho on this project.

Creating a laser beam of doom

In this task you will create a laser beam, which the evil MechBot uses to evaporate the guards. Once again you will be using a stock effect in Premiere Pro CS6; the Lightning effect. This is part of the generator effects and you will need to heavily customize it, straightening it out and taming it down, in order for it to look like an effective laser beam of doom.

In this project you have masks on two of the clips that would cause problems if you tried to add an effect directly to either clip. To get around this you will create a transparent video clip to avoid having the laser bolt interact with the masks, and in this task you'll also learn how to automatically add Timeline tracks on the fly.

Engage Thrusters

Create a laser beam using the Lightning effect and a transparent video clip. Perform the following steps to do so:

1. Set the **Project** panel as active and create a new transparent video clip by clicking on the **New Item** button at the bottom of the panel. Accept the defaults (these should match your current sequence settings) and click on **OK**.

2. Add the transparent video clip to the Timeline and at the same time create a new track by dragging-and-dropping the transparent video clip just above **Video 3** to add a new Timeline track, **Video 4**, to the Timeline.

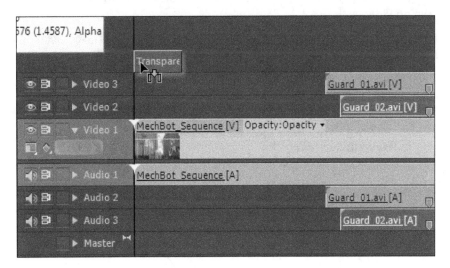

3. Use the mouse to move the clip on **Video 4** so the start of it lines up with the **Guard_02.avi** clip reacting to a laser beam (around **50;14**). Use the mouse to shorten the duration of the transparent video clip to around 10 frames.

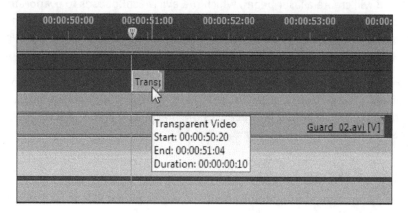

 A laser beam of around 10 frames is just under half a second for this project (PAL = 25 frames per second), however as this is science fiction, your beam could last as long as you want it to, although you need to make sure it ends before the MechBot moves its 'head'.

4. Open the **Effects** browser and search for the word **Lightning** (not lighting effects). Drag-and-drop this effect from the `Generate` folder onto the transparent video clip on **Video 4**.

5. As it stands the Lightning effect doesn't look very much like a laser beam of doom. To get that effect you need to straighten out the lightning and tame some of its more wild variables. This can be done in a number of different ways, but to start with, try the suggested parameters given next in order to get something like the effect shown in the next screenshot:

   - **Segments**: 3
   - **Amplitude**: 0.000
   - **Branching**: 0.000
   - **Speed**: 20
   - **Width**: 20
   - **Width Variation**: 0.100
   - **Outside Color**: Change to suit yourself (dark blue suggested)
   - **Inside Color**: Change to suit yourself (dark red suggested)
   - **Blending Mode**: Normal

6. Click on the **Lightning** text in the **Effect Controls** panel. The start (left) and end (right) cross hairs will appear. Move the start cross hair to the laser gun and the end cross hair to the guard nearest the MechBot.

 The start of the Lightning effect is always on the left of the screen and the end is always on the right, no matter what's happening in your scene, when you add the Lightning effect, these start and end positions will always be the defaults. In this example you need to move the start and end points to the opposite ends of the screen in order to achieve the correct effect.

7. Now you need to keyframe the laser beam so that it zaps out of the MechBot's gun and strikes the guard as he reacts. Start by zooming in on the Timeline using the + (plus) key on the main area of the keyboard (not in the number pad area).

8. Move the Timeline indicator so that it is about halfway through the transparent video clip. Realign the start and end points of the laser beam if necessary.

 You may find it easier to use the zoom function on the Program Monitor for accurate placement of the start and end points. When you have finished, your Program Monitor should look something like the next screenshot.

9. Set the **Effect Controls** panel as the active panel, then make **Toggle Animation** ON for the start and end points of the Lightning effect. This will create a keyframe at the dead center of the transparent video clip.

10. Use the right arrow key to move the Timeline indicator inside the **Effect Controls** panel to the last frame of the transparent video clip. If you stop seeing the effect, move one frame back so that it shows up again.

11. Move the start point (at the MechBot) downwards to join the end point (at the guard). Now use the left arrow key to move the Timeline indicator to the very start of the transparent video clip and move the end point (at the guard) to join the start point at the MechBot's gun.

12. Set the Timeline as the active panel and play back this area of the Timeline by pressing *Shift + K* (don't forget to reduce the zoom setting of the Program Monitor). Alter the start and end points as you see fit (try to only use the three keyframes you have already created) and move onto the next step when you are finished.

13. Create a second laser beam for the **Guard_01.avi** clip by holding down the *Alt* or *option* key, then use the mouse to click on the transparent video clip, and drag it upwards to create a duplicate of this clip. This will also create a new Timeline track called **Video 5**.

14. Reposition the transparent video clip on **Video 5** so that it times with the reaction of the guard being shot in **Guard_01.avi** (around **54;01**).

> You will have to zoom the Program Monitor out (use Fit) and alter the zoom levels of the Timeline to complete steps 13 and 14. You may also find it a timesaver to use a marker to locate the exact moment when "Guard_01" is shot.

15. Delete all start and end keyframes for the Lightning effect by making **Toggle Animation** OFF for the start and end points (deselect the stopwatch icons). Click on **OK** when the warning window appears for both the start and end stopwatch icons.

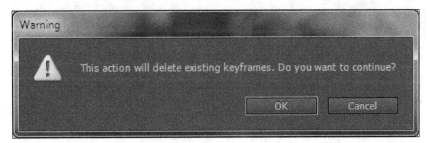

16. Now repeat what you have learned in the previous steps to align the start and end points of the laser beam to the MechBot's gun and the guard. Start by placing the Timeline indicator in the middle of the transparent video clip on **Video 5** and then make **Toggle Animation** ON (select the stopwatch icons) for the start and end points to set a middle keyframe. Now set the final and first keyframes for this version of the laser beam. When you are finished, your Program Monitor should look something like the following screenshot:

17. Finish this section by shortening the two guard clips on **Video 2** and **Video 3** so that they line up with the end of the transparent video clips on **Video 4** and **Video 5**. Press *Shift + K* to playback this area of the Timeline. When you are happy with the results, render the Timeline, then save your project before moving on to the next task.

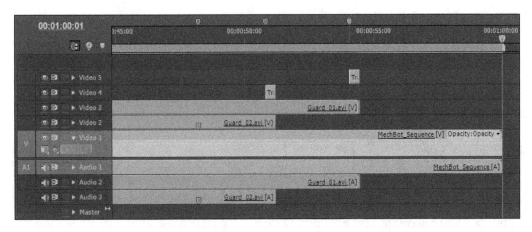

 Animation of effects using keyframes is a tricky business and there is no real right or wrong workflow. In previous projects you have keyframed from the start of the clip working forward and the other way around. In this example you started in the middle, before creating the last then the first keyframe. How you work and which method you choose will depend greatly on the project, and the methods you feel most comfortable using. Here it was essential to first set the whole duration of the laser beam using the middle keyframe, to create a Star Trek type phaser effect. If you're more of a Buck Rogers fan, then you can skip the middle keyframe and have the beam chase itself to the target.

Objective Complete - Mini Debriefing

In this task you have encountered yet another element of the Premiere Pro Timeline, the transparent video clip. This is a handy element that can be used as a placeholder for special effects. The advantages are simply that adding a special effect, such as lightning, to say for example, the **Guard_01.avi** clip would have been easy enough, but the mask you placed in an earlier task would have restricted its movement. Similarly, if you now want to improve on the laser effect (as you will do later in this project) by adding a blur or glow or any of the other Premiere Pro effects, you would have blurred the video of the guard as well as the lightning. By using a transparent video clip you can stack effects to your heart's content and you can experiment with the various blend modes available in the **Opacity** settings. For this particular effect, why not try a few blend modes to see which one you think makes this laser bolt look cool (hint – try **Linear Dodge (add)**).

You also learned how to add a Timeline track on the fly and without right-clicking on the track header area. This is particularly useful when you are creating a copy of an existing Timeline clip using the *Alt* + click + drag or *option* + click + drag method.

Classified Intel

Step 15 showed you how to delete keyframes from an effect all in one fell swoop. Sometimes it's just easier to erase the previous keyframes and start again, especially when, as in this case, there are only three keyframes to worry about. Consider this next time you start working on a duplicate clip that contained keyframed effects. How much time are you really saving by attempting to tweak pre-existing keyframes?

Creating a lightning spectacular (freeze frame and lightning ball)

In this task you will create a set of effects to show the guards being erased from time and space by the evil MechBot's laser beam of doom. You'll do this using the export frame function, a Track Matte effect, some very untamed and nonstraight lightning, and a simple White Matte. And you'll finish by wrapping up the entire effect in a fresh nested sequence. The effects and methods being used in this task shouldn't hold any mysteries to you, but you might be surprised by the variation on workflow used to create the illusion of a guard being consumed by heaving bundles of deadly lightening!

Engage Thrusters

Use the Lightning effect again to create an untimely end for the guards. Perform the following steps to do so:

1. Use any of the keyboard shortcuts to move the Timeline indicator to the end of the **Guard_02.avi** clip. The guard needs to be visible in the Program Monitor, if he has vanished, move back one frame.

2. With the Program Monitor as the active panel, use the keyboard shortcut *Ctrl + Shift + E* or *command + Shift + E* to start the process of creating a single exported frame from your Timeline. When the **Export Frame** window appears, change the **Name** field to Guard_02_Frame_Export and alter the **Format** field to **PNG**. Use the **Browse...** button to find a location to save the frame, ideally this would be in the Images folder inside Project 5 on your video drive. Click on **OK** or press *Enter* to close this window.

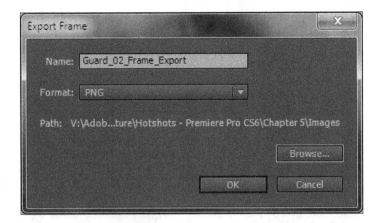

 If pressing *Ctrl + Shift + E* or *command + Shift + E* does nothing, check to see that the Program Monitor is the active panel and not the **Timeline** panel!

3. Return to the **Project** panel and move out of the `Video` folder to the main project area. Open the `Images` folder without creating a separate window and then import the `Guard_02_Frame_Export.png` file.

4. Right-click on the **Guard_02_Frame_Export.png** file and select **New Sequence from Clip** from the context menu. When the clip appears on the new Timeline sequence, use the \ (backslash) key to zoom to the clip length.

5. Create a New Color Matte by clicking on the **New Item** button in the **Project** panel. Accept the defaults and then drag the color picker down to the lower-left corner to select pure white (**R**: 255, **G**: 255, **B**: 255). Click on **OK** to exit the color picker and type in `White_Matte` in the **Name** field. Press *Enter* and `White_Matte` will appear in the `Images` folder.

6. Drag-and-drop **White_Matte** onto **Video 2** and then open the **Effects** browser and locate **Sixteen-Point Garbage Matte**. Place this effect on **White_Matte** on **Video 2**.

7. Open the **Effect Controls** panel for **White_Matte** and then click on **Sixteen-Point Garbage Matte** to show the Matte's bounding box in the Program Monitor. Use the mouse to create a Matte all the way around the guard until you have something like the next screenshot.

You may find it easier to temporarily turn down the opacity of **White_Matte** (around 40 percent should be enough) while you set the **Sixteen-Point Garbage Matte** in place. Don't forget to turn it back up again when you're finished.

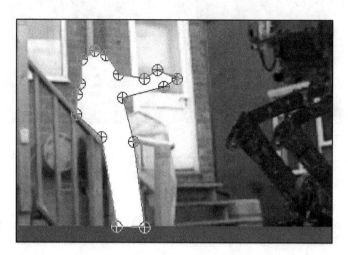

8. Locate the **Lightning** effect in the **Effects** browser and apply it to the **Guard_02_ Frame_Export.png** clip on **Video 1**. Open up the **Effect Controls** panel and using techniques you practiced in the last task, place the start point of the lightning at the head of the guard and the end point at his feet.

9. In the last task you tamed lightning; in this step you are going to make it go crazy by turning up the various controls to create a ball of crazy fast moving, multi-forking lightening. Don't alter the **Width** or **Width Variation** parameters, but do change **Blending Mode** to **Normal** before finishing this step.

You don't need to "max" out every setting in the last step, but now would be a good chance to see what effect each one has by first bringing it up to the max, then taking it slowly back down to something you can actually use. Don't take amplitude much beyond 25 as any lightning that falls outside of **White_Matte** will not be visible at the end of this task.

If the White Matte is restricting your view of how to set up the lightening, temporarily toggle the video off for the **Video 2** track by clicking once on the eyeball in the **Video 2** header area. Don't forget to toggle it back ON again when you are finished.

10. You now need to restrict the lightning to the dimensions of the guard (inside the White Color Matte); to do this you will use an effect from *Project 3*, the Track Matte Key. Locate the Track Matte Key effect in the **Effects** browser and then add it to the **Guard_02_Frame_Export.png** clip on **Video 1**.

11. Open the **Effect Controls** panel for this clip and alter the **Matte** setting to **Video 2**. Then change **Composite Using** to **Matte Luma**.

12. Playback the clip and you will see the lightning now restricts itself to **White_Matte**.

13. Finish this section by selecting both clips on the Timeline by dragging a bounding box around them, then shortening them both to around 2 seconds in length. Click on the name of this sequence in the **Project** panel and change it to **Guard_02_Nest**.

14. Now you understand the complete workflow for creating this type of effect, return to the **Main_Project** sequence and repeat what you have learned to create the same effect for the last frame of the **Guard_01.avi** clip on **Video 3**. If you are feeling confident enough, try to do it without reading steps 1 to 13.

15. When you have created another sequence containing the Guard_01's demise, rename that to **Guard_01_Nest**, then drag each of **Guard_01_Nest** and **Guard_02_Nest** onto the Timeline of the **Main_Project** sequence to create something similar to the following screenshot:

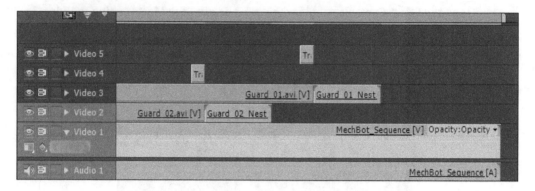

16. Render and save your project when you are happy with the effects created so far.

Objective Complete - Mini Debriefing

In this section you used some old and new workflows, the Track Matte and the Lightning effect to create a fiery demise for both guards, first of all utilizing the export frame function in order to create a still image for you to work on. The combination of these effects creates the illusion of the guard being consumed by a fiery storm of lightning. If you want to show a slow fadeout during the fiery death scene, you could return to the nested sequence and set an **Opacity** keyframe of 100% at 1 second, then a second **Opacity** keyframe of 0% at 2 seconds.

Classified Intel

Track Matte Key must appear second in the list of effects, in this case underneath the **Lightening** effect. If the effects are stacked the other way around, the containment would not work and the lightening would be unaffected by the Garbage Matte. Similarly, you might want to add a **Gaussian Blur** effect to the White Matte on **Video 2** in **Guard_01_Nest** and **Guard_02_Nest** in order to soften the edges of the Garbage Matte. In this case, the **Gaussian Blur** should be below **Garabage Matte**. Adding the blur to those sequences will automatically show up on their nested twins in the **Main_Project** sequence.

Creating a muzzle flash

In this task you will add some muzzle flashes to the pistol and rifle, as they are fired by the guards. This will be accomplished using a multilayered sequence, some Color Mattes, and the Garbage Mattes. All of these should be familiar friends to you by this stage in the book, but here you will use them in a slightly unusual fashion.

Engage Thrusters

Use Color Mattes to create a muzzle flash. Perform the following steps to do so:

1. Start by creating a new sequence and call it **Muzzle_Flash**. Use the **DV Pal Widescreen** settings that are used by the majority of the clips in this project.

2. In the **Project** panel, open up the `Images` bin if it has been closed from the previous section, and create three new Color Mattes — one red, one yellow, and one white. Name them appropriately.

3. Drag-and-drop **Red_Matte** onto **Video 1** and press \ (backslash).

4. Locate **Sixteen-Point Garbage Matte** and add it to **Red_Matte** on **Video 1**, then create a shape roughly the same, as shown in the following screenshot:

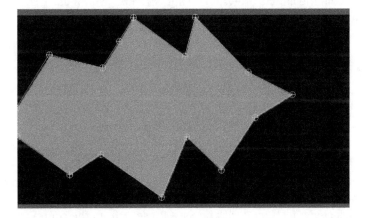

5. Repeat the preceding steps to add **Sixteen-Point Garbage Matte** to **Yellow_Matte** (placed on **Video 2**) and then to **White_Matte**, (placed on **Video 3**), but make each successive Garbage Matte slightly smaller until you have something similar to the next screenshot.

Save time here by copying and pasting the Sixteen-Point Matte from Red Matte to Yellow Matte and White Matte and reduce as instructed in step 5.

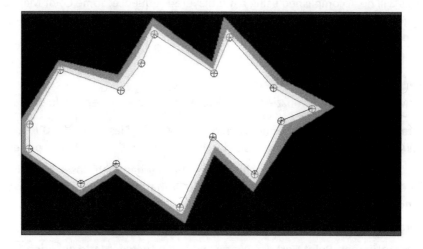

6. Now add some effects to **Red_Matte** to soften the edges. Locate the **Directional Blur** effect in the **Effects** browser and add it to **Red_Matte** using the following parameters:

   □ **Direction**: 275

   □ **Blur Length**: 9

7. Locate the **Gaussian Blur** effect in the **Effects** browser and add it to **Red_Matte** using the following parameters:

   □ **Blurriness**: 11

   □ **Blur Dimensions**: Vertical

8. With the *Ctrl* or *command* key held down, click on the titles of the **Directional Blur** and **Gaussian Blur** effects to select them both, then right-click on the title of either of the selected effects, and click on **Save Preset...** from the context menu, as shown in the following screenshot:

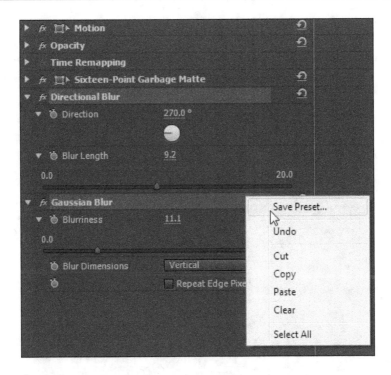

9. Type in `Muzzle Flash Blur` into the name field, then click on **OK** to save the effect.

10. Make sure there are no letters or words in the search field of the **Effects** browser, then open up the `presets` folder. In here you should find the `Muzzle Flash Blur` effect you just created. Add this effect to the **Yellow_Matte** and **White_Matte** on **Video 2** and **Video 3**.

11. Select all three tracks using a bounding box, then reduce the video clips to a duration of just two frames (it's called muzzle flash for a reason). You will probably have to zoom in on the Timeline to accurately achieve this.

12. Return to the **Main_Project** sequence and add the **Muzzle_Flash** sequence to the Timeline to create a new **Video 6** track.

13. Zoom in on the Timeline to accurately see where the muzzle flash should be placed (try **50;05**). Click on the **Muzzle_Flash** clip on **Video 6** to select it, then open up the **Motion** parameters for this sequence clip, and adjust **Scale** and **Position** so that it looks something like the next screenshot (**Scale** of 5 should be about right). You may also want to add a touch of rotation (-4.9 should do it).

14. Add as many muzzle flashes, as you think, are needed to be added to **Video 6** for both the **Guard_01.avi** and **Guard_02.avi** clips (listen for the sound of the guns being fired).

[If you see a black border on the edges of the muzzle flashes, use the Crop filter to remove it.]

15. Render and save your project once you are happy with the results.

Objective Complete - Mini Debriefing

In this task you've used some simple tools inside Premiere Pro CS6 to create an often used asset of special effects films, the much loved muzzle flash. In this example you also created a preset effect from one video track that was used to save time when adding it to the other Color Mattes. The effect is pretty cool, it won't replace an actual muzzle flash effect that you can buy online, but it does prove that with a little imagination and not much effort, you can save yourself some money and create a very passable imitation of a muzzle flash. And all of this is done with just the stock effects that come with every copy of Adobe Premiere Pro CS6.

Classified Intel

In this task you created a preset of stacked effects, namely Directional Blur and Gaussian Blur. Theoretically, there is no limit to the amount of effects that can be included in a user preset effect; however, you cannot include the **Motion**, **Opacity**, or **Time Remapping** parameters into a saved preset.

Adding sound effects

This is a short and sweet section where you will simply add some of the sound effects that came with your download package, and some that you downloaded yourself. This is just to give you an idea of the huge difference that adding a few simple effects can make to your projects.

Engage Thrusters

Spruce up the action with some well-timed sound effects. Perform the following steps to do so:

1. Set the **Project** panel as active, and then navigate to the Audio folder. Import all the sound FX you have stored in the Audio folder on your designated video drive (those that came with the download for this book, plus any others you have collected).

2. Move to the **Timeline** panel and move the Timeline indicator through the sequence until you come to where the laser is about to fire. Use the *J*, *K*, and *L* keys to get the exact position.

3. Press *M* on the keyboard to place a marker at this position, then double-click on the marker to open it up, and give it the name **Laser Beam 1**.

4. Repeat this to place a marker for the second laser burst, name this **Laser Beam 2**.

5. Locate the **Laser_Beam.mp3** sound effect in the `Audio` folder of the **Project** panel, then drag-and-drop it onto **Audio 4**, make sure it lines up with the **Laser Beam 1** marker. Repeat this for the **Laser Beam 2** marker.

6. Continue through the Timeline creating markers for sounds and adding the **Laser_Beam.mp3** sound effect and your own sound effects, as you see them fit.

7. Render and save your project before moving on to the next task.

Objective Complete - Mini Debriefing

As promised, this section was short and sweet, but necessary to enhance the overall feel of your project. In the real world of editing, the job of adding sound effects would be passed onto an actual sound engineer, however, if you are making your own projects that person will probably be you. In that case it's good to practice using markers and adjusting the volume levels whenever you can. Never underestimate the importance of a well-placed sound effect!

Adding various effects to polish the scene

Another short and sweet task here. In this task you will tidy up the sequence, chop out some material that's not needed, alter the look of the MechBot so that it blends in a little better with the scene, add a glow to the muzzle flashes, and finish by adding a movie look to the whole scene. It might not sound much, but you will be surprised what difference these small steps can make.

Engage Thrusters

Use various workflows to add the final polish to this Timeline sequence. Perform the following steps to do so:

1. Time now to tidy up this project and you will start by removing the excess material at the start of the **Main_Project** sequence. Begin this by clicking on each light gray track to turn it dark gray. Press the \ (backslash) key to zoom to the longest clip.

2. Use the up and down arrows to place the Timeline indicator at the start (the In point) of the **Guard_02.avi** clip on **Video 2**. Press *O* on the keyboard to set this as the Timeline Out point.

3. Move the Timeline indicator to the start of the Timeline using the *Home* key, then press *I* on the keyboard to set this as the Timeline In point.

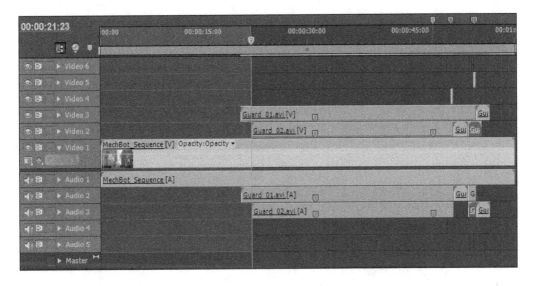

4. Extract this section of the Timeline by pressing the hash (#) key.

5. Double-click on the **MechBot_Sequence** to open it out and select the **Mechbot_01.avi** clip.

6. Locate the **Median** effect in the **Effects** browser and then drag-and-drop it on to the **MechBot_01.avi** clip. Open up the **Effect Controls** panel for this clip and set the **Median** effect to a value of 1. Return to the **Main Project** tab on the Timeline to see the difference this filter makes.

The Median effect, introduced in Premiere Pro CS5.5, has been used in the above example to slightly blur the edges of the MechBot. Although used at its lowest value (1), this video filter 'places' the 3D object in the scene by dulling the sharp edges often associated with 3D models.

7. Locate the **Alpha Glow** filter in the **Effects** browser and add it to the muzzle flashes and the laser beams on the Timeline. Adjust as you see them fit.

For the muzzle flashes a setting of 40 for **Glow** and 180 for **Brightness** will make the effect pop so long as you also set the start color to red. For the laser beams, a slightly lower setting of 12 for **Glow** and 160 for **Brightness** will work better with the start color set to blue.

8. Finally, you will add a movie look to the scene to give it a gritty SF film look. Start by using \ (backslash) to zoom the Timeline to show all the clips. To get a good idea of the changes you are about to make, move the Timeline indicator to an action-packed part of the scene (around **30;19** should be fine).

9. In the **Project** panel, create a new adjustment layer, accept the defaults, then drag-and-drop the clip onto the Timeline to create a new track above **Video 6**. Trim the duration of the adjustment layer with the mouse so that it covers the whole of the sequence clips.

10. Locate the following effects in the **Effects** browser and add them in this order to the adjustment layer using the following settings:

   - **Unsharp Mask**
   - **Amount:** 80
   - **Radius:** 80
   - **Luma Curve**
   - **Output: Composite**
   - Describe a curve as shown in the next screenshot.
   - **Noise**
   - **Amount of Noise:** 15%
   - **Noise Type:** Uncheck **Use Color Noise**
   - **Brightness & Contrast**
   - **Brightness:** 15%
   - **Contrast:** 10%

11. Make **Toggle Animation** for **Opacity** OFF (deselect the stopwatch icon) and set **Opacity** to 50% and **Blend Mode** to **Hard Light**.

12. Render and save your project when you have finished adjusting the settings.

Objective Complete - Mini Debriefing

In this section you added some polish to the various effects and also created a variation on the classic bleach bypass look that tends to be favored by film makers describing on screen a stark futuresque look.

Classified Intel

The addition of noise also creates a slightly voyeuristic view point, as though we are looking at the scene through a security camera. If you were to keyframe this effect to increase and decrease during the scene, you could also have created the illusion of a malfunctioning screen. Perhaps turn the noise up to the maximum setting at the end of the scene to suggest the MechBot has, in some way, disconnected the camera!

Mission Accomplished

The techniques you have learned here are valuable enough, but you probably will still favor expensive third-party plugins and pre-composed muzzle flashes and explosions, as used in the next project. That's fine, but at least now you have the option of using the effects that come with Premiere Pro CS6 and you will realize by now how much you can accomplish by customizing those effects to your needs.

You Ready To Go Gung HO? A Hotshot Challenge

The project looks pretty good in its current form, but there's still room for improvement. Experiment now on your project by looking through the various video filters and taking note of what effect (if any) they have on your effects. Can the laser beam be improved? Are there any other effects to add some polish to the muzzle flashes? How can the masks be tweaked for absolute perfection?

Move on to the next project only when you have spent at least an hour or two being creative with this one. The only way to really learn with Adobe Premiere Pro is to get in there and get your hands dirty. Here with this small 38-second scene, you have the ideal chance to let your creative ideas flow to their maximum!

Project 6

Visual FX Using Real Media

In the last project, you managed to put together a special effects scene using only those tools and effects available in the standard version of Adobe Premiere Pro CS6. In this project, you're going to look at the other extreme of visual-effect creation by using composited versions of muzzle flashes, fire, smoke, and really big explosions. You'll also play out a scenario where your director comes to you with a change of plan, and you as the editor have to make it happen with the materials to hand!

Mission Briefing

Your objective in this project is to take the scene you created in *Project 5, Visual Effects – Muzzle Flashes, Laser Beams, and Clones* and replace the muzzle flashes and laser beams with composited effects. You'll also replace the MechBot clip with one film against a green screen in order to gain some experience of using the **Ultra Key** effect. In addition, the director also wants one of the guards to be blown out of shot by the explosion, but this shot will have to be constructed using only the materials you have available. The next screenshot shows the sort of complex Timeline you will be creating:

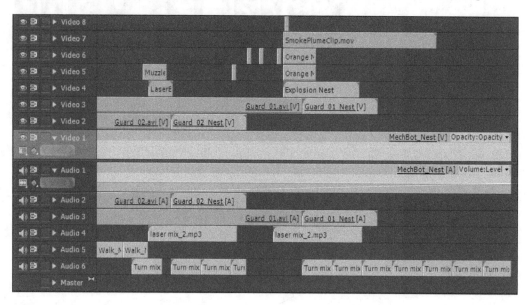

Why Is It Awesome?

This project will show you how to source free effects and keyframe them into your videos to create an awesome science-fiction battle scene. It will also demonstrate how you can rework the existing material in *Project 5* to show a totally different ending to the scene. You'll do all this without having to go through many of the steps you went through in *Project 5* simply by adapting your original project.

Your Hotshot Objectives

The following tasks have been divided up to represent the sort of workflow you would likely use when creating a special-effects scene:

- ▸ Organizing your media
- ▸ Adding in a new three-dimensional object to your scene
- ▸ Adding an explosive clip
- ▸ Manually tracking the explosion
- ▸ Adding a heat glow and smoke
- ▸ Adding muzzle flashes and laser beams
- ▸ Creating an explosive tremor and flying figure effect

Mission Checklist

Before you start this project, there are a number of preparations you need to make. Firstly, open your designated Video drive and access the Hotshots folder you created in *Project 1, Creating a Movie Montage – the Easy Way*. Here, you should find the Project folders you created in the previous projects. Create a new folder next to them called Project 6, and inside that new folder, create three folders called Video, Images, and Audio.

Video

Access the folder containing the content you downloaded from *Packt Publishing* in Project 2. You should find a folder called Project 6. Copy the contents to the Video folder you created in the first paragraph of this section. There are two files in total from the downloaded pack for this book; however, you will need to download and organize four more files (see the next *Third-party effects* section). Once you have the media copied to the correct location on your computer, proceed to the first task.

Third-party effects

Muzzle flash and explosion effects are freely available for download from various sources on the Internet. However, if you want to follow the instructions in this project, you might like to visit www.detonatiomfimls.com to download the files listed in the next items. To help you locate these files, use the tiny URL address, which should prompt you to download the files you need without having to search the detonation website:

- ▸ Detonation03.avi (tinyurl.com/beqprzq)
- ▸ SmokePlumeClip.mov (tinyurl.com/aw7occz)

▶ Muzzleflashes_UnitK.mov (tinyurl.com/aadnaa7: it is inclusive in the
   MuzzleFlashes_UnitK4.zip file)

▶ SMG_Gaudy_Sample.mov (tinyurl.com/a56tko1: it is inclusive in the
   SMG_Gaudy_Smaple.zip file)

All of these effects should be placed in your Video folder of Project 6. These effects are
free for you to use in your own projects.

Organizing your media

Organizing your media for this project is going to be a departure from what you've covered
in previous projects. Here, you will take *Project 5*, save it under a new file name, then
delete some of the effects in preparation for adding the new ones. If you haven't attempted
Project 5, it is strongly advised that you do so now. Although you may have no interest in
creating effects using Premiere Pro's stock filters, you will gain valuable information on the
use of masks.

Prepare for Lift Off

Once you have completed all the preparations detailed in the *Mission Checklist* section of
this project, you are ready to go. Launch Adobe Premiere Pro CS6 in the usual way, and then
proceed to the next part.

Engage Thrusters

Organize your project by following these steps:

1. Once Premiere Pro CS6 has finished launching and the **Recent Projects** splash
    screen appears, select Hotshots - Special Effects 1. When the project
    has finished loading, select **File | Save As**, and save under the project named
    Hotshots Special Effects 2.

2. If it is not already selected, chose the **Editing Optimized Workspace** option
    you created in *Project 1*, and then close any sequences that are open in the
    Timeline panel.

3. Select the **Project** panel, and create a new bin called Archive. Press *Esc* to exit the
    renaming function.

4. Use *Ctrl* + click or *command* + click to highlight all items in the **Project** area except
    the following files:

    ❑ Main_Project

    ❑ MechBot_Sequence

❏   `Archive` (the bin you just created)

5. Drag all the highlighted files into the `Archive` bin, and then collapse the bin to hide these files from view.

6. Create three new bins (*Ctrl+ /* or *command + /*): `Video`, `Images`, and `Audio`. Each time you create a bin, you will need to click in an empty area of the **Project** panel to deselect that bin; otherwise, the next bin you create will be a sub-bin of the previous one.

7. Import the following to the `Video` bin:

   ❏   `Detonation03.avi`

   ❏   `SmokePlumeClip.mov`

   ❏   `Muzzleflashes_UnitK.mov`

   ❏   `SMG_Gaudy_Sample.mov`

   ❏   `MechBot_dies.avi`

   ❏   `LaserBeam_1.avi`

8. If you have downloaded additional sound effects, these should be imported into the `Audio` bin (see *Project 5* for details on required `Audio` files).

9. Right-click on the `Main_Project` sequence in the **Project** panel, and select **Duplicate** from the context menu. This will create a sequence called `Main_Project Copy`. Double-click on this new sequence to open it in the Timeline.

10. Move the Timeline indicator near to the end of the sequence (around **31;00**), and then zoom in on the Timeline (**+**) so that you are able to clearly see the muzzle flash clips you created in the last project.

11. Make sure that only the tracks that contain the muzzle flash and laser beams are light gray (active), that is, **Video 4** and **Video 5**, and that all the other tracks are dark gray (inactive). Now use the up and down arrows to move the Timeline indicator to the start of the first muzzle flash. Press *M* on the keyboard to mark this position.

12. Repeat step 11 to place a marker at the start of each muzzle flash and each of the two laser beams.

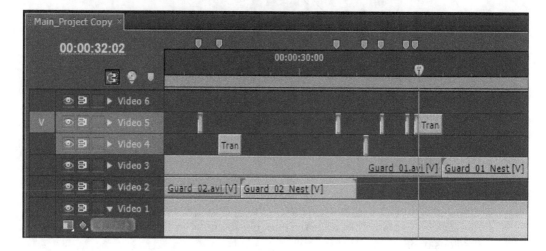

13. Drag a bounding box around the muzzle flash clips and the two transparent video clips that contain the laser beams to select all of these clips. Be careful not to accidently select the Guard_01.avi clip on the track below. Press *Delete* on the keyboard to remove these elements from the Timeline.

14. Save your project before moving on to the next task.

Objective Complete - Mini Debriefing

With careful use of **Save as** and **Duplicate**, you can adapt your old projects without losing the original. In this task, you also covered multiple selection methods using *Ctrl* + click or *command* + click and also the alternative method of dragging a bounding box around the elements you want to move or delete. Both of these methods can be used on the Timeline or in the **Project** panel.

Classified Intel

Although, you have moved the location of the files in the **Project** panel, Premiere Pro CS6 still knows where they are. It's only when you move the files on your hard drive, or rename them, or do either to their folders that Premiere Pro CS6 starts to get a little lost. The actual project file resides in your `Documents` folder, and that's good too, as it means you are not placing all your data eggs in one hard drive basket.

Adding a new 3D object to your scene

In this task, you will replace the `MechBot.avi` file you used in *Project 5* with the `MechBot_dies.avi` file. As well as looking at the Ultra Key to remove the `MechBot_Dies.avi` file's green screen background, you will learn how to copy and paste attributes from one clip to another in order to save time when updating or replacing clips of a similar nature. You will also use masking techniques to get rid of any on-screen garbage that might have been left on the set during filming; in this case, a ladder and a chair!

Engage Thrusters

Add a new MechBot to your scene by following these steps:

1. Make sure the **Project** panel is the active panel, and open the `Archive` bin without creating a new window. Then, double-click on the `MechBot_sequence` file to open it in the Timeline. Click on the backslash key to zoom the Timeline to the duration of the longest clip.

2. Right-click on the **Track Header** area of the Timeline, and select **Add Tracks** from the context menu. Leave the defaults of adding the `1 Video` and `1 Audio` tracks, and press *Enter* on the keyboard or click on **OK**.

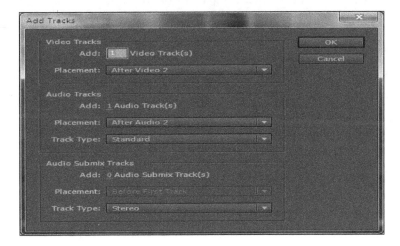

3. Use the down arrow to send the Timeline indicator to the end of the `Background.avi` clip, and press *O* to set an Out point on the Timeline.

4. Return to the **Project** panel, and open the `Video` bin without creating a new window. Send the `MechBot_dies.avi` clip to the **Source** monitor using your preferred workflow. A **V** label should appear in the track header area next to **Video 1** and an **A1** label should appear next to **Audio 1**. Drag the **V** label in the track header area upwards to **Video 3** and the **A1** label downwards to **Audio 3**.

 The **V** and **A1** labels will not appear if there is nothing in the Source Monitor!

5. Set the **Video 1** and **Audio 1** tracks as inactive by turning them dark gray (click once on each). Then set **Video 3** as active (click once on the **Video 3** track header) to make it light gray. Move on when your Timeline looks something like the following screenshot:

6. Return to the **Project** panel, and if you have closed it, then open the `Video` bin without creating a new window. Right-click on the `MechBot_dies.avi` clip, and select **Overwrite** from the context menu. Your Timeline should look something like the next screenshot, and if it does not, review the previous steps before continuing:

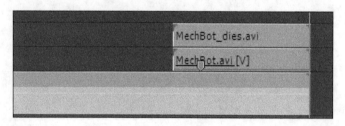

7. Return to the Timeline and send the Timeline indicator to the start of the `MechBot_dies.avi` clip using the up arrow. You need to remove the green-colored background from the `MechBot_dies.avi` clip, and get rid of some of the rubbish that has been carelessly left on set. This will be done using the Ultra Key and a garbage matte. Start by opening the **Effects** browser (*Shift + 7*) and typing `Garbage` into the **Find** field.

8. This will reveal the garbage matte effects. Make sure the `MechBot_Dies.avi` clip is selected on **Video 3**, then double-click on the **Four-Point Garbage Matte** option in the effects panel to send it to the `MechBot_Dies.avi` clip on **Video 3**. Use *Shift + 5* to open the **Effect Controls** panel, then click on the title area of **Four-Point Garbage Matte** to show the garbage matte's bounding box in the Program Monitor. You may have to use the Program Monitor's zoom function in order to see the bounding box.

 Effects can be dragged and dropped onto a clip, or you can double-click on an effect to send it to the selected clip on the Timeline. Just make sure you have the correct clip selected when you attempt this workflow.

9. Adjust the bounding box so that it cuts out the ladder and the chair that were carelessly left in frame, such was the hurry of the director to film this new exciting sequence. Your bounding box should look something like the following screenshot; be careful not to clip any of MechBot's motion:

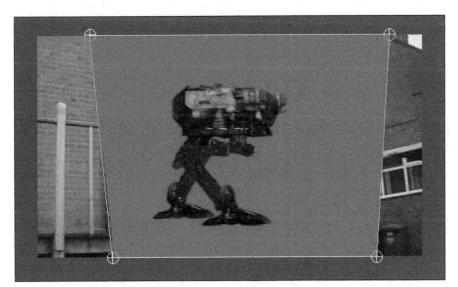

10. Return to the **Effects** browser (*Shift + 7*), and type `Key` into the **Find** field. This will reveal the Ultra Key filter in the `Keying` folder. Drag-and-drop this effect onto the `MechBot_Dies.avi` clip on **Video 3** (or double-click it). Set the **Effect Controls** panel as active, then dial open the Ultra Key parameters.

11. Click on the ink drop icon to activate that feature, and then collect a color sample from any part of the exposed green area by placing the ink dropper over that area and clicking once. This should create a pretty good key all on its own, but you should also play with the other parameters to see if you can enhance the extraction.

 Set output to **Alpha** in order to show the Mechbot as a white silhouette. This will help you see how much of the outline is being obscured as you adjust the various parameters in this filter. Some experimentation is needed to get the best from the Ultra Key, so spend some time here to optimize this key removal.

12. Return to the Timeline, and select the original `MechBot.avi` clip on **Video 2**. Press *Shift + 7* to open the **Effect Controls** panel, then right-click on the word **Motion**, and select **Copy** from the context menu.

13. Click once on the `MechBot_dies.avi` clip on **Video 3** to select it. Right-click anywhere in the **Effect Controls** panel and select **Paste**. The motion keyframes from the old `Mechbot.avi` clip will now be copied across to the new `MechBot_dies.avi` clip.

14. Repeat steps 12 and 13 to copy the **Median** effect to the `MechBot_dies.avi` clip.

15. Deselect the video output for **Video 2** by clicking once on the eyeball icon in the track header area to toggle **Track Output** to **OFF**.

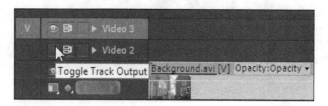

16. Render and save your project before moving on to the next task.

Objective Complete - Mini Debriefing

At the end of this section, you have replaced the original MechBot clip and used **Copy** and **Paste** options to replicate the animation of the old clip. This is a great time-saving way to set up an animation. In this section, you also used the Ultra Key, which many Premiere users regard as the only way to remove a colored background. It certainly has a lot of power, but it can also be overkilling, so don't ignore the other types of keys that come as standard with Adobe Premiere Pro CS6.

Finally, you added the garbage matte in order to remove rubbish that had accidently been left in a shot (a ladder and a chair). Garbage mattes can also be used to remove areas of a green screen that have been badly lit and will cause your keying filter to become confused and create a poor key. A standard workflow for most green or blue screen removal is to take out any unused areas of the key before you apply whichever keying filter you intend to use.

Adding an explosive clip

In this section, you will add an explosion to the `Main_Project Copy` sequence using one of the pre-composited explosions from Detonation Films. You'll then improve its look using two filters that come as standard in Premiere Pro CS6: **Median** and **Gaussian Blur**. You'll then duplicate this clip, turn it upside down, and use the combined effort to create a much bigger explosion.

Engage Thrusters

Add an explosion to your Timeline by following these steps:

1. Set the **Timeline** panel as active, and use the *J*, *K*, and *L* keys to find a spot where the MechBot reacts to being hit by a bullet for the last time (around **31;24**). Zoom in on this spot using the plus (+) key.

2. Press *M* on the keyboard to set a marker at this position, and then double-click on the marker to open its properties screen and call it `Explosion`.

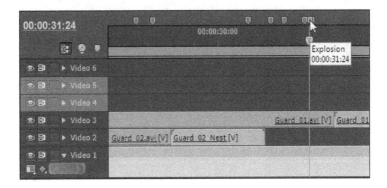

3. Set the **Project** panel as active, and open the Video bin without creating a new window. Locate the file Detonation03.avi (which you downloaded from the Detonation Films site at the start of this project), and send the clip to the Source Monitor using your preferred method.

4. Use the *J*, *K*, and *L* keys to find the point where the Detonation Films logo is no longer visible (around **00;11**). Press *L* on the keyboard to set this as the In point for this clip.

5. Make sure the Timeline indicator is on the explosion marker you created in step 2 of this task, and then set the Timeline mapping to **Video 4** (move the **V** label down onto this track). Insert the Detonation03.avi clip onto the Timeline using **Overwrite** mode.

6. Click on the Detonation03.avi clip to select it, and then use the left and right arrow keys to move the Timeline indicator 1 frame into the Detonation03.avi clip (Timeline: **32;00**), so the start of the explosion can be seen.

7. Press *Shift + 5* to open the **Effect Controls** panel, and click on the word **Motion** to show the bounding box around the Detonation03.avi clip. Use the mouse to move the bounding box, so the bottom of the clip area sits on top of the MechBot's head (**Position X = 548.1** and **Y= -46.7**). In the **Effect Controls** panel, enter a **Rotation** value of **13.6**. Deselect the **Uniform Scale** checkbox, and enter a **Scale Width** value of **120**. The bounding box in your Program Monitor should then look something like the following screenshot:

8. Remove the sky-blue background of the Detonation03.avi clip on **Video 4** using the **Blue Screen Key** option. Try the following values:

   ❑ **Threshold: 13%**

   ❑ **Cutoff: 7.3%**

9. Locate these listed filters in the **Effects** browser, and add them to the
   `Detonation03.avi` clip on **Video 4** using the following values given
   with them:

   - **Median**: **3**

   - **Gaussian Blur**: **5.0**

10. This looks okay; however, the explosion has a line at the bottom that rather spoils
    the effect. To solve this, click on the `Detonation03.avi` clip on **Video 4** to select
    it, then with the *Alt* key held down, drag a copy of the clip upwards onto **Video 5**.

11. Select this duplicate clip on **Video 5**, and press *Shift + 5* to set the **Effect Controls**
    panel as active. Open up the **Motion** parameters and type `-166.4` into the **Rotation**
    parameter to flip the clip on **Video 5** upside down. With the mouse, move this clip
    so the two clips overlap and no line can be seen (**Position** X = **693.2** and Y=**479.3**).
    Refer to the following screenshot:

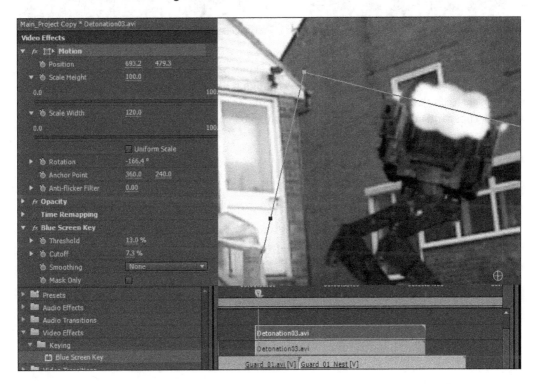

12. Render and save your project before moving onto the next task.

Objective Complete - Mini Debriefing

In this section, you used workflows that you should now be very familiar with to trim a clip, send it to a specific spot on the Timeline, and remove the background color. You then saved yourself the trouble of doing it all over again by simply duplicating the clip on the Timeline, flipping it 180 degrees, and resetting the position. The result is a very large explosion created with the minimum of effort.

Classified Intel

When dealing with the accurate positioning of clips inside the Program Monitor, you should use the zoom function to zoom out for a rough idea of where the clip should be, then zoom all the way in to get the positioning dead right. This can be fiddly and time-consuming, but the end results will always be worth it.

Manually tracking the explosion

Play back this short clip now, and you will see a large explosion that has a certain reality to it; however, as the explosion happens, the two explosive halves do not line up correctly. The explosion also has a slightly flat feel to it, as though it's not really part of the scene (which technically it isn't). In this section, you will manually alter the track (keyframe the position) of both clips, and add a garbage matte, so the explosion appears to go behind the corner of the house.

Engage Thrusters

Keyframe the explosion to match the scene by following these steps:

1. Set the Timeline as the active panel, and move the Timeline indicator to one frame into the `Detonation03.avi` clips on **Video 4** and **Video 5**.

2. Select the `Detonation03.avi` clip on **Video 4** and toggle **ON** key frames for **Position** to set a keyframe at this point.

3. Move the Timeline indicator to 7 frames from the start of the `Detonation03.avi` clip on **Video 4**. Here, you can clearly see the two clips are misaligned. Solve this by selecting the `Detonation03.avi` clip on **Video 4**. Set the **Position** to the following values:

   - X = **673.2**
   - Y = **-16.7** (minus)

4. Repeat steps 2 and 3 for the `Detonation03.avi` clip on **Video 5** to set a keyframe at the start of the clip, then set a keyframe **7** frames into the clip using the following **Position** values:

   ❑ **X = 619.1**

   ❑ **Y = 441.3**

5. Locate the **Eight-Point Garbage Matte** in the **Effects** browser and add it to the `Detonation03.avi` clip on **Video 5**.

6. Open the **Effect Controls** panel for this clip, then dial open the **Eight-Point Garbage Matte** option (if it is not already open). Make sure the Timeline indicator is at the first frame of the `Detonation03.avi` clip on **Video 5**, and then toggle on keyframing for all parameters.

7. Move the Timeline indicator **7** frames into the `Detonation03.avi` clip on **Video 5**.

8. Click on the title of the **Eight-Point Garbage Matte** option to show the bounding box in the Program Monitor. Adjust the left-hand points, as shown in the following figure; don't forget to drag the top-center point upwards so that it does not cut off that area of the explosion:

9. Tidy up the Timeline now by dragging a bounding box around the Detonation03. avi clips on **Video 4** and **Video 5**. Right-click on either selected clip, and choose **Nest** from the context menu to create a single clip on your Timeline.

10. Right-click on the nested sequence that you have just created, and select **Rename** from the context menu. When the **Rename Clip** window appears, type in Explosion Nest, and then press *Enter* to close this window.

When you rename a nested sequence on the Timeline, the version in the **Project** panel retains the name it was given by Premiere Pro. Change this as well when you have time in order to retain your sanity on larger projects.

11. Finish this section by rendering the Timeline, then save your project before moving onto the next task.

Objective Complete - Mini Debriefing

In this task, you animated a clip and a garbage matte in order to enhance the illusion of the explosion moving behind the building. You finished this section by creating a single nested clip. The advantage of doing this when working with **Effects** is that you end up with a much less-cluttered Timeline and have a much smaller chance of accidently putting things out of alignment as you work. Nested clips will keep your Timeline tidy. Use this function whenever you can.

Classified Intel

All of the mask effects in Premiere Pro CS6 can be animated over time; an animated crop, for example, could be used to reveal an object or a person over time as well as hiding it from view.

Adding heat glow and smoke

In this task, you will finish off the explosion effect by adding a heat glow to the objects nearest to the source of the explosion and a little after-explosion smoke. A heat glow is a reaction of elements in the shot, walls, doors, and so on, to the expanding ball of flame; it's used to create the illusion that real-world objects are interacting with the pre-composited explosion you added in an earlier task. Once again, you will use keyframes, a mask, and the new Blend Modes feature of CS6 to complete this section. You will also make good use of Blend Modes to turn an ordinary smoke clip into something a little cooler.

Engage Thrusters

Add a heat glow to enhance the explosion effect by following these steps:

1. Start by setting the **Project** panel as active, and open the `Images` bin without creating a new window. In this bin, create new **Color Matte** (**File** | **New** | **Color Matte...**). Accept the default frame settings by clicking on **OK**, and the **Color Picker** window will appear. Here, you need to choose a deep orange (such as **#DE5705**). Click on **OK** to exit the **Color Picker** window when you are happy with your choice and name it `Orange Matte`.

2. Drag-and-drop the color to the **Video 5** (create a new video track if this does not yet exist), and align it with the start of the explosion at around **32;00**. Trim the duration of the clip to be slightly shorter than the nested explosion clip beneath. Ideally, it should end at around **32;21**.

3. Select the color matte on **Video 5** by clicking on it, then open up the **Effect Controls** panel. Dial open the **Opacity** parameters and change the **Blend Mode** to **Color Dodge**.

4. Locate the **Sixteen-Point Garbage Matte** clip in the **Effects** browser, and add it to the **Orange Matte** clip on **Video 5**. In the **Effect Controls** panel, click on the title of the **Sixteen-Point Garbage Matte** clip to show the bounding area in the Program Monitor. Adjust the points, as shown in the following screenshot:

5. Locate the **Gaussian Blur** filter in the **Effects** browser, and add it to the **Orange Matte** clip on **Video 5**. Set the **Blurriness** to **50**.

6. Make sure the Timeline indicator is at the very start of the **Orange Matte** clip on **Video 5**, and then set the **Opacity** to **0.0%**. By default, **Opacity** has **Keyframes** toggled **ON**, so a keyframe will be created at this point in the effect.

> **Opacity** is the only effect where **Keyframes** are on by default, which can catch out the unwary, who are experimenting with different opacity levels.

7. Move the Timeline indicator to the height of the explosion (about seven frames into the **Orange Matte** clip), and then set the **Opacity** effect to **65%**. Move the Timeline indicator to the end of the explosion (around **32;15**), and reduce the **Opacity** effect to **0.0%**.

8. Duplicate this clip by holding down the *Alt* or *option* key and use click + drag to create a new track and a new clip above the one you have just been working on.

9. Reset the **Sixteen-Point Garbage Matte** clip using the **Reset** button for this effect (the looped arrow to the right-hand side of the title of the effect), and place the Timeline indicator at the first frame of the duplicate **Orange Matte** clip on **Video 6**. Adjust the points of the **Garbage Matte** clip to create a mask around the front of the guard similar to the one shown in the following screenshot:

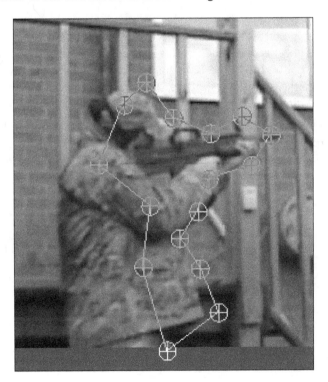

10. In the **Opacity** settings area, click on the **Go to Next Keyframe** button to move the Timeline indicator to the middle keyframe. Reduce the **Opacity** effect for this keyframe to **50%**. The guard is further away than the wall and doesn't require such an intense exposure to the heat effect.

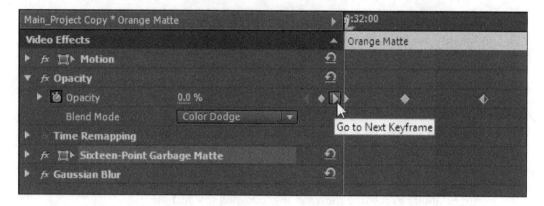

11. Finally, locate and open the `Video` bin and send the `SmokePlumeClip.mov` to the Source Monitor. Trim the start of the clip to remove the Detonation Films header. You only need a section of this clip, so you can set the In point at **01;10**. Drag-and-drop this clip to the Timeline, so that it appears about two-thirds the way through the explosion sequence. Add it to the Timeline by creating a new track above **Video 6**.

12. Using the various workflows you have learned in this book, reposition the `SmokePlumeClip.mov` clip to look something like the following screenshot. Change **Blend Mode** to **Color Dodge**. Note that, in this example, the **Uniform Scale** check box has been deselected.

The effect **Rough Edges** could also be added to the `SmokePlumeClip.mov` clip on **Video 6** in order to smudge away the straight line at the bottom of the smoke plume. But, this will all depend on your placement of the clip.

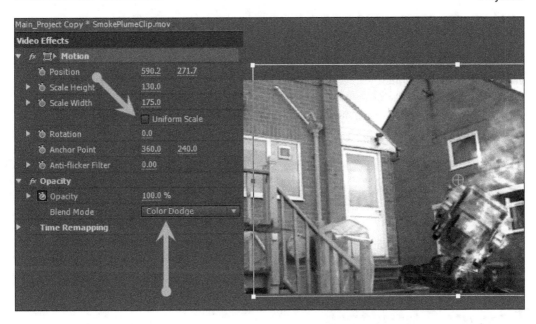

13. Render and save your project once you are happy with the results.

Objective Complete - Mini Debriefing

In this section, you combined a color matte with a garbage matte to create depth to your explosion; now the explosion appears to shed a wave of heat and light onto the walls and to a lesser extent the guard. A simple effect and easy to do, but one that will add a great deal of realism to your scenes.

This same heat glow effect can also be used with muzzle flashes to add a brief source of color to the face and hands of the person firing the weapon. The smoke plume you added at the end of this task is there simply to give a sense of the MechBot sinking into a burning heap of its own circuitry. Experiment with the smoke plume, perhaps adding more than one and using Blend Modes and rotation to differ the way they are presented on screen.

Classified Intel

If you try to nest clips that have altered opacity levels, you will find that the nested sequence will not reflect the changes or keyframes you have made. This appears to be a bug in the current version of Premiere Pro CS6, so please don't try it, otherwise, you might have to restart this section of the project to correct it. You can, however, get around this by nesting the two clips with another that has no opacity changes. You'll see a demonstration of this right at the end of the project.

Adding muzzle flashes and laser beams

In this next section, you will add some real-world muzzle flashes to the pistol and rifle, and also a pre-composited laser beam effect created in **After Effects**. Both of these effects replace the ones you created in *Project 5*, enhancing the overall look of this project.

Engage Thrusters

Add a muzzle flash and a laser beam to your Timeline by following these steps:

1. Use any of the keyboard shortcuts to set the **Project** panel as active, then open the Video bin, and locate the LaserBeam_1.avi clip. Move the Timeline indicator to the point where the laser should fire (around **28;11**).

2. Drag-and-drop the LaserBeam_1.avi clip from the **Project** panel onto **Video 4**. The clip lasts a little too long, rather than trim it; press *X* on the keyboard to activate the **Rate Stretch** tool. Place the cursor over the right-hand edge of the clip, and drag it to the left, so the clip's overall duration is just 14 frames.

[Using the **Rate Stretch** tool to trim the clip in this way speeds up the action to give a more dramatic look to the laser beam.]

3. Move the Timeline indicator to around halfway through the `LaserBeam_1.avi` clip. Press the *V* key to return the cursor to **Selection** mode, and click once on the clip to select it. Open the **Effect Controls** panel for this clip (*Shift + 5*), and then dial open the **Opacity** settings. Change **Blend Mode** to **Screen**.

4. It's time now to add a pistol muzzle flash to the scene. Return to the **Project** panel, and send the `Muzzleflashes_UnitK.mov` clip to the Source Monitor, and set an In and Out point for the muzzle flash (**36;10** and **36;29** for the suggested example). Then drag that clip onto **Video 5**, line it up with the marker you placed on the Timeline earlier in this project (for the pistol firing).

5. Select this clip on the Timeline, and then open the **Effects Controls** panel, dial open the **Opacity** parameters, and alter **Blend Mode** to **Lighten**.

6. With the black background removed, move the Timeline indicator so that you can actually see the muzzle flash, then use all the various workflows and techniques you have learned in this book so far to reposition the muzzle flash, reduce the scale, and alter the rotation to get the correct angle. The suggested settings will work, but try to spend time finding your own perfect combination:

   ❑ **Position** of X: **372.3** and Y: **252.0**

   ❑ **Scale: 67.1**

   ❑ **Rotation: 8.7**

7. Repeat the previous steps to set up a muzzle flash for the rifle fired by guard 01. This time use the SMG_Gaudy_Sample.mov clip from the Detonation Films website. Try it with the suggested settings (this particular muzzle flash effect appears to work better if it straddles the muzzle flash marker):

- ❑ Source Monitor: Assign In point as **00;11** and Out point as **00;14**
- ❑ Drag to Timeline onto **Video 5**
- ❑ Change **Opacity Mode** to **Color Dodge**
- ❑ Assign **Position** of X as **292.8** and Y as **346.0**
- ❑ **Scale**: **37.0**
- ❑ **Rotation**: **179.5**

8. Add another muzzle flash to the rifle by zooming in on the clip, selecting it, then holding down the *Alt* or *option* key, and dragging a copy of the clip up onto **Video 6**. Release it to allow the duplication to complete, and then slide it across to line up with the next point the rifle fires, dropping it back down onto **Video 5**.

9. Keep doing this until you have all muzzle flashes in place. You can use **Video 5** or **Video 6** for most of the muzzle flashes and line them up with the rifle being fired by guard 01 (use the wave file indicators on **Audio 3** or the Timeline markers you placed earlier in this project). The very last muzzle flash will have to be placed on a newly created **Video 8**.

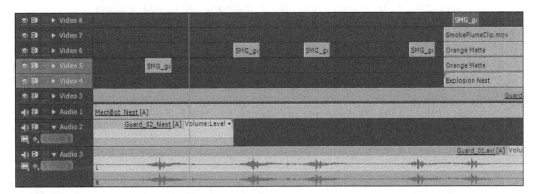

10. Render and save your project when you are happy with the effects created so far.

Objective Complete - Mini Debriefing

In this project, you added a pre-composited laser beam created in After Effects and two muzzle flash clips downloaded from Detonation Films. And, yes, it really is that easy. Once you have mastered the art of the **Motion** parameters for each clip, you can set up muzzle flashes and pre-composited effects with ease. Don't forget to play around with the Blend Modes to find the distinctive look you are after.

Classified Intel

The **Laser Beam** clip was created in After Effects using the **Beam Effect** and to help with the positioning, a single frame was exported from Premiere Pro (using the **Export Frame** function) and used as a temporary backdrop.

Creating an explosion tremor and flying figure effect

In this task, you will finish the visual effects of this scene by sending the guard flying out of shot, then adding a little shake to the camera in order to imply how violent the explosion is. All of this will be accomplished using the **Motion** filter (added by default to every clip on the Timeline) combined with keyframes. This is something you have achieved many times in different scenarios, so this section should be a breeze for you.

Engage Thrusters

Add a tremor effect and the illusion of a flying figure by following these steps:

1. Start by double-clicking on the **Guard_01_Nest** clip at the end of **Video 3**, and open up the nested sequence. Once it has opened, click on the `Guard_02_Frame_Export.png` clip on **Video 1**, and open the **Effect Controls** panel.

2. Click once on the fx symbol next to the **Lightening** effect to toggle the effect off for this clip.

3. Return to the **Main_ProjectCopy** sequence either by clicking on the tab or by using *Shift + 3* to cycle through the open sequences. Move the Timeline indicator to the start of the **Guard_01_Nest** clip and click on it to make sure it is selected. Open up the **Effect Controls** panel, and then dial open the **Motion** parameters.

4. Toggle animation **ON** for the **Position** and **Scale** parameters.

5. Move the Timeline indicator 10 frames into the **Guard_01_Nest** clip, and then use the mouse to move the clip out of shot. Ideally, the bounding box would look something like the following screenshot:

6. Alter the **Scale** level at this point in the clip to around **150%**.

7. Now for the camera shake, use the backslash key to zoom the Timeline in order to show all the clips on all video tracks.

8. Drag a bounding box around all the clips on the Timeline, then right-click on any clip, and select **Nest** from the context menu.

 If you needed to create a larger vertical space for your Timeline in step 7, you should return your Timeline to the normal proportions now.

9. Click once on the nested sequence on **Video 1** to select it, then open the **Effect Controls** panel area, and dial open the **Motion** parameters.

10. Place the Timeline indicator to the start of the explosion (around **32;00**) and toggle on **Keyframes** for the **Position** parameters. Move two frames into the scene, then alter the **Y** parameter (the one on the right-hand side) to **280**.

11. Move another two frames into the scene, and alter the **X** parameter to **352**. Move another two frames and alter the **Y** parameter to **295**. Move another two frames and alter the **X** parameter to **360**.

12. Zoom in on the area that contains the keyframes in the **Effects Controls** window so that you can see the keyframes you have created. Drag a bounding box around them, then click on any keyframe and select **Copy** from the context menu.

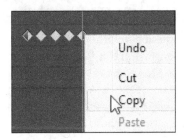

13. Click anywhere in the keyframe area to deselect the keyframes, then move the Timeline indicator two frames further into the scene. Right-click on the red line in the keyframe area, and select **Paste** from the context menu.

14. You now have the keyframes you need to create camera shake, but this also creates an annoying black border that shows up the movement. Cancel this out by increasing the **Scale** to **103%**.

15. Render and save your project once you are happy with the results.

Objective Complete - Mini Debriefing

In this task, you used some simple keyframing techniques along with a little bit of copying and pasting to create the final visual effects of this scene. Most of your effects work will involve in some way; the use of keyframes and simple exercises, like this, allow you to understand their use before you move on to even more complex projects. Now, our mission is accomplished.

Creating special effects takes a long time, getting them to look cool takes even longer, and getting to a point where you are ready to release them to the world takes longer still. In this section, you've had a look into the world of adding composited special effects to a Premiere Pro timeline. In many ways, this project makes it easy; for a start, the view point never changes, and the camera was mounted on a tripod. Take away either of those factors, and the process of creating a special-effects scene becomes that much harder! However, the workflow will nearly always be something similar to what you have accomplished in this project.

You Ready To Go Gung HO? A Hotshot Challenge

Special effects can always be improved. In other words, it's the ideal place to go Gung Ho! Using the techniques you have learned in this Project, work your way through the Timeline to add effects, such as a heat glow to the hands of anyone using a weapon, perhaps, a fuzzy heat glow to the laser barrel of the MechBot. Also, check out the Action Essentials 2 pack from Video Copilot (www.videocopilot.net) for some amazing explosions, smoke, and dust clouds that can add great realism to your scenes. They are designed to work in After Effects, but with a little imagination and by following the instructions in this project, you should be able to adapt them to your needs with very few problems.

Project 7

The Ultimate Do-over – Correcting Visual and Audio Problems

Working in color correction and sound are art forms in their own right, almost a separate career path from video editing. However, if you are making your own films on a budget, you probably don't have the money to spend on getting color imperfections professionally corrected or indeed on getting better sound. In these next tasks, you will see how you can use some of the filters and effects that come as standard with Premiere Pro CS6 to correct a few of these problems.

Mission Briefing

Your objective in this project is to take elements from previous projects and a few clips that you haven't yet seen, and apply various effects to them in order to create a much better visual and auditory experience. Some of these changes need time and work to get them just right, but others are available to you with just a few mouse clicks. By the time you finish this project, you should have a much better understanding of how to fix your visual and audio problems.

Why Is It Awesome?

You might think that a video editor like Premiere Pro CS6 absolutely needs **Adobe After Effects** and **Adobe Audition** to remedy or enhance visual and audio problems. In this project, you will see that this isn't necessarily so; in fact, out of the box Premiere Pro CS6 is capable of fixing many of the problems that you will encounter while either editing other people's footage or creating your own projects. Remember, fixing in post-production is always the cheaper option; getting the crew and cast back for re-shoots is often a logistical nightmare.

Your Hotshot Objectives

These tasks have been divided up to represent the sort of workflow you are likely to use when correcting visual and audio mistakes:

- ► Correcting white balance issues
- ► Correcting color issues
- ► Creating an isolated color effect
- ► Using Rolling Shutter Repair for DSLRs
- ► Using Warp Stabilizer as a virtual tripod
- ► Improving audio quality of a sound track
- ► Removing coughs and other disturbances
- ► Trashing audio – altering the sound of a voice
- ► Globally adding audio filters to your Timeline clips

Mission Checklist

Before you start this project, there are a number of preparations you need to make. Firstly, open your designated `Video` drive and access the `Hotshots` folder you created in *Project 1, Creating a Movie Montage – the Easyway*. Here, you should find the project folders created for the previous projects you have worked on. Create a new folder next to it called `Project 7`, and inside that new folder, create three folders named `Video`, `Images`, and `Audio`.

Video

With the new folders created, access the folder containing the content you downloaded and extracted in *Project 2, Cutting a Short Film without Getting Stung*. You should find a folder inside called `Project 7`. Copy the contents of this folder to the `Video` folder you created in the Mission Checklist section. There are four files in total:

- ► `Boat_Night.avi`
- ► `Cough_Clip.avi`
- ► `IMG_2081.MOV`
- ► `Rain_In_Greece.avi`

Proceed to the first task once you have these media files copied to the correct location on your computer.

Correcting white balance issues

Poor white balance is a problem that occurs when the camera is not set correctly for the color temperature of the lights under which the media is being filmed. Often this is because the automatic white balance function in the camera has been incorrectly adjusted to the available light; predominantly, this can be seen under certain types of indoor lighting or under low light conditions. It can also occur, as in the next example, when the camera is confused by conflicting natural elements; in this case, both rain and sun occur at the same time. Fortunately, fixing an incorrect light balance is a simple matter in Premiere Pro CS6.

Prepare for Lift Off

Once you have completed all the preparations detailed in the *Mission Checklist* section of this project, you are ready to go. Launch Premiere Pro CS6 in the usual way, and then proceed to the next part.

Engage Thrusters

Learn white balance correction by following these steps:

1. Once Premiere Pro CS6 has finished launching and the **Recent Projects** splash screen appears, select **New Project** from the splash screen, and name this project, `Film Adjustments`.

2. If it is not already selected, choose **Editing Optimized Workspace** you created in *Project 1*, and then close any sequences that are open in the **Timeline** panel.

3. Select the **Project** panel, and import the file `Rain_In_Greece.avi` from the `Video` folder on your designated video drive into the `Video` bin.

4. Create a new sequence. Don't worry about the settings, but rename it `White Balance Adjustment`.

5. Drag-and-drop the `Rain_In_Greece.avi` file from the **Project** panel onto **Video 1**, click on **OK** if the **Change Sequence Settings** window appears, then press backslash to zoom the Timeline to the duration of this clip.

6. Switch to the **Effects** browser (*Shift + 7*), and type the word `Fast` into the **Search** field.

7. Locate the **Fast Color Corrector** effect and drag it onto the `Rain_In_Greece.avi` clip on **Video 1**.

8. Open the **Effect Controls** panel (*Shift + 5*), and scroll down to show the controls as shown in the next figure.

9. Click once on the **White Balance** eyedropper tool to select that tool, then in the Program Monitor, select an area of white by clicking on the **Eyedropper** tool on it (the upright pole in the foreground would be ideal).

10. Scroll the **Effect Controls** panel down until you can see the **Saturation** parameter. Drag it out to a value of around **147**.

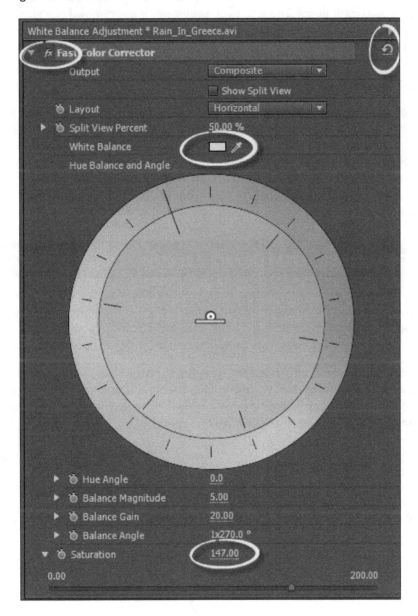

11. Save and render your project when you are happy with the image quality.

Objective Complete - Mini Debriefing

With any kind of color correction, you need to be restrained in your efforts, particularly when it comes to correcting a white-balance problem. To see the changes you have made, toggle the **Fast Color Corrector** effect to **ON** and **OFF** using the fx button (see the previous screenshot). This shows the results of just a couple of simple changes you have made using the **Fast Color Corrector** effect. The result you should see is the removal of a glaze on the image and the colors (in particular the greens) should now punch out a little more, but the rain should still be clearly visible.

Classified Intel

Avoid sampling an area of white that is overexposed, as this can lead to unpredictable and unwanted color casts. If you get into trouble with this, just reset the **Fast Color Corrector** effect using the **Reset** button to the left-hand side of the effects title bar. If this project is for playback on a TV via DVD or Blu-Ray, color correction is best undertaken with a secondary feed from the TV-out of your graphics card (Component and S-Video are common sockets on most graphic cards). If you are going to show your project on the Internet, this is not strictly necessary.

Correcting color issues

In this next task, you are going to attempt to correct the color balance of an image that is far too warm, which means the image contains too much of red color. Images that are described as being too cold have (guess what?) too much blue in them. It's that simple. Too much green in the image is a clear sign of the cameraperson drinking too much!

The clip you will be working with in the next task (`Boat_Night.avi`) is too warm, because it was shot under a light that gave out an orange hue; as such, simply trying to adjust the white balance will probably not result in an ideal adjustment. Instead, you will use the **Three-Way Color Corrector** effect in an attempt to remedy this problem.

Engage Thrusters

Use the three-way color effect to correct the color in this clip by following these steps:

1. Select the **Project** panel, and import the file `Boat_Night.avi` from the `Video` folder on your designated video drive.

2. Create a new sequence. Don't worry about the settings, but rename it `Color Balance Adjustment`.

3. Drag-and-drop the `Boat_Night.avi` file from the **Project** panel onto **Video 1**, and allow Premiere Pro to adjust **Timeline Settings** to match the clip. Press backslash to zoom the Timeline to the duration of this clip.

4. Switch to the **Effects** browser (*Shift + 7*), and type the word `Color` into the **Search** field.

5. Locate the **Three-Way Color Corrector** effect, and drag it onto the `Boat_Night.avi` clip on **Video 1**.

6. Open the **Effect Controls** panel (*Shift + 5*), and scroll down to show the controls as shown in the next screenshot:

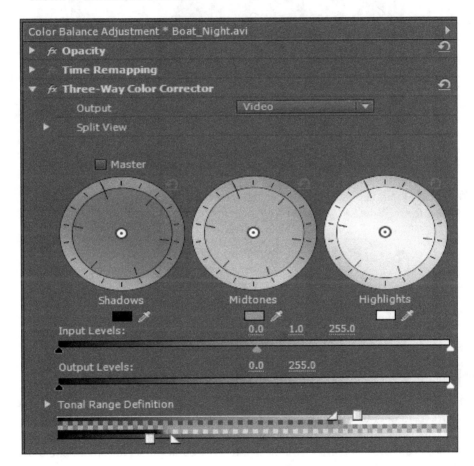

7. An easy way to correct a color problem is to add the opposite color; in this clip, you want to correct the orange hue, so you need to add the opposite, which is blue. The problem is seen starkly in the **Shadows** and **Midtones** areas, so click inside and drag the dot towards the blue, as shown in the next screenshot:

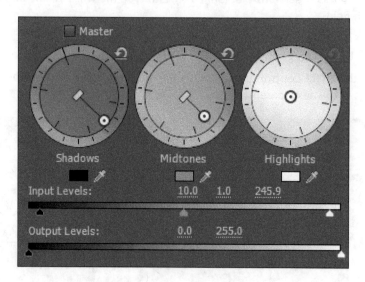

8. Locate **Input Levels** below these dials, and adjust to around **10.0** for the black and **245** for the white.

Remember to be restrained when making adjustments, otherwise, you could lose the detail from the image during the pursuit of a perfect color correction!

9. Save and render when you are happy with the adjustments you have made to this image.

Objective Complete - Mini Debriefing

At the end of this section, you have seen how easy it is to utilize the power of the **Three-way Color Corrector** effect to enhance or repair an image. Obviously, if the image had been too cold (too much blue), then you would have added reds to the **Shadows** and **Midtones** areas. Stylistic looks can also be created with the **Three-Way Color Corrector** effect; one of the simplest methods is to move the **Shadows** and **Midtones** areas in opposite directions to each other.

Classified Intel

If you want to make quick adjustments to the **Three-Way Color Corrector** effect, select the **Master** checkbox; any changes you make in the **Master** area, selecting circle (the dial under the **Master** checkbox) will be reflected in the **Midtones** and **Highlights** selection circles. If you want to make a bigger adjustment to the color in your images, move the center yellow bar towards the outer rim.

Creating an isolated color effect

The isolated color effect has been used in many films over the years, from Schindler's List to Sin City. The idea is to create a stark black and white image, but have one specific color show through the monotones. This effect is something most people think only Adobe After Effects can accomplish; however, it is possible to do this within Premiere Pro using the **Black and White** and the **Leave Color** filters. In this section, you will take the `Rain_In_Greece.avi` file and attempt to show only the green colors on screen.

Engage Thrusters

Isolate a single color on the Timeline by following these steps:

1. Create a new sequence. Don't worry about the settings, but rename it `Color Isolation Effect`.

2. Drag-and-drop the `Rain_In_Greece.avi` file from the **Project** panel onto **Video 1** and allow Premiere Pro to adjust **Timeline Settings** to match the clip. Press backslash to zoom the Timeline to the duration of this clip.

3. Switch to the **Effects** browser (*Shift + 7*), and type the word `Black` into the **Search** field.

4. Locate the **Black and White** filter, and drag it onto the `Rain_in_Greece.avi` clip on **Video 1**. The image should now be monochrome.

5. Now add some color back in again. Start by returning to the **Project** panel to drag-and-drop a second copy of the `Rain_In_Greece.avi` file onto **Video 2**. Place it directly above the first.

6. Switch to the **Effects** browser again (*Shift + 7*), and this time type the word `Leave` into the **Search** field.

7. Locate the **Leave Color** filter, and drag it onto the `Rain_in_Greece.avi` clip on **Video 2**.

8. Open the **Effect Controls** panel (*Shift + 5*). Using the **Color to Leave** eyedropper, take a sample of the color green in the image; somewhere around the tree on the left-hand side of the frame would be ideal.

9. On its own, just sampling the color green does nothing. To see the effect in action, you need to increase the **Decolor** parameter. Ideally, around **100%** is a great starting point to get a clear idea of what you are adjusting.

10. Next, fine-tune the effect using the **Tolerance** slider. If you feel that you are not getting the result you are looking for, try re-sampling another area of green with the eyedropper tool.

11. Save and render your project when you are finished.

Objective Complete - Mini Debriefing

In this section, you've created something that Hollywood once paid millions of dollars to achieve, and you've done it with just a few mouse clicks. Not all colors can be removed completely from the screen or indeed kept in view. If you study the previous example carefully, you will see that some areas of green have filtered out to black and white, in particular the trees in the background. You can attempt to retrieve these colors by increasing the **Tolerance** levels of the **Leave Color** filter, but in this case, any adjustment in excess of 25 percent will start to show the other colors in the frame; specifically the yellow wall.

Classified Intel

Primary colors such as red, green, yellow, or blue work best with this type of effect. The iconic image, of course, is the single red rose on a haunted black and white graveyard, or of course, a banana skin on an urban street.

Using Rolling Shutter Repair for DSLRs

A rolling shutter defect is a problem produced by devices that capture footage progressively scanning the frame from top to bottom. DSLRs and mobile phones that use this method of capture can show a poor image in which vertical lines appear against an oversaturated background. In this example, blinds at a window, the vertical lines distort as the camera moves from the left-hand side to the right-hand side, moving ahead of the progressively scanning method. In this task, you will use the new filter in Adobe Premiere Pro CS6, the Rolling Shutter Repair, to help alleviate that problem.

Engage Thrusters

Correct a common DSLR camera problem by following these steps:

1. Select the **Project** panel, and import the file `IMG_2081.mov` from the `Video` folder on your designated video drive.

2. Create a new sequence. Don't worry about the settings, but rename it `Rolling Shutter Correction`.

3. Drag-and-drop the `IMG_2081.mov` file from the **Project** panel onto **Video 1** and allow Premiere Pro to adjust **Timeline Settings** to match the clip. Press backslash to zoom the Timeline to the duration of this clip.

Play this clip back now, and you will be able to see a slight judder as the horizontal lines of the blinds pass from the left-hand side to the right-hand side. This is caused by the camera capturing the clip progressively from the top of the frame to the bottom, meaning that by the time the scan line has moved from one part of the image to the next, the horizontal lines would have changed.

4. Drag-and-drop a second copy of the `IMG_2081.mov` clip onto **Video 2**.

5. Switch to the **Effects** browser (*Shift + 7*), and type the word `Crop` into the **Search** field.

6. Locate the **Crop** filter, and drag it onto the `IMG_2081.mov` clip on **Video 2**.

7. Click on the `IMG_2081.mov` clip on **Video 2** to select it, then open the **Effect Controls** panel, and set the left **Crop** parameter to **50%**.

The **Rolling Shutter** filter takes a long time to render, even on a small clip such as this. To show you the effect it's having, it is necessary to add a second unrefined clip to the timeline, and then add the **Crop** filter in order for you to see the difference. Normally, you would not include this in your workflow to remove the **Rolling Shutter** effect, unless you wanted to make sure you are getting the correct result.

8. Locate the **Rolling Shutter Repair** filter in the **Effects** browser by typing `Rolling` into the **Search** field.

9. Drag-and-drop this filter to the clip on **Video 1**.

10. Open the **Effect Controls** panel, and adjust the settings to suit the device this clip was captured on. In this example, the `IMG_2081.mov` file was captured with an iPhone 3GS, so Adobe recommends the **Rolling Shutter Repair** parameter be set to **100%**. The shot was taken in portrait mode, so the **Scan Direction** can be left at **Top->Bottom**.

 To find the best **Rolling Shutter Repair** settings that suit your camera will require some time searching the Internet, although the first place to check would be one of the many Premiere forums. In particular, the Creative Cow forums for Premiere Pro are to be recommended (`forums.creativecow.net/adobepremierepro`).

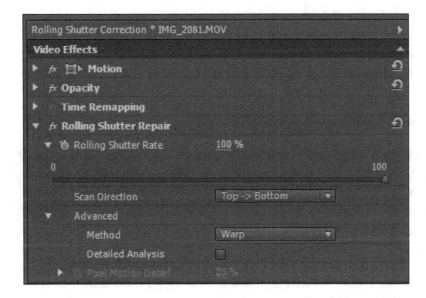

11. Press *Ctrl* or *command* + *S* to save your project. Then press *Enter* on the keyboard to render the Timeline.

12. Once the render has been completed, view the final result; remember that the **Rolling Shutter Repair** filter results will only show on the left-side of the screen; adjust as you see fit.

13. Save your project before moving onto the next section. DSLR's

Objective Complete - Mini Debriefing

The actual process of applying the **Rolling Shutter Repair** filter is simple enough, but setting the various parameters to correctly eliminate the problem is always going to be time-consuming. Especially, as you need to render the timeline in order to get a clear idea as to how the changes you have made have affected the clip. The best use for this filter would be to use *Ctrl* or *command* + *K* to split the clip, where the problem can be seen, and only apply the **Rolling Shutter Repair** filter to those short sections of the Timeline that most show the problem. However, despite the limitation of a slow render time, the **Rolling Shutter Repair** filter is a welcome addition to Premiere Pro CS6, particularly as this was once a filter that could only be found in After Effects. Stand-alone versions of this type of correction tool once cost many hundreds of dollars!

Classified Intel

Each device that suffers with the rolling shutter problem will perform in a specific way, and it's important that you find out how your device performs in order to get the most from this filter. Specifically, you are looking for information on the direction of scan your device uses during filming (top to bottom, bottom to top, left-hand side to right-hand side, or right-hand side to left-hand side). Once you know that, you can alter the **Scan Direction** parameters for this filter to suit the footage your device has captured.

Using Warp Stabilizer as a virtual tripod

Warp Stabilizer is one of those filters that you will probably use a lot more than you think you might. Anytime a shot is made without a tripod, you'll probably need to add this filter to smooth out the small hand movements of the cameraperson that look large on the screen. In this task, you will revisit the `Rain_in_Greece.avi` clip in order to smooth out the obvious hand-held jitters in this short clip.

Engage Thrusters

Stabilize your footage by following these steps:

1. Create a new sequence. Don't worry about the settings, but rename it `Warp Stabilizer`.

2. Drag-and-drop the `Rain_In_Greece.avi` file from the **Project** panel onto **Video 1**, and press backslash to zoom the Timeline to the duration of this clip.

3. Switch to the **Effects** browser (*Shift + 7*), and type Warp into the **Search** field.

4. Locate the **Warp Stabilizer** filter, and drag it onto the Rain_In_Greece.avi clip on **Video 1**.

5. As soon as you drop the **Warp Stabilizer** filter on the clip, it will begin to analyze the content of the clip.

If you know the default settings for the **Warp Stabilizer** filter are not going to work well with your clip, click on the **Cancel** button in the **Effect Controls** panel.

6. Play back the footage after the analysis has completed, and you should see a smoother presentation. However, on systems lacking full Mercury Playback support, you may need to render to see the full effect. Render now by pressing the *Enter* key when the Timeline is the active panel.

7. For this particular clip, you may find that increasing the **Smoothness** to **75%** will help smooth out the footage.

If you prefer **No Movement**, then you can select that from the **Result** parameter, although in this case that may lead to undesired effects. Try it, and you will see the pole wander about as though it is not attached to anything.

Objective Complete - Mini Debriefing

In this task, you've solved the dilemma of a cameraperson not using a tripod. Sometimes that's an inevitable part of being a cameraperson; sometimes it's just laziness, and occasionally it's a style choice (some directors hate anything that's shot on a tripod and for good reasons). If the camera has been suitably stabilized during the shoot using an alternative method (some kind of hand rig), then it's all good! However, if the cameraperson was a little too jittery during filming, that coveted hand-held look, a good shot can look amateurish.

The cool thing is Adobe Premiere Pro CS6 now has an excellent tool to solve the problem; no more shuffling the clip off to After Effects to get the job done. The render time, although not amazingly fast, is much better than the **Rolling Shutter Repair** filter, making this a more viable option when working on longer clips.

Classified Intel

Your footage should only need to be analyzed once. After that, any changes you make will only need to pass through the second stage, stabilization, saving you a little bit of time when using this filter. Some important facts about the **Warp Stabilizer** filter: firstly, the **Warp Stabilizer** filter will analyze the whole of the clip on the Timeline, even if some of it has been trimmed away while on the Timeline. Get around this by making sure you set the correct duration in the Source Monitor before sending the clip to the Timeline. Secondly, using the **Warp Stabilizer** filter on lots of clips on a Timeline can make your project file huge. Get around this by adding **Warp Stabilizer** to each clip in a separate project, exporting it through the Media Exporter, and then re-importing that clip(s) into your actual working project. Lastly, **Warp Stabilizer** will only work on clips that match the Timeline settings. Some significant restrictions there, but now that you are aware of how to work around them, they shouldn't pose you too many problems.

Improving audio quality of a sound track

The problem with the real world is the various real-world stuff that conspires against you on a moment-by-moment basis to ruin your shot, or that of the cameraperson providing the video for you to edit. Nowhere is that more true than in the world of sound. Even the camera being used can be a pain, as the sound of it whirring away makes an unwanted contribution to the video being produced.

In this short task, you will take one of the clips from *Project 3, Protect the Innocent – Interview Edit Techniques* and attempt to remove a slight hiss in the background; actually, it's the noise of a tiny motor inside the camera feeding the tape through the recording head. Tiny it might be, but the background hiss is enough to detract from the overall presentation. Here you will use the **Lowpass** filter to combat this noise, which includes one of the many audio filters available to you in Premiere Pro CS6.

Engage Thrusters

Remove background hiss from your clip by following these steps:

1. Select the **Project** panel, and import the file `Intro_Shot.avi` from the `Video` folder of *Project 3* on your designated video drive.

2. Create a new sequence. Don't worry about the settings, but rename it `Hiss Reduction`.

3. Drag-and-drop the `Intro_Shot.avi` file from the **Project** panel onto **Video 1**, and press backslash to zoom the Timeline to the duration of this clip.

4. Dial open the Waveform on the **Audio 1** track by clicking on the small triangle to the left-hand side of the word **Audio**.

5. Expand the **Audio 1** track by placing the mouse cursor under the bottom line of the **Audio 1** header so that it forms a vertical double-headed arrow and then drag downwards.

6. Switch to the **Effects** browser (*Shift + 7*), and type the word `Low` into the **Search** field.

7. Locate the **Lowpass** filter, and drag it onto the audio section of the `Intro_Shot.avi` clip on **Video 1**.

8. To make more sense of this next section, you will add the **Loop Playback** button to the controls of the Program Monitor. Start by clicking once on the small plus sign (**+**) in the lower-right corner of the Program Monitor. This will display **Button Editor**. Drag the **Loop Playback** button from **Button Editor** so that it sits next to the **Export Frame** button.

9. With the new button installed to your Program Monitor, toggle loop **ON** by clicking on it once, then press *Space bar* to begin looped playback.

10. Monitor the sound as the clip plays. You will notice the **Lowpass** filter has removed the hiss, but the voice of the newsperson is a little flat (too much bass). Toggle the **Lowpass** filter **ON** and **OFF** using the fx button to hear the difference.

 New to Premiere Pro CS6 is the ability to toggle (most) effects on and off without stopping a looped playback. This is, of course, a huge advantage when you want to make changes to the audio of a clip, as you will be able to hear the results fed back to you in real time.

11. When toggling this effect on and off, it becomes all too apparent how bad the camera hiss actually is. With the **Lowpass** effect toggled **ON**, adjust the **Cutoff** parameter until you reach the sweet spot, where the newsperson's voice is not flattened, but the hiss has been reduced enough to be less annoying. A value of around **4600** should do it.

12. Toggle the **Lowpass** effect **ON** and **OFF** again using the fx toggle to hear the difference as the timeline performs a looped-playback.

 Most **Sound** filters in Premiere Pro CS6 do not need rendering and will give real-time feedback on the changes you make.

13. Save your project once you're satisfied with the changes you've made.

Objective Complete - Mini Debriefing

Although Premiere Pro CS6 is a video editor at its core, it has a surprising number of really good filters to help out when repairing your sound files. Yes, of course, it's never going to be as good as a dedicated sound editor such as Adobe Audition, but it does have the advantage that all your audio edits can be performed on the Timeline, without any time-consuming swaps between applications. And now that you can make adjustments while the Timeline loops the playback, Premiere Pro is even more attractive as the first-stop solution for your sound problems.

Classified Intel

The **Lowpass** filter is primarily used to reduce background hiss from your footage. If you want to reduce the impact of wind, then try the **Highpass** filter, which can block out some of the nastier noise problems you will encounter. Mixing **Highpass** and **Lowpass** is not recommended! As an alternative, you can try using the **DeNoiser** filter instead of the **Lowpass** filter if you are not getting the results you want.

Removing coughs and other disturbances

Background coughs, sneezes, or car horns sounding from afar are off screen noises that any cameraperson can do without but can do little to prevent. That's where you, as the trusty video editor, come in to reduce their impact. In this task, you will remove an isolated cough from a backing audio track, and replace the deleted sound area with a sympathetic copy and paste.

Engage Thrusters

Get rid of nasty coughs by following these steps:

1. Select the **Project** panel, and import the file `Cough_Clip.avi` from the `Video` folder of this project, on your designated video drive.

2. Create a new sequence. Don't worry about the settings, but rename it `Cough Removal`.

3. Drag-and-drop the `Cough_Clip.avi` file from the **Project** panel onto **Video 1**, and press the backslash key to zoom the Timeline to the duration of this clip.

4. Dial open the **Audio 1** track using the small triangle, then expand the track by placing the mouse cursor under the bottom line of the **Audio 1** header so that it forms a vertical double-headed arrow; drag downwards to expand the track.

5. Use the *J*, *K*, and *L* keys to identify the point where the cough interrupts the background noise (at around **02;11**).

6. Use the *I* and *O* keys to set an In and Out point on either side of the cough. Make a note of the duration of this selection area (displayed on the lower-left side of the Program Monitor).

7. Set the **Video 1** track as inactive by clicking on it once to turn it light gray. Make sure the **Audio 1** track is set to active (it should be dark gray).

8. Press the lift key (semicolon) to remove the section between the In and Out points.

9. Switch to the **Project** panel, and send the `Cough_Clip.avi` clip to the Source Monitor.

10. Find a point you think would make a good substitution for the sound you just removed and set an In and Out point around that area; make sure the duration of this new selection is the same duration you made a note of in step 6.

You may find it easier to switch the Source Monitor to display the Waveform of the clip. Right-click anywhere inside the Source Monitor, and from the context menu select **Display Mode | Audio Waveform**.

11. Return to the Timeline and use the up and down arrow keys to set an In and Out point around the gap on **Audio 1**.

Because the **Audio 1** track is set to active, the up and down arrow keys will take the Timeline indicator to the start and end of the gap you have created, making it easier for you to define the third and fourth point of this four-point edit.

12. Send the clip in the Source Monitor to the Timeline using **Overwrite** mode.

13. Search for **Exponential Fade** in the `Audio Effects` bin, and add the fade to the two sides of the clip you just inserted.

14. Save your project when you are happy with the solution.

Objective Complete - Mini Debriefing

This short task is an excellent example of how to use the core functions in Premiere Pro CS6 to your advantage. Here, the Lift function, explored in *Project 3*, is used to accurately discard an area of the audio track that is causing a problem. You then filled the gap with footage taken from elsewhere in the clip. Imagine if you had a lot of different noises in the background you needed to get rid of; having a simple but effective workflow like this will be a great way to solve those problems.

Classified Intel

When you film any material, you should try to shoot what's often referred to as the room's absolute silence. In fact, few rooms have absolutely no noise in them, but what you should be recording is the ambience of the room when no one is there and with as few background noises occurring as possible. This clip of absolute silence can then be used to patch up areas of the footage, where you need to remove coughs and other distractions (directors giving instructions, for example). If you don't have such a clip, then you will need to scavenge your absolute silence clip from somewhere in the audio as you have done in this task.

Trashing audio – altering the sound of a voice

This task will add some finishing touches to the interview you edited in *Project 3*. If you did that project, you might remember the so-called eyewitness from the interview requested his identity to be hidden. Although, in *Project 3*, you hid his face well enough, his voice remained unaltered.

To give a quick example of how to achieve a voice-altering effect, you will work on just one small clip from that project, adding the **Pitch Shifter** effect and the **Bass** filter. You will then save this cumulative effect as a custom preset for you to add to your version of *Project 3* once you are done here.

Engage Thrusters

Alter the sound of a voice by following these steps:

1. Select the **Project** panel, and import the file `OS_at_Witness.avi` from the `Video` folder of *Project 3* on your designated video drive.

2. Create a new sequence. Don't worry about the settings, but rename it
   `Voice Changer Effect`.

3. Send the `OS_at_Witness.avi` clip to the Source Monitor, and use the *J, K,* and *L* keys to define an In and Out point using the following parameters:

   ❑ In point: **08;23**

   ❑ Out point: **14;23**

4. Send the `OS_at_Witness.avi` onto **Video 1**, and press the backslash key to zoom the Timeline to the duration of this clip.

5. Switch to the **Effects** browser (*Shift + 7*), and type the word `Pitch` into the **Search** field.

6. Locate the **PitchShifter** filter, and drag it onto the `OS_at_Witness.avi` clip on **Video 1**.

7. Switch back again to the **Effects** browser (*Shift + 7*), and type the word `Bass` into the **Search** field.

8. Locate the **Bass** filter, and drag it onto the `OS_at_Witness.avi` clip on **Video 1**.

9. At the moment, both filters are inert at zero; change this by opening the **Effect Controls** panel (*Shift + 5*) and dialing open the **PitchShifter** parameters. Ignore **Custom Setup** and open **Individual Parameters**. Alter the semitone to **-8**, leave **Fine Tune** at **0**, and set **Formant Preserve** to **OFF**.

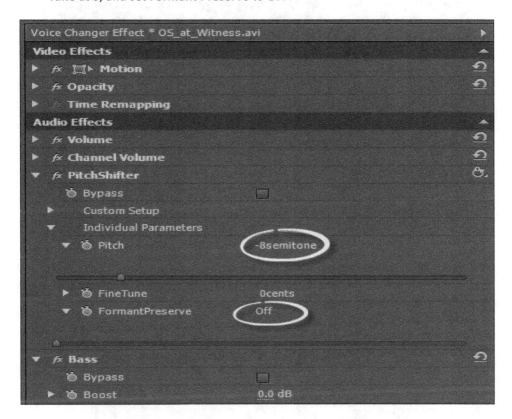

 To create a high pitched secret squirrel type of voice, use plus values in the **Pitch** parameter.

10. This alters the sound of the voice, but adds some hard edges to the higher sounding vowels in the actor's words. Change this by dialing open the **Bass** parameters in the **Effect Controls** panel and changing **Boost** to 10.0 dB.

11. If you want to experiment with these settings, set the loop toggle button in the Program Monitor to **ON**, press space to perform a looped playback, then experiment with the settings.

12. Once you are happy with the effect you have created, press the Spacebar key to stop playback, then hold down the *Ctrl* or *command* key, and click once on the title of the **PitchShifter** and **Bass** filters to select them.

13. Right-click either of these effects and select **Save Preset** from the context menu.

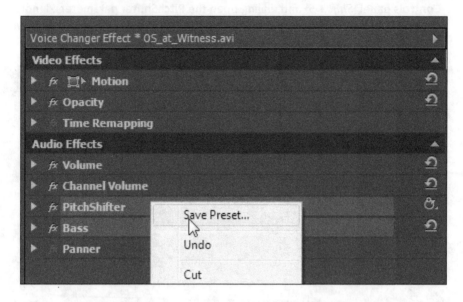

14. When the **Save Preset** window appears, type `Voice Changer` into the **Name** field, and press *Enter* to save this filter. The voice changer will now be available in the **Effects** browser inside the `Presets` folder (make sure there are no letters in the **FIND** field, otherwise, you might not see all your presets).

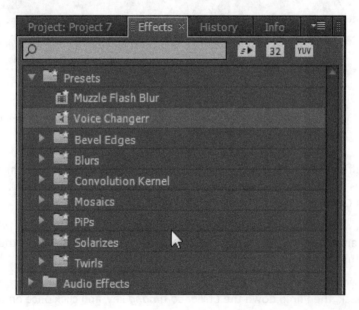

Objective Complete - Mini Debriefing

You have now created a preset to change voices whenever you need to, and by a happy coincidence, you need to do so to complete *Project 3*. Once you have worked your way through all the tasks in this project, reload *Project 3*, save it as another file name (Project 3 - Voice Change, for example), then use this saved preset to alter the voice of the eyewitness. You will need to use *Ctrl + K* to slice up the audio tracks of the various clips; otherwise, you will add this **Preset** filter to the newsperson's voice. When slicing up the audio tracks in *Project 3*, make sure the relevant audio track is the only dark gray (active) track on the Timeline!

Classified Intel

You can also use the **EQ** filter to alter the way a voice sounds; there are a lot more parameters to play with, and you can create some amazing effects, but for something simple like this, the **PitchShifter** filter in combination with the **Bass** filter is probably the quickest and simplest solution.

Globally adding audio filters to your Timeline clips

Adding audio filters to your clips can be a somewhat time-consuming affair, particularly if you have a known problem such as camera hiss. If you need to remove this problem from all the clips on **Audio 1**, you could either add the **Lowpass** filter to each clip, or you could copy and paste it once you have the right setting. Even with a custom-saved preset, this can be time-consuming, although you could select lots of clips and drag an effect onto them all. Alternatively, this task will show you a way to add any filter to all the clips on any audio track using the Audio Mixer.

Engage Thrusters

Globally add audio filters to audio tracks by following these steps:

1. Select the **Project** panel, and import the file Reconstruction_1.avi from the Video folder of *Project 3* onto your designated video drive.

2. Create a new sequence. Don't worry about the settings, but rename it Global Audio Effects.

3. Drag-and-drop the Reconstruction_1.avi clip from the **Project** panel onto **Video 1**.

4. You should already have the Cough Removal sequence in your **Project** panel. Drag-and-drop this sequence from the **Project** panel to the **Global Audio Effects** sequence you created at the start of this sequence. Press the **backslash** key to zoom the Timeline to the duration of these clips.

5. Switch the workspace to **Audio** by pressing *Alt* or *option + Shift +1*. Press *Shift + 6* to open the **Audio Mixer** window if it is not already shown.

6. Both of these clips could do with some hiss noise reduction. To accomplish this, you will add the **Lowpass** filter to the entire **Audio 1** track. Start by toggling open the **Effect and Send** box by dialing down that area using the small triangle, as shown in the next screenshot:

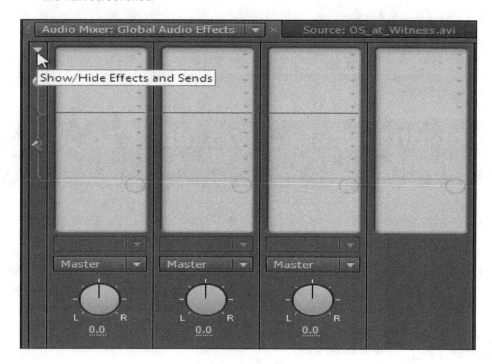

7. Click on the downward arrow, and select the **Lowpass** filter.

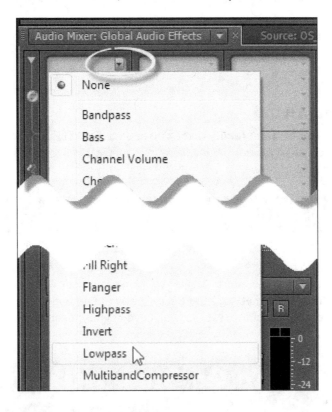

8. Alter the settings to **4600.00 Hz** using either the dial or by entering the value directly.

9. Play back using the looped-playback option toggled **ON**. To toggle the effect off and on, click on the italic f in the audio effect.

10. Save your project when you are happy with the effect.

Objective Complete - Mini Debriefing

In this task, you discovered another way to add filters to the timeline, one that will globally affect all clips on that audio track. If you wanted to add an effect to all the audio tracks at the same time, no matter how many there are, you should click on the arrow in the **Master Volume** column.

Classified Intel

To remove an audio effect from **Audio Mixer**, you need to select **None** from the drop-down list. Filters added to **Audio Mixer** do not appear in the **Effect Controls** area and therefore, cannot be used to save as presets.

Mission Accomplished

In this project, you have seen how accomplished Premiere Pro CS6 can be when it comes to fixing visual and audio problems. You've also seen how you can use those same effects to create stylized visual and audio effects to alter your clips in artistic directions. Premiere Pro CS6 comes with a mountain of effects, and the only way to find out what they all do is to try them one at a time on some of the test clips you have at your fingertips courtesy of the *Packt Publishing* download material.

You Ready To Go Gung HO? A Hotshot Challenge

You should now consider returning to *Project 3*, and repair camera hiss on all the clips that were filmed especially for this book. Then you need to to disguise the voice of the eyewitness in all shots where he speaks. After that, why not try some experimental work using the three-way color corrector to create some unusual color casts on the finished projects in this book? Combine it with the nested sequence and adjustment layer workflow to add that color cast to the whole movie. The scope of these filters and others found in Premiere Pro CS6 is really only ever limited by the scope of your imagination, and your patience to find out what combinations are possible and indeed beautiful.

Project 8

Reach the World – Export to DVD, the Internet, and Beyond

Crafting away at an edit for hours on end is all well and good, but for the work to have any point at all, eventually you need that video to reach the world. In this project, which is the final project of this book, you will look at the various ways of exporting your material using Premiere Pro's vast array of media export options.

Mission Briefing

Your objective in this project is to learn how to export your projects to whatever output you require. There's not a whole lot of mystery behind how to do this, so in a break from the various projects you have completed so far, this section of the book will be a mixture of instructions and a look at some of the export options that Premiere Pro CS6 offers you.

Why Is It Awesome?

This project will explore a number of different export options, starting with the simplest, the creation of an animated GIF file, through to setting up a Timeline so that it's ready to be imported into Encore.

You'll also find valuable advice on working with final assembly Timelines, archiving your finished project, and just for fun, how to create an animated GIF for creating a more interesting forum avatar.

Your Hotshot Objectives

The following tasks look at the various export options available to you when using Premiere Pro CS6:

- ▶ Exporting audio for refined post work
- ▶ Creating an animated GIF
- ▶ Assembling multiple Timelines for final output
- ▶ Adding markers and creating an Encore CS6 compatible export
- ▶ Export options for uploading to the Internet
- ▶ Creating archive copies of your work

Mission Checklist

Before you start this project, you need to be aware that some of the tasks use at least two or three of the previous projects in this book. If you haven't done any projects so far, it's strongly recommended that you do so now. You don't have to complete all the projects, but it is best to prioritize *Project 2, Cutting a Short Film without Getting Stung*; *Project 3, Protect the Innocent – Interview Edit Techniques*; *Project 4, See the Bigger Picture – Edit Multiple Cameras*; and *Project 6, Visual FX Using Real Media*. These detail some great workflows that you will be able to put into everyday use in your editing projects. The other projects also contain some cool workflows, but if you just want to do the minimum, those are the ones you should focus on before continuing with the tasks in this project.

Prepare for Lift Off

Once you have read the advice in the *Mission Checklist* section, you are ready to go. Launch Premiere Pro CS6 in the usual way and then proceed to the first task.

Exporting audio for refined post work

In *Project 7, The Ultimate Do-over – Correcting Visual and Audio Problems*, you looked at ways in which audio can be edited, for example to remove the sound of someone coughing. It was mentioned in that section that sometimes you do need a little more audio muscle than Premiere Pro CS6 can provide; although what it can do is excellent, sometimes you will need more options. In this task you will look at a relatively simple workflow to export only the audio from your video so that you can start working on it with your dedicated audio software. To accomplish this you will reuse **Cough_Clip.avi**, which you have stored in the Video folder under Project 7.

Engage Thrusters

Export only audio by performing the following steps:

1. Once Premiere Pro CS6 has finished launching, the **Recent Projects** splash screen appears. From here, select **Hotshots Template – Montage** from the list.

2. When the project has finished loading, select **File | Save As...** and save this file as `Hotshot - Project 8 - Reach the World`. If a sequence was automatically created, close it now by clicking on the small X next to the name of the sequence. You should now be looking at a **Project** panel containing three empty bins – `Audio;` `Video`, and `Images`.

> If you used the Hotshot Template instead of saving the file as a separate project, then delete the content of the bins and close any sequences that are open. Do this *after* you have saved the project in step 2! Once you have done this, create a new sequence by using *Ctrl + N* or *command + N*.

3. Make sure the workspace you created in *Project 1* is active by going to **Window | Workspace** or **Premiere | Workspace**, and then select the **Editing Optimized** workspace you created in that project.

> You can also try using the keyboard shortcut assigned to your workspace by Premiere Pro in *Project 1* (hint – if you saved the workspace as the suggested name `Editing Optimized`, it would probably have been assigned the shortcut *Alt + Shift + 5* or *option + Shift + 5*).

4. Select the **Project** panel by using the keyboard shortcut *Shift + 1*.

5. Use *Ctrl* + double-click or *command* + double-click to open the `Video` bin without creating a separate window.

6. Import the **Cough_Clip.avi** clip from the `Video` folder under `Project 7` by pressing *Ctrl + I* or *command + I* to open the **Import** window.

7. Press *Ctrl + N* or *command + N* to create a new sequence and name it **Audio Export**. Pick any settings at random.

8. Drag-and-drop the **Cough_Clip.avi** video clip from the `Video` bin to the Timeline. Premiere Pro CS6 should now tell you that this clip does not match the sequence settings and prompt you to match them up. Click on **Change sequence settings** and allow the match to happen.

9. Press backslash (\) to zoom the Timeline to the clip.

10. Click on **Cough_Clip.avi** to select it, then right-click inside the ruler bar area and choose **Mark Selection** from the context menu. The clip should now have the In and Out points selected for the duration of the clip. If the **Mark Selection** option is gray, check that you do have the clip selected on the Timeline.

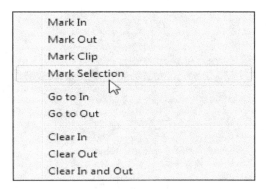

 Pressing *Shift + /* (forward slash) marks the clip directly under the Timeline indicator without having to click on the clip to select it.

11. Press *Ctrl + M* or *command + M* to bring up the **Media Export** window.

12. Locate the **Format** menu in the upper-right area of the window and select **MP3** from the choices available. Leave the **Preset** option for the MP3 at the default of **128 kbps**.

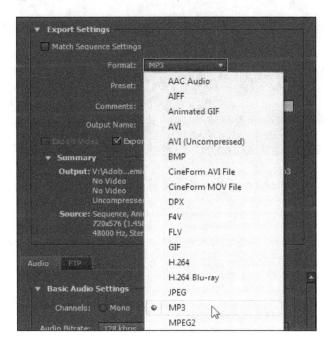

13. Click on the MP3 filename next to the **Output Name** parameter (marked in the next screenshot). Browse to your designated video drive and locate the `Project 8/Audio` folder. Enter a filename of `Cough_Clip_Audio_Only.mp3`. Ensure the **Channels** option is set to **Stereo**, as shown in the following screenshot:

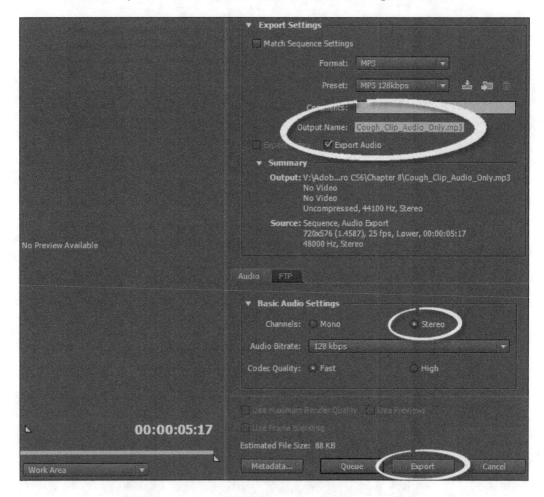

14. Click on the **Export** button to begin the export process. Do not press *Enter*! See the following tip.

Back in earlier incarnations of Premiere Pro the only way of exporting a sequence would have been through the Media Encoder. This application has been sidelined slightly in later versions of Premiere Pro, but Adobe still seem keen for you to use it, so much so that the default *Enter* response inside the **Media Export** window is set to open the Media Encoder.

15. The file will be exported to the folder you selected in step 13. Using your computer's file browser, right-click on the clip and open it in the audio application of your choice.

 If you don't have an audio application and if you cannot afford Adobe Audition, you can obtain a free audio editor from `audacity.sourceforge.net/download`. Audacity is a fully functional application with a thriving user base. If you need to edit sound on a budget, this is probably going to be your best choice.

Objective Complete - Mini Debriefing

In this task you've seen just how easy it is to export a section of your audio for working on it in another application. Using a similar method you could also export just the video to Adobe After Effects or one of the various color grading applications that are currently available. The workflow is blissfully simple, the only caveat is to remember to *name* the file before you begin export, otherwise you'll just end up with the Premiere Pro default name, which is usually less informative than it could be.

If you have the Adobe Production Premium, you can export clips (audio and video) to other applications using Dynamic Link. Dynamic Link allows you to send clips directly from the Timeline, edit them in other applications, then have the results of those edits automatically updated when you switch back to the Premiere Pro Timeline.

Classified Intel

One huge advantage that Media Encoder has over Media Export is the ability to store jobs in a list, allowing you to add various sequences to a render queue. Hit the **OK** button and you can go and do something less boring instead of watching a render progress bar.

Creating an animated GIF

Animated GIF files are video sequences that have been turned into a single image file that is capable of playing back the relevant video data. They are often used in forums where you can set your profile image to be an animated GIF file, which will play in an endless loop in most browsers. As you will see, the workflow for creating such a file is simple and the output can be a lot of fun; it's certainly a lot more interesting to have an animated GIF as your profile image than a boring still image!

Engage Thrusters

Create an animated GIF from your Timeline by performing the following steps:

1. Set **Timeline** as the active panel and check that the `Audio Export` sequence you created in the last task is still active and that the In and Out points you defined are still set around **Cough_Clip.avi**.

2. Press *Ctrl + M* or *command + M* to bring up the **Media Export** window.

3. Locate the **Format** menu in the upper-right area of the window and select **Animated GIF** from the choices available.

4. Change the **Source Scaling** option to **Change Output Size To Match Source**.

5. Leave the **Preset** option set to **Custom**.

6. Click on the filename **Audio Export.gif** next to the **Output Name** parameter. Browse to your designated video drive and locate the `Project 8/Images` folder. Enter a filename of `Cough_Clip_Animated.gif`.

7. Alter the **Width** and **Height** parameters to those required (check your forum guideline pages to see what the maximum sizes should be, as images that exceed these specifications will be rejected by the forum software).

8. Click on the **Export** button to begin the export process.

9. The file will be exported to the folder you selected in step 6. Using your computer's file browser, locate the `Cough_Clip_Animated.gif` file, then double-click on the file to open it in your default Internet browser. Once the browser opens, you should see a preview of how the animated GIF will play. You can now upload this file to your forum profile page.

 Some forums may show a better animated GIF file if **Field Order** is changed to **Progressive** and **Aspect** to **Square Pixels**. Experimentation is the only real way to find the right settings for the forum you are using.

10. Save your project once the export has completed.

Objective Complete - Mini Debriefing

At the start of this task you were told how easy it is to create an animated GIF and you probably were not disappointed to find confusion levels set quite lowish during this task. Now that you have created the animated GIF as a single file, you will be able to use it for uploading to any forum that supports the use of this file type. Bear in mind that the longer the Timeline you use, the larger the rendered file will be! Lowering the **Quality** settings and reducing the **Width** and **Height** parameters will render a file of a smaller size.

Classified Intel

The only slight piece of puzzlement is of course setting the correct scaling for your clip. This function is not available where you would probably expect to find it; in the **Preset** menu, instead you need to alter **Source Scaling** as detailed in step 4. This forces the **Preset** option to become **Custom**, and then renders out your GIF without any black borders or any disproportionate stretching of the image's aspect ratio.

Assembling multiple Timelines for final output

This task is all about preparing your Timeline for the final output of a major or large project. As mentioned in previous projects, most films, documentaries, or whatever it is that you are making, are created as separate scenes on separate Timeline sequences.

One Timeline sequence should always equal one scene.

This helps the video editor when trying to cope with an unwieldy 60 to 90 minute Timeline, where small changes at one end can have a drastic knock-on effect at the other. Even if your movie is just 10 or 15 minutes long, you should consider separating each scene into different Timeline sequences simply to avoid frustrating errors from creeping in. If you want to play mega-safe, you can create a separate project for each scene to combat the dreaded 'Scene failed to load' error message.

The preferred method of editing is to create separate Timeline sequences or separate projects with each one representing a separate scene. In this next task you will look at how to assemble these scenes back together in order to create the entire master project. In this case you will be importing sequences from the various different projects you have created in this book.

Prepare for Lift Off

To complete this section of the book you will need access to one or more projects created in projects 1 to 6. Check now that you know the locations of those projects. If you have followed the directions in this book, you should find the project files (*not* the media files) in your Windows or Mac `Documents` folder and then inside the subfolders `Adobe/Premiere Pro/6.x/Hotshot` (x will equal the version you are using). Once you have confirmed the location of your project files, proceed to the start of this task.

Engage Thrusters

Create a master Timeline from previous projects by performing the following steps:

1. Select the **Project** panel as the active panel, and ensure that you are not inside any bins. If you are, move up one level using the Folder icon in the upper-left corner of the panel, as shown in the following screenshot:

2. Choose **File** | **Import** from the menu or press *Ctrl + I* or *command + I*. Browse to the location of your Premiere Pro projects (by default they live in the Documents folder) and select the **Hotshots_Movie_Montage.prproj** file.

3. Click on **Open** to see the **Import Options** window. From here, select **Import Selected Sequences** and then click on **OK**, as shown in the following screenshot:

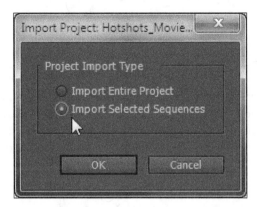

4. Premiere Pro will bring up the **Import Premiere Pro Sequence** window.

 Loading the elements from a project can take some time, so be a little patient while waiting for the data to be displayed.

5. Once the project information has finished loading, select the sequence containing your montage and click on **OK**.

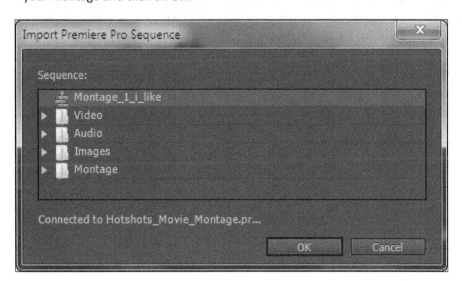

6. Premiere Pro will import the project, placing it inside its own Bin7. Repeat steps 1 to 5 and import the following project sequences:

- ❏ Project 2
- ❏ Project 3
- ❏ Project 4
- ❏ Project 5
- ❏ Project 6

7. Create a new sequence and name it **Combined Projects**.

8. Locate the main sequence you used to create the Montage Project, then drag-and-drop the sequence clip from the **Project** panel to the new **Combined Projects** Timeline sequence. Place it on **Video 1**. Premiere Pro CS6 should now tell you this clip does not match the sequence settings and prompt you to allow the program to match them up. Click on **Change sequence settings** and allow the match to happen.

9. Press backslash (\) to zoom the Timeline to the duration of the sequence clip.

10. Repeat steps 8 and 9 to add the rest of the imported sequence clips to your Timeline.

11. When you have finished, press *Ctrl + S* or *command + S* to save your project, then render it by making sure **Timeline** is the active panel and pressing the *Enter* key on the keyboard.

Objective Complete - Mini Debriefing

This task has effectively shown you how to combine any number of projects together into a single film. This is particularly useful if you have several editors working on different scenes that need to be combined into a single Timeline sequence. Workflows like this are fairly common in today's commercial editing world, so it would be good if you could fully understand the concept behind it.

Keep this project safe; you will be using it in the remaining tasks.

Classified Intel

If you followed the naming conventions suggested in each and every project in this book, you should have had no trouble identifying and importing the correct projects. The final assembly of your Timeline sequences relies on you having a documented workflow for creating and naming your projects and your sequences. If you fail to do this, then your final assembly is going to be that much harder to accomplish. Create good logical names now; don't wait for that last minute deadline!

Adding markers and creating an Encore CS6 compatible export

Now that you have all your work from this entire book combined onto a single Timeline, it's time to start finding ways to share it with the world. In this task you will look at a simple but effective way of preparing this final assembly Timeline sequence before sending it to Encore for the creation of a DVD. You'll do this by placing markers on the Timeline, then naming them and flagging them as DVD chapter points.

> Encore in this case is used as an example; you could in fact send it to any DVD authoring application on your computer. However, as Encore CS6 is bundled with Premiere Pro CS6, it's probably a safe assumption that you will use Encore CS6 for your DVD authoring. Also, you should be aware that the marker workflow used in this task will not work with any other program except Encore.

Engage Thrusters

Create a DVD export-ready Timeline by performing the following steps:

1. Make sure **Timeline** is the active panel and then place the Timeline Indicator at the very start of the Timeline.

2. Press *M* on the keyboard to set a marker at this point or click on the **Add Encore Chapter Marker** icon, which can be found in the upper-left corner of the **Timeline** panel.

> You can also define a keyboard shortcut for adding **Encore Chapter Marker** by selecting **Edit | Keyboard Shortcuts...**, then entering `Encore` into the search field. The *E* key is possibly a memorable choice.

3. Double-click on the marker to bring up the **Marker Properties** window.

4. In the **Name** field, enter `Montage Project`.

5. In the **Options** section, select **Encore Chapter Marker**, as shown in the following screenshot:

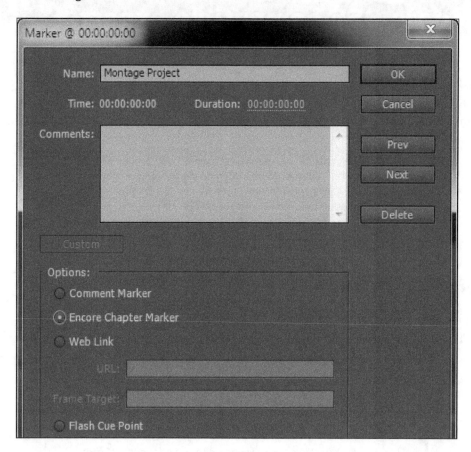

6. Repeat steps 1 to 5 and place, name, and flag as **Encore Chapter Marker** for each of the sequences on the Timeline. They are as follows:

  ❑ Film Project

  ❑ Interview Project

  ❑ MultiCam Project

  ❑ Native Effects Project

  ❑ Commercial Effects Project

Use the up and down arrows to move to the start of each new sequence on the Timeline. DVD chapter markers will show up as red on the Timeline, just to let you know that you have the right flag for each marker.

7. Once you have these markers set, you are ready to export the Timeline in a format that will be compatible with Encore CS6. Press *Ctrl + M* or *command + M* to open the **Media Export** window.

8. To clearly see all the options available to you, click-and-drag the bottom of the **Media Export** window so that it covers the screen, as shown in the next screenshot.

9. Click on the **Format** menu and select **MPEG2-DVD** from the menu and then change **Output Name** to **Hotshot – DVD Project**.

The parameter changes given next are used to create a DVD of maximum visual quality without compromising the DVD's compatibility with the type of DVD players you are likely to encounter. If you do have trouble playing a DVD you created with these settings, try lowering each setting until you find the one that works for you.

10. Make sure the **Video** tab is displayed and **Quality** is set to **5**.

11. If you live in a PAL area, leave **TV Standard** and other settings in this section set to **Automatic (based on source)**. If you live in another area, change these to suit the TV standard you will be using to play this DVD.

12. In the **Bitrate Settings** area, change the following parameters:

    ❑ **Bitrate Encoding: VBR, 2 Pass**

    ❑ **Minimum Bitrate [Mbps]: 7**

    ❑ **Target Bitrate [Mbps]: 8**

    ❑ **Maximum Bitrate [Mbps]: 9**

The preceding parameters are shown in the following screenshot:

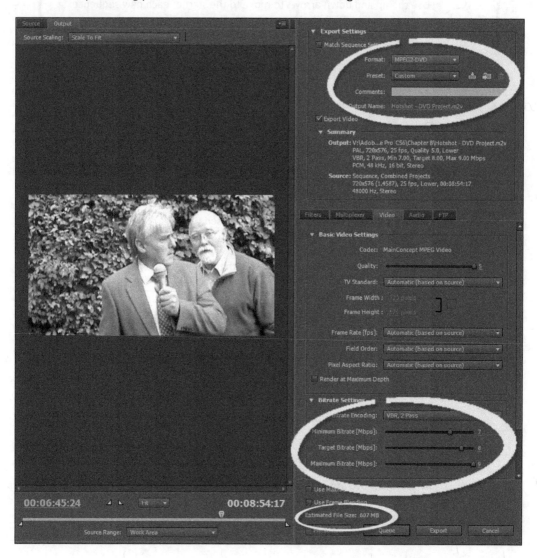

A DVD can only hold around 4.5 gigabytes of information; this will include any DVD menus you create, plus any music those menus might use. When you set up your render in Premiere Pro CS6, an estimated file size is displayed just above the **Queue** button. This should not exceed 4 GB if you are to have any chance of creating a halfway decent menu system inside Encore. If you are creating a Blu-ray Disc, you will of course have a greater overhead to play with.

13. Click on the **Export** button when you are ready to create an export to be used in Encore CS6.

14. Save your project when you are finished.

Objective Complete - Mini Debriefing

As this is a combined sources Timeline (with both PAL and NTSC sources in the sequence) and with the quality set to maximum, the render may take some time. That being said, the actual process of creating a high quality DVD output with Encore compatible chapter markers is relatively simple. That is of course only half the story, working in Encore CS6 being the other half. The use of Encore CS6 is outside the scope of this book, so please refer to the Adobe handbook for further help on this subject.

One thing that you might have noticed when playing around with the Timeline is that the film project shows up with a border around it on a PAL Timeline. That's because you created this project on an NTSC Timeline. If you select that clip on the Timeline, then enter the **Effect Controls** panel, altering the **Scale** parameter to a value of 122% will get rid of the black border without too much graphical loss.

Classified Intel

The **Marker Properties** window can also be used to add a web link and a Flash cue point to your videos so that they open web pages or set off interactive events at certain points during playback. These types of markers really need third-party applications to make the most of them. Simply adding a web link marker to your video and then opening that up in a video player on your PC will not cause a web page to open. More details on these types of markers can be found in the Adobe Premiere Pro handbook (helpx.adobe.com/pdf/premiere_pro_reference.pdf).

Exporting options for uploading to the Internet

In this task you will look at the workflow for exporting a video that will be ready to upload to the Internet, with the *Classified Intel* section of this task containing some information on what options you have available to you when rendering a file for the Internet using Premiere Pro CS6.

That being said, this task is very simple and has been included here to complete your knowledge on export choices rather than to amaze you with a new workflow. However, it's worth looking at this section as there may be information here that surprises or helps you with your future projects.

Engage Thrusters

Create an export for uploading to the Internet by performing the following steps:

1. Use any of the keyboard shortcuts to set the **Project** panel as the active panel.

2. Locate the sequence containing the nested version of `Project 2`. If you have been following the other tasks in this project, you should see this sequence in your **Project** panel named as **Film Project**.

3. Open this project in the Timeline by double-clicking on the **Film Project** sequence file in the **Project** panel.

4. Press *Ctrl + M* or *command + M* to bring up the **Media Export** window and drag out the window so that it occupies most of your computer screen.

5. In the **Format** menu, select **H264** and leave the **Preset** option at **NTSC DV Widescreen** (the native resolution of the clips on the Timeline).

6. In the **Bitrate Settings** area, alter the following parameters:

   ❑ **Bitrate Encoding: VBR, 2Pass**

   ❑ **Target Bitrate [Mbps]: 8**

   ❑ **Maximum Bitrate [Mbps]: 10**

   The preceding settings are shown in the following screenshot:

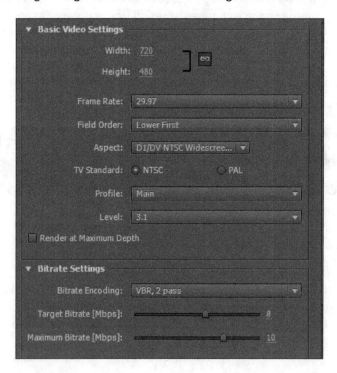

As you are encoding for the Web, the maximum bitrate can exceed the recommended maximum for DVD players (9).

7. Note the estimated file size and ensure this is a size you can comfortably upload using your available broadband setup.

 To quickly access the YouTube and Vimeo presets, make sure the format is set to **H264**, then click on the **Preset** list to open the long list of options. Pressing *V* on the keyboard will take you directly to the first Vimeo setting; similarly, pressing *T* will take you to the first YouTube setting.

8. When ready, click on the **Export** button to begin the render process. At the end of the process, locate the file you have created and upload it to the video hosting site of your choice.

Objective Complete - Mini Debriefing

In this task you have successfully encoded your short film ready to be uploaded to the video hosting site of your choice. Yes, it really is that easy; however before you actually export anything, take a quick look at the following *Classified Intel* section. Here you will find some render choices that may save you time when encoding and uploading.

Classified Intel

The preceding workflow is the simplest way to create a video that will work with the video hosting site you intend using. However, when you do upload your video, it's likely the host (be that YouTube or Vimeo or whomever) will transcode your video so that it works in an optimal fashion with their site.

There is nothing wrong with this other than the fact that an extra transcode may cause some loss of video quality. On top of that it can also be time consuming while you wait for their servers (often busy machines) to finish the conversion process. To help maintain the quality you want and reduce the possibility of waiting for an extra transcode, you should click on the **Preset** tab, and then scroll all the way down to the bottom. Here you will find various options, including specific presets for Vimeo and YouTube. This should create a file that will offer higher quality with minimal transcoding time when uploaded to the video host of your choice.

Creating archive copies of your work

Exporting your work is the final stage. It says you are done with the editing process and you are ready for the world to see your work! Or it could say that you have run out of time or you are sick to death with making single frame adjustments to your film and you want to move on to the next project.

Whichever is true, you will probably create a DVD or you will find a format you want to use with a video web hosting site. However good these formats are for their specific function, they will in some way create a slight degradation in quality. Re-renders will compound the problem.

If you want to work on your final project again at some point in the future, you need to create a safety backup and the best format for that is an uncompressed AVI. In this task you will do just that.

Engage Thrusters

Create archive copies of your work by performing the following steps:

1. Make sure **Timeline** is the active panel.
2. Select the **Film Project** tab on the Timeline and make sure the work area bar covers the whole of the Timeline.
3. Press *Ctrl + M* or *command + M* to open the **Media Export** window.
4. To clearly see all the options available to you, click-and-drag the bottom of the **Media Export** window so that it covers the screen, as shown after step 6.
5. Click on the **Format** menu and select **AVI (Uncompressed)** from the menu and then change **Output Name** to **Hotshot – Uncompressed Film Project**.

6. Make sure the **Video** tab is displayed and **Quality** is set to **100**, as shown in the following screenshot:

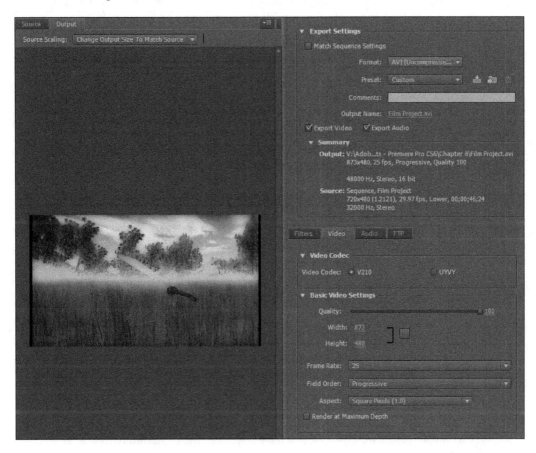

7. Click on the **Export** button when you are ready to create an uncompressed AVI. Make sure the amount of space on the target drive is sufficient for this export.

> If you are working with HD files, a better option would be simply to back up the working folder on your designated video drive. This is another reason why all assets, be they video, music, or images, should be stored in one place. Alternatively, you could export an HD-finished Timeline in using the native settings of that sequence.

8. Save your project when you are finished.

Objective Complete - Mini Debriefing

In this final task you created an uncompressed AVI of the film project. The process is again very simple, but is here to show you the importance of creating such a backup, just in case you need that final edit at some point in the future.

Classified Intel

An uncompressed AVI will take up an enormous amount of hard drive space. If you intend archiving everything you create, then you should think about buying an external drive, probably one that has the maximum amount of space that you can afford and that is network enabled (NAS drive). Using something like this will enable you to create archived material of your projects that is not limited to use only on one computer.

Mission Accomplished

And with this final workflow for backing up your work, you have finished this book. In these last pages you have seen how to create an animated GIF, build Timeline sequences that contain multiple scenes imported from other projects, and add markers to the Timeline to help with DVD creation in Encore. You have also created an uncompressed AVI for you to safe guard your final renders, if not for future projects, then for posterity. Who knows what you could learn by looking back at what you have done!

I hope that you have enjoyed this book and that you have learned a number of useful workflow techniques to make your editing tasks that much easier. Keep this book handy by your desk; as well as being a project book, it will also come in useful as a reference guide if you want to quickly recall how a specific workflow should function.

Good luck with your future edits, and if you have any videos you created with the techniques you have learned in this book, please contact me at PaulEkert@PaulEkert.com.

Thank you for reading this book. If you wish to find out about any other Packt Publishing books, please visit their website at www.packtpub.com.

Index

Thank you for buying
Mastering Adobe Premier Pro CS6 HOTSHOT

About Packt Publishing

Packt, pronounced 'packed', published its first book "*Mastering phpMyAdmin for Effective MySQL Management*" in April 2004 and subsequently continued to specialize in publishing highly focused books on specific technologies and solutions.

Our books and publications share the experiences of your fellow IT professionals in adapting and customizing today's systems, applications, and frameworks. Our solution based books give you the knowledge and power to customize the software and technologies you're using to get the job done. Packt books are more specific and less general than the IT books you have seen in the past. Our unique business model allows us to bring you more focused information, giving you more of what you need to know, and less of what you don't.

Packt is a modern, yet unique publishing company, which focuses on producing quality, cutting-edge books for communities of developers, administrators, and newbies alike. For more information, please visit our website: www.packtpub.com.

Writing for Packt

We welcome all inquiries from people who are interested in authoring. Book proposals should be sent to author@packtpub.com. If your book idea is still at an early stage and you would like to discuss it first before writing a formal book proposal, contact us; one of our commissioning editors will get in touch with you.

We're not just looking for published authors; if you have strong technical skills but no writing experience, our experienced editors can help you develop a writing career, or simply get some additional reward for your expertise.

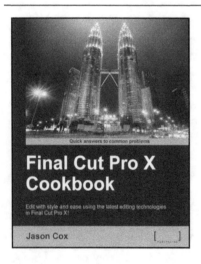

Learning Adobe Edge Animate

ISBN: 978-1-849692-42-7   Paperback: 368 pages

Create engaging motion and rich interactivity with Adobe Edge Animate

1. Master the Edge Animate interface and unleash your creativity through standard HTML, CSS, and JavaScript

2. Packed with an abundance of information regarding the Edge Animate application and related toolsets

3. Robust motion and interactivity through web standards

4. Those approaching Edge Animate from Adobe Flash Professional will find many references and tips for a smooth transition

Learning Adobe Muse

ISBN: 978-1-849693-14-1   Paperback: 268 pages

Create beautiful websites without writing any code

1. Plan a website from scratch.

2. Create a functioning website prototype

3. Use master pages to apply a common look and feel across the website

4. Apply effects such as drop shadows, bevel, and glow

5. Add interactive elements to your site including an image slideshow

Please check **www.PacktPub.com** for information on our titles

www.ingramcontent.com/pod-product-compliance
Lightning Source LLC
LaVergne TN
LVHW062309060326
832902LV00013B/2129